DARK TALES

FROM THE LONG RIVER

Aboriginal and Torres Strait Islander readers are respectfully advised that this book contains the names of people who have died. Some of the historical quotes reproduced in this book contain language now considered offensive.

In memory of
Greg Nicolay
(1957–2012)

First published 2021 by
FREMANTLE PRESS

Fremantle Press Inc. trading as Fremantle Press
PO Box 158, North Fremantle, Western Australia, 6159
fremantlepress.com.au

Copyright © David Price, 2021

The moral rights of the author have been asserted.

This book is copyright. Apart from any fair dealing for the purpose of private study, research, criticism or review, as permitted under the *Copyright Act*, no part may be reproduced by any process without written permission. Enquiries should be made to the publisher.

Cover images by Callum Robbins, John Carnemolla, David Whitemyer, and Ensure / Shutterstock
Cover design by Carolyn Brown, tendeersigh.com.au

 A catalogue record for this book is available from the National Library of Australia

ISBN 9781925816631 (paperback)
ISBN 9781925816648 (ebook)

Fremantle Press is supported by the
Western Australian State Government through the
Department of Cultural Industries, Tourism and Sport.

Fremantle Press respectfully acknowledges the
Whadjuk people of the Noongar nation as the Traditional Owners
and Custodians of the land where we work in Walyalup.

DARK TALES
FROM THE LONG RIVER

A BLOODY HISTORY OF
AUSTRALIA'S NORTH-WEST
FRONTIER

DAVID PRICE

David Price is an Australian writer who grew up in the small north-western town of Carnarvon. He has been a teacher and principal in many parts of the state and influential in public education innovation and reform. Although now living in Perth, David has long been intrigued by the hidden history of his home town and the sometimes wilful amnesia of his country in relation to the treatment of Aboriginal people and Asian migrants by early waves of white colonists. He has two children and continues to work in the field of educational leadership and executive coaching.

CONTENTS

The Frontier on the Long River		7
Prologue	Player of the Game	10
Chapter 1	Death and the 'Dusky Venus'	16
Chapter 2	The Lonesome Death of Thackabiddy	36
Chapter 3	A Bush Beating	52
Chapter 4	The Shark Bay Stand-off	74
Chapter 5	The Yankee Town Murders	100
Chapter 6	Affray at Monkey's Well	113
Chapter 7	In the Shadow of the *Cleopatra*'s Pearl	135
Chapter 8	Spargo the Killer	144
Chapter 9	How Topsy Died	162
Epilogue	The 'Grand Old Man of the Gascoyne'	187
Endnotes		190
References		200
Acknowledgements		202
Index		203

THE FRONTIER ON THE LONG RIVER

In the beginning there was no frontier. There was only a place by the sea where a long, sandy river flung its tail eastwards towards the centre of a silent continent. In the west, the river's tongue split in two, licking the salty lip of an indifferent ocean that sometimes slapped, sometimes caressed the mangrove-littered shores and the empty beaches of the shimmering land.

Each day, the ocean tide slid slowly, quietly in and out of the river's moist throat. Sawfish, stingrays and flathead basked in the warm, shallow water left behind. On hot summer afternoons seagulls and pelicans hung in the eddy of salty sou'westers that blustered in across the waves. The wind brought with it cooler air that bent the gum trees on the riverbanks.

Sometimes cyclones tore into the north-western reaches of the continent. When they had spent their fury, they moved dark and sullen towards the inland where they dropped rain on the river's eastern tributaries. Then a great stream of water would race brown, blind and mute towards the land's end, spewing into the ocean, staining its waves and littering the beaches with logs and branches and dead animals.

A dark people lived there. Those people were owned by that land. It was their place, their birthright. They left no scar on that country's skin, raised no fences, moved silently through its silence. They called the place by the ocean Kuwinywardu, the neck of the river, and along its length they knew every secret, every sacred place and the names of everything in it.

Once, thousands of years before there was a northern frontier, there was only a river, a sea, a sky, and a place that owned a people.

****

I now turned off west by south, quitting the bed of the river, which I named the Gascoyne in compliment to my friend, Captain Gascoyne, and found that we were in a very fertile district, being one of those splendid exceptions to the general sterility of Australia which are only occasionally met with: it apparently was one immense delta of alluvial soil covered with gently sloping grassy rises, for they could scarcely be called hills; and in the valleys between these lay many freshwater lagoons which rested upon a red clay soil that tinged the water of its own colour and gave it an earthy taste.
—Journal of Lieutenant George Grey, 1839

Sir, I am directed by the Governor to inform you that you have been appointed to direct the exploring expedition about to proceed northwards [from Perth] ... The party under your direction, it is intended, should proceed northward as high as the Gascoyne River ... You will examine that river as far as it may be practicable to do, with the view of tracing its course; of ascertaining, if possible, the nature of the bar at the mouth of it, and the question of its being practicable for boats, to what distance from the bar, and the nature of the soil in the vicinity of either bank.
—Letter from Colonial Secretary's Office to R.T. Gregory, 1848

The Gascoyne here divides into several broad sandy channels, sometimes as much as a mile apart. Towards evening we came upon a native encampment; few of the men appeared to have returned from their day's hunting, but we observed upwards of thirty women and children, who ran into the bed of the river to hide, some of the women immersing their children completely under water occasionally to prevent their cry of alarm attracting our attention.
—Journal of R.T. Gregory, 1848

A town-site named Carnarvon has been laid out at the mouth of the Gascoyne River. The boundaries and the upset prices of the lots in the new town-site are specified in the last Government Gazette.
—The Herald (Fremantle, WA), Saturday 27 January 1883

Nothing in the shape of a townsite could be more unprepossessing to a stranger than Carnarvon: low shores, treeless, houseless, giving one at first that he was in squatting country; background made up of ridges and raw sand bearing stunted scrubs; the same thing being alive with natives in a state of nature; a number of houses, include two hotels and three stores.
—Reverend John Brown Gribble, Dark Deeds in a Sunny Land, *1886*

... they found no serious difficulties in handling the natives and keeping on friendly terms with them during the early days when only those experienced in pioneer work and new countries had to do with them, but on the advent of strangers and new settlers from other parts, and the natives being spoilt and their heads turned by a policy of over-indulgence at one time and inexperienced methods of treatment and correction at another, with much ignorance of their ways, customs, habits, language, dispositions etc., the natives began thence to acquire a familiar kind of contempt for their white employers and ceased to look on them with the proper respect and reasonable fear that the superior race should have inspired, and soon showed a disposition and intention to measure strength and a determination to throw them out of their country, and then there was no end of trouble from them for some years ...
—Alexander Robert Richardson, Early Memories of the Great Nor-West, *1909*

The appointment of Mr. Charles Denroche Vaughan Foss, to the lately-created post of itinerant magistrate for the Gascoyne district, will, doubtless, be hailed with much satisfaction by all the settlers of that locality, many of whom have, since their arrival there, been sufferers, to a greater or less degree, from the thievish propensities of the aboriginals. The selection of Mr. Foss to fulfil the important duties pertaining to such a post, is a most happy one, as he is eminently qualified therefore, in every way, being still in the vigour of life, a shrewd observer, a fearless and experienced bushman, and one well acquainted with the peculiarities and customs of the nomadic race, in dealing with which, his principal work will lie.
—The Victorian Express (Geraldton, WA), *Wednesday 27 September 1882*

PROLOGUE
PLAYER OF THE GAME

> We, the undersigned, on behalf of the residents of the town of Carnarvon and the Gascoyne District, on the eve of your retirement from the position of Resident Magistrate of the said District after 33 years of continuous service in that capacity, desire to convey to you our feelings of respect and goodwill, and our regret that the Regulations of the Public Service make your retirement imperative.
> —*The Northern Times* (Carnarvon, WA), Saturday 25 September 1915

'IT IS A STRANGE THING'

One mild Monday morning in September 1915, in the seventy-fourth year of his life, Magistrate Charles Denroche Vaughan Foss sat and gazed around at the group of dignitaries who had gathered to pay their respects to him. A relic of a bygone age, he was a man who had, for more than three decades, willed law and order into a wilderness where he saw only lawlessness and strife. The figure of the magistrate had long towered over the pioneer town struggling to gain a foothold among the mangroves, salt plains and arid bushland that marked a bleak, windswept line of defence between the western edge of a great continent and the relentless waves of a great ocean.

Preparations for his farewell had been underway since April, when Mayor Frank Whitlock had convened a planning committee at the office of the Vermin Board to make sure suitable testimonials and presentations would crown the old man's departure after thirty-three years of service. There had been a good turnout and no problem raising money for the send-off. When that first meeting adjourned there was already one hundred pounds in the kitty; by September there was double that amount.[1]

Now the long-anticipated day had arrived. In front of the old man sat a cross-section of Carnarvon's establishment. Foss knew all the faces well. There was the mayor, Frank Whitlock, who had started out humbly enough on the staff of Dalgety and Company in the mid-1880s, when the Aboriginal troubles were at their height. The affable Whitlock now ran his own prosperous business supplying merchandise to the local sheep stations—so successfully that word on the street was that Dalgety's was considering buying him out and making him manager of a new store.

Above the general murmur, Foss could hear the Lancashire tones of solicitor Ed Holden, rumoured to be on the run from a messy divorce down south and already talking about shooting through to join the war effort. Not far away sat Fitzroy Francis Marmion, Holden's opposing solicitor in many a case brought before the local court.

Also present was the council secretary, Bill Newman, who plied his trade as a storekeeper among the Afghan, Chinese and Aboriginal residents of Yankee Town, the settlement's unkempt eastern backblocks. If Newman still held a grudge against Foss for rejecting his application for a liquor licence back in 1906,[2] he kept it well hidden these days.

As the old man took to his feet to speak, a silence descended on the group. C.D.V. Foss cleared his throat and began:

> It is a strange thing that it was on the same day, the 20th [of] September, in 1882, in the Governor's office in Perth, that I was told they had appointed me as Magistrate at Carnarvon. They said they were quite sure I would be a success in that position, and wished me good luck. Now, on the anniversary of that appointment, you have come and said the same thing; that I have been a success, that I have your goodwill, respect, and esteem, and that I have played the game since I have been in the district.[3]

A murmur of approbation passed through the gathered assembly, even though few had been there when the game had begun.

'THE NECESSARY LEGAL AMMUNITION'

Charles Foss had just turned forty when he took up his appointment as itinerant stipendiary magistrate to the new settlement at Carnarvon. Born in County Cork, Ireland, he had arrived with his family in the fledgling

British colony of Western Australia in 1849, aged just seven. By the time he was fourteen he was working on farms in the Irwin and Greenough districts, eventually rising to become a stock inspector before managing pastoral leases in the Murchison, including Irwin House for more than ten years.

By the time of his posting to the northern reaches in 1882, he had served a useful apprenticeship as a pastoralist and was a respected figure in farming circles in the Midwest of the colony. When the opportunity arose to become the chief lawman in the new port town of Carnarvon, Foss sold his share of the cattle station he part-owned at Gooroonoo on the banks of the Irwin River to his business partner, Charles Fane.[4]

Thus disencumbered of his old life, Foss could now turn his gaze towards the new challenges that lay to his north. As itinerant magistrate he would be responsible for applying Her Majesty's law along the length of the Gascoyne River, an 865-kilometre line in the dust beyond which lay the farthest reaches of the nation's largest colony.

Foss's reputation preceded him. But while Carnarvon's pastoralists celebrated the elevation of one of their own to this most powerful of positions, a Geraldton newspaper keenly spelled out the exact nature of the game that the new magistrate was expected to play in that wild country:

> Mr. Foss, the newly appointed itinerant magistrate for the Gascoyne Districts, is now en route for the sphere of his future duties. We have, before, in noting the selection by the Government, of Mr. Foss, taken the opportunity of congratulating the authorities upon their choice, as we know that Mr. Foss will be the right man, in the right place ... His constabulary, armed with the necessary legal ammunition, in the shape of warrants, will be despatched in pursuit of offenders, who, upon capture, will be summarily arraigned, and, if necessary, punished by sentence of imprisonment— five hundred miles away [on Rottnest Island]. All this is very well, and satisfactory proof that the Government is alive to the necessity for taking vigorous steps to put a stop to the ever recurring audacity of aboriginal depredators, and to deal with peculiar circumstances in a manner which, while certainly unusual, is partially calculated to have the desired effect.[5]

The newspaper's allusions would not have been lost on Charles Foss. He would have been keenly aware himself of the hothouse he was entering. Since the early 1870s it had seemed almost inevitable that the slow but steady arrival of pastoralists and the establishment of a small settlement at the mouth of the colony's longest river would soon bring conflict between the new claimants of the land and the peoples they dispossessed.

The settlers of the distant Gascoyne frontier into which Foss and his small band of police constables would ride that year felt themselves outnumbered and frustrated at every turn by an Indigenous people who would not melt quietly into the countryside of which they had been divested. Rather, refusing to pliantly cede their land to the white newcomers, they expressed resistance in myriad ways that disrupted and exasperated the fledgling settler society. It wasn't long before stories of theft, murder and 'frontier justice' began to abound across the district.

Adding to this already volatile atmosphere, increasing numbers of Chinese, Malays and Afghans were taking up work as cooks, gardeners, cameleers and launderers in the small port community and on outlying sheep stations. While no-one doubted that these workers were a critical source of labour without which the settlers' survival would have been impossible, many white pioneers also viewed them with suspicion and disdain. Most saw them as a necessary but temporary evil, who must never be allowed to gain more than a transitory foothold in the Australian community.

Of even more concern to many was the possibility that friendly relations between Asians and Aborigines would lead to a new and ultimately dominant 'mixed' population that would marginalise the white population and exploit the economic opportunities offered by colonisation.

The settlers in the small white outpost of Carnarvon and in the station homesteads dotted sparsely across the vast plains, scrub and grasslands of the surrounding bush grew increasingly restless. As their fears, anger and ambition began to assert themselves in the form of increasing violence against Aboriginal people and ongoing strife with Asian workers, the colonial government, fearing a loss of the rule of law, intervened.

So it was that the new itinerant magistrate was dispatched with his party of five constables—comprising two white men and three Aboriginal assistants—to pacify the troubled district.[6] This mobile team would be complemented by the four policemen who had arrived at Port Gascoyne six months earlier and four more at Mount Wittenoom,[7] half of each contingent being made up of Aboriginal assistants.

In Foss the Gascoyne settlers had a man who, from personal experience, understood the existential nature of the fears that confronted them and who could use the 'ammunition' of the law to protect their interests, justify their causes and legitimise their material ambitions.

The new lawman set to work immediately, and within two months the colony's major newspaper would report with satisfaction that:

> Mr. C.D.V. Foss, the itinerant magistrate for the 'disturbed' districts, has been doing sound work in bringing to justice more native offenders. On Tuesday morning last, P.C. Smith arrived in town with a batch of twenty, sentenced to various terms of imprisonment on charges of sheep and ration stealing. They proceed to their temporary island home [Rottnest Island Prison] by the Otway, leaving here this evening.[8]

Not all of the settlers were happy, however. For some, the diligence of the new magistrate was too little, too late. As one correspondent to a Geraldton newspaper wrote at the end of Foss's first year:

> In spite of the presence in our district of an itinerant law-wielder and his posse, in spite of the deportation of scores of their fellow robbers, and in direct contradiction of the assertions of Perth wiseacres, who say the outcry against the natives is without foundation of excuse, the aboriginal pests are still at their old game.[9]

Despite—or perhaps because of—such occasional criticism, Foss became increasingly tenacious, simultaneously rounding up Aboriginal 'pests' and dealing with growing unrest about Asian immigrants. The colony-wide newspaper reported happily on his progress towards the latter goal:

> Chinese labourers in the Gascoyne and Sharks Bay [sic] districts are causing a great deal of trouble, both to their employers and the police. More than a dozen cases of absconding have come before the Resident Magistrate, and one of assault, and also a case of suicide. It seems that the Chinese in this district prefer a month's imprisonment to going to the employ of their masters. It is a difficult thing to conjecture why they abscond. I do not think it is because their food is insufficient, because they are well looked after in that respect.[10]

The game was afoot, and there is little doubt that C.D.V. Foss was aware of the high stakes at play. He was to be instrumental in defining, by use of law, the nature of the Gascoyne–Murchison: who would win, who would lose, who would stay, who would go, and where people would fit in the hierarchy of a new social order. If the responsibility worried him, it didn't show. Foss was a man with the confidence, the energy and the backbone to see the game through to its conclusion. He would do so unrelentingly for the next thirty years.

CHAPTER 1
DEATH AND THE 'DUSKY VENUS'

… nor did it appear as if the police would have more difficulty in bringing offenders to justice on the yet thinly settled wilds of the Gascoyne than in the most thickly peopled portions of the colony. The recent trial therefore goes to prove two things: first that to keep down crime among the natives of new districts there must be sufficient police force to impress them with the belief that, if they destroy life and property, they will be pursued and punished, and secondly, that the State is quite able by taking reasonable precautions to protect both the life and property of its subjects even in places distant from the seat of Government and among tribes comparatively new to the white man's rule; and enable the settlers to pursue their avocations in peace and keep on terms of amity with the native inhabitants.

—*The Herald* (Fremantle, WA), Saturday 28 April 1883

WHITE LAWS AND WIRE FENCES

From as early as 1876, settlers had begun journeying northwards by land and sea to the mouth of the Gascoyne River in search of new land and fresh fortune. In 1881 a Geraldton newspaper would report on the:

> departure by the Ocean Queen of Mr Charles Crowther, jun., and Mr George Baston, jun., who are about to commence business at the Gascoyne mouth, as merchants and shipping agents, under the style of Crowther and Baston. They bear with them every material and requisite for the necessary buildings, including labourers. These young gentlemen will thus be the first settled inhabitants of the new townsite shortly to be surveyed at the

mouth of the river, and the establishment of their store will mark the birth of another town to Western Australia.[1]

This store was to prove a much-needed stimulus to the small port community. Crowther and Baston were both from well-known pioneering families in the Geraldton region and they quickly established themselves in Port Gascoyne. By 1883 they had commissioned the building of a twenty-four ton schooner named *Pioneer* to bring goods ashore from Fremantle and Geraldton for their expanding businesses.[2] The two men were also instrumental in lobbying the government to build a jetty for the coastal settlement, where lack of a suitable facility meant that 'every pound landed or shipped [had] to be carried ashore through shallow water'.[3] The pair dissolved their partnership in 1885 and set up separate businesses; Baston would go on to become the town's first mayor.[4]

By the end of the following year—1882—the settlement at Port Gascoyne was developing quickly to meet the needs of the increasing numbers of settlers, drovers and squatters passing through the region. Three stores were already plying their trade, although, as one resident complained, there was still no hotel, 'a want which is very much felt, both by strangers landing in the district and by people coming in from the country'.[5] This lack was soon remedied when Thomas Bird built the Port Inn, which by early 1883 had become a thriving part of the community.[6] A year later a telegraph line was completed linking the tiny port to Perth, some nine hundred kilometres south. A fledgling sandalwood trade had also sprung up, and there was hope for a prosperous pastoral industry that would grow as colonists laid claim to thousands of acres of surrounding bushland.

One traveller described in early 1883 how the port town, now known as Carnarvon, was beginning to take shape:

> I set out for Carnarvon, which I succeeded in reaching just in time for lunch. This new port cannot be said to present a picturesque appearance. The townsite is situated on the bank of a salt creek, while the town itself consists of the Police Station, a store which is kept by Messrs. Crowther and Baston, and a public-house which is 'run' by Mr. Bird. There are also to be seen about a dozen other buildings of a nondescript kind, and, voila! there is the flourishing port of Carnarvon before you. As all the wood and water required for domestic use have to be carted to the town from a distance of about two miles, the inhabitants can hardly be said to live exactly at their

ease; and yet a great deal of business is done there, and the town promises to soon rise to some degree of importance.[7]

Despite such appearances, however, the optimism and enterprise of the first settlers was tempered by their increasing frustration with the local Aboriginal people. Those tribes whose homelands spread the length of the long river showed little respect for the white laws and wire fences that had begun to spring up on their ancient lands, and stories of stock loss, petty theft and the occasional murder of a shepherd or drover had begun to circulate widely as early as 1879.

Police had reported to parliament that year that skirmishes between Aboriginal people and settlers were becoming commonplace in the Gascoyne region, mainly due to the former's theft of supplies from settler huts and killing of livestock. The situation was difficult to police, given the vast distances involved and the isolation of the settlers. The colony's chief of police advocated establishing a permanent constabulary in the area and, in the meantime, granting the settlers authority to deploy 'castigation' in the form of corporal punishment against Aboriginal people where deemed necessary. The police chief acknowledged that such authority would merely add legal sanction to existing practice. As he admitted to parliament, 'This course [corporal punishment] I have reason to believe has been adopted more than once, without sanction certainly, but with a very beneficial effect.'[8]

There is little doubt that some settlers took this advice to heart and began openly taking the law into their own hands. Even a decade after the chief of police's observations, the Sydney *Bulletin* reported on the punishment in Carnarvon of:

> two natives, convicted of sheep-stealing and sentenced by two Justices of the Peace to imprisonment and 25 lashes apiece. The two niggers [*sic*] were triced up to the corner-post of a stockyard, their hands made fast to the top rail, and their legs bound with stirrup-leathers to the bottom rail. The flagellators were two brawny bullock-drivers, who used 14 wattle-sticks, each 6ft. long and two inches round the thickest end, striking blow for blow. The highly-respectable J.'s P. superintended the castigations.[9]

This incident prompted the attorney-general to issue tighter guidelines to magistrates overseeing such floggings:

> Under no circumstances whatever should any other instrument than the Cat o' nine-tails be used, unless it be some description of whip (other than a stock whip), or a birch rod; a rope, or a stick of any kind or sort must not on any account be used …[10]

One of the J.P.s involved in the Carnarvon punishment was reportedly so offended by this implied criticism that he resigned from the role.[11]

In 1882, even corporal punishment appeared to be having a limited effect on the reactions of Aboriginal people to the arrival of the new settlers. The southern newspapers reported rumours that two shepherds on the Minilya River had been murdered, resulting in eight Aboriginal people being shot dead and a number wounded in reprisal.[12]

That same year, the violent death of a Swan River Settlement Aboriginal man in charge of his master's shearing shed was reported in the district. The disappearance of a local Chinese man was also rumoured to be the sinister work of northern tribes, with one correspondent to the colony-wide newspaper declaring: 'probably the natives have eaten him. And yet there are no police to investigate these matters!'[13]

The rumours of Aboriginal cannibalism fed into the prevailing fears of the isolated settlers and heightened their sense of vulnerability. Eminent pastoralists such as Robert Edwin (Bob) Bush[14] had no doubt about the veracity of these rumours, even claiming personal experience:

> Whoever says the Australian Aboriginal is no cannibal knows not of what he is talking about. I have seen the skulls of people that have been eaten.[15]

Hearsay, ignorance and isolation were fuelling an air of hysteria that gave licence to increasingly extreme reactions. When Crowther and Baston's Carnarvon store was broken into, 'Mr. Baston is said to have been obliged to fire upon them, wounding two.'[16]

Meanwhile, the general atmosphere of disquiet continued. One angry citizen of the port wrote:

> The natives continue to be troublesome, and are in fact more daring than ever, killing sheep in daylight and defying the settlers. Some severe check must be put upon their malpractices or there will be wholesale slaughter. It is a wonder the settlers, when they find their property attacked and stolen from them, do not take steps to arrest the depredators; if a white man were to break into my house I should have no hesitation in dealing with him, why not the same with the black fellow?[17]

Despite there being no evidence of a coordinated Aboriginal resistance to the vastly outnumbered population of the settlement and its pastoral outposts, the situation was becoming a tinderbox. Simmering anger among the white population was coalescing into organised agitation for something to be done by the authorities in Perth.

Finally, in 1882, demands for action were met in the form of the indomitable Magistrate C.D.V. Foss and his small entourage of mounted police. Soon hundreds of Aboriginal people from one end of the Gascoyne River to the other would find themselves in neck chains, walking towards ships that would carry them south to the prison on Rottnest Island, offshore from the mainland port of Fremantle. In 1884, for example, 'prisoners from the Murchison and Gascoyne regions accounted for more than half of the Rottnest prisoners, with the most convictions for stock killing'.[18]

In the meantime, violence and retribution continued to mar the early interactions between blacks and whites on the northern frontier. It seemed inevitable that the tension would eventually explode into murder.

'A VERY SAVAGE CANNIBAL'

The year 1882 had not begun well for the pastoralists who eked out a living east of Carnarvon. Despite plentiful rains further north there had been few falls along the Gascoyne River, stockfeed was scarce and apprehension was growing that it would be a poor lambing season.[19]

Into this mix, rumours began circulating about the murder of a teamster called Charlie Redfern who had been making his way westwards from the junction of the Gascoyne and Lyons rivers.[20] The alleged murderer was purported to be 'the chief of the tribe ... a very savage cannibal named Wangabiddy, who is known to have a particular penchant for plump young women, and fat children'.[21] This crime, and the subsequent calls for the punishment of its perpetrator, became a rallying point of the settlers for more police and harsher penalties. Maitland Brown, the irascible parliamentary member for the Gascoyne at the time, addressed the legislative council that same year, expressing no doubt about the identity of the guilty party:

> When I was at the Gascoyne last year this very man, Wangabiddy, had openly threatened that the first white fellow he came across, he would murder him; in fact, he was the terror of the district ... Wangabiddy had always declared that the white man should not occupy that part of the country in peace, at any rate, so long as he lived ...[22]

Sartorially elegant and incisively eloquent,[23] Brown was no stranger to the frontier or to the fractious relationship that existed between the settlers and local Indigenous peoples. He had been a member of one of the first European exploratory expeditions of the southern Pilbara, led by Francis (Frank) Gregory back in 1861. Later he had led his own deadly punitive action against a group of Aboriginal people near La Grange Bay for the murder of three explorers some months earlier, leaving at least six dead and twelve wounded in retribution.[24] In 1882, his sympathies were firmly with the white settlers around the port on the Gascoyne River.

'THE NATIVE QUESTION'

In an effort to stave off the increasing agitation of the settlers, the colonial secretary finally decided in early 1882 to appoint respected resident magistrate Robert Fairbairn as a commissioner to travel to the region and 'inquire into the native question'.[25]

Fairbairn was well credentialled for the job. Born in Bunbury, he had been educated privately and had joined the civil service after a short career as a schoolteacher. His talent and fairness had lifted him through the ranks until, in 1873, he was appointed resident magistrate at Greenough, a role he later also served at Toodyay.[26]

Fairbairn's new task as commissioner was spelled out clearly by His Excellency the Colonial Secretary, who hoped that:

> you will be able to report, from a disinterested side of the question, the true state of the relations that exist between the settlers and the aboriginals, whether the former have acted in any way harshly towards the latter and thereby forced them to the hostile attitude that it is reported they have assumed towards the settlers, or whether the natives have, without receiving provocation, taken upon themselves the position which they are said to occupy, from, a belief that they will not be punished, and from a mistaken notion of our inability to cope with them successfully.[27]

From the beginning, though, Fairbairn's mission was viewed sceptically by pastoralists, who thought the commissioner's brief was framed to find fault with them rather than the Indigenous people they complained about.

Indeed, Fairbairn soon found evidence that at least some settlers were meting out their own extrajudicial form of justice. In one of his reports to the colonial secretary, he related:

> I received a report of the murder of Charles Brackle [*sic*; the victim's surname was Brackell] on the 8th instant, and as soon as the horses had a day's rest, of which they were in much need after their long journey from the Murchison, I dispatched two police and a native to the Minilia [*sic*], with instructions not to return till the murderers were arrested. Three days after the police had started, a man arrived with a letter from Messrs. Gooch and Wheelock, reporting that they had shot the native [Nanacaroo] in attempting to arrest him; also five or six others.[28]

Fairbairn's findings won him few friends in the north. He reported that many of the pastoralists' claims about theft were exaggerated, that misuse of Aboriginal women by shepherds and teamsters was rife and that the killing of stock was related to the loss of traditional food sources due to sheep grazing.

While the new commissioner proved tenaciously conscientious in carrying out his mission, his investigations and subsequent reports received a constant stream of indignant criticism from the region's settlers, much of it appearing in the colony's newspapers. After one such criticism, Fairbairn fired off an uncharacteristically angry riposte to *The West Australian* newspaper, in which he not only asserted the veracity of his previous claims but also recounted a conversation in which a white man had allegedly suggested that the government allow settlers to give the 'natives a good dressing', as had been done at the De Grey River to the south and at Champion Bay to the north where they were 'shot right and left for sheep and cattle stealing'.[29]

Whatever the full truth of the matter, Fairbairn's reports did little to settle the tensions and violence that continued to smoulder on either side of the long river. And while the government ostensibly supported his findings, it came under more and more pressure to act decisively in the interests of keeping the peace in the far-flung northern regions.

A FATEFUL MEETING ON THE TRACK

Meanwhile, the Redfern affair continued to fester. As part of his northern expedition, Fairbairn had looked into the death of the teamster, exhuming the body and carrying out an inquest in which the jury had little trouble establishing that the dead man had been murdered.[30] It is possible that this finding of the much-maligned Fairbairn provided the beleaguered colonial government with just the excuse it needed to temporarily appease the angry settlers and bring some form of order to the troubled bush.

As the crime's sole suspect, Wangabiddy—a powerfully built but ageing Aboriginal man[31] described by the press as an 'extraordinary and most repulsive looking object'[32]—was duly arrested and charged with wilful murder in early 1883, and transported to Perth for trial.

The Crown's case was brought by no lesser personage than the colony's acting attorney-general, George Leake QC. In turn, Wangabiddy's defence lawyer was the formidable Frank Mends Stone. Stone was a blue blood of the colony's legal establishment, his father having served as attorney-general on two different occasions and his older brother as the colony's chief justice. Stone himself would become a politician the following year, representing the newly delineated North Province from 1894 to 1906.

Acting as interpreter was Henry Pass, who translated for the defendant and the Aboriginal witnesses.

Gazing around the alien courtroom, the man in the dock, if the proceedings meant much to him at all, might at least have assumed that he was to be ably prosecuted and defended. Mr Pass reported that the prisoner pleaded not guilty.

During the course of that autumn day in Perth, the story emerged of what had allegedly taken place in the shadow of the distant Kennedy Ranges in May of 1882. That month, the Crown asserted, the teamster Charlie Redfern had set off from James Drummond Mackintosh's station a few kilometres from the junction of the Gascoyne and Lyons rivers. Redfern, who had been working on the station for about a year, was bound for the Gascoyne port some ten days' travel to the west, most likely transporting goods for shipping south.

Travelling in the cart with Redfern was an Aboriginal woman named Kaluman, who had also been working on the property. Mackintosh thought nothing of sending her off with his teamster, there having been no boy available to lend for the job.[33] Redfern was, according to his employer, 'a very good-tempered man, and usually got on very well with the natives'.[34]

Redfern and Kaluman carried enough rations for the journey—mainly flour, meat, tea and sugar—as well as practical equipment, spare clothing and a few personal items. For protection, the teamster also carried a rifle, powder and shot, and a revolver with about forty cartridges.

The small party had been travelling westwards for three days when they camped on sunset for dinner at a site called Willy Willy.[35] It was just as the horses were being turned out for the evening that the figure of Wangabiddy emerged silently from the bush. He whispered to Kaluman that she was wrong to desert her Aboriginal husband, Dickie, for the white teamster. 'Go and join Dickie,' Wangabiddy told her. 'I'll stay with Redfern.'

Kaluman stayed where she was until, after their meal, Redfern told her to go and bring in the horses. She walked away into the scrub, leaving Redfern and Wangabiddy alone together.

The Aboriginal woman was moving cautiously through the darkening bush when Dickie, who had been watching from the shadows, suddenly appeared silently before her. She had only just enough time to see him raise his arm before she felt a sharp pain in her leg where a spear had pierced her flesh. The wounded Kaluman fled into the night, too afraid to return to the camp.

A BLOODY DISCOVERY

As dawn approached the next day, first light revealed Wangabiddy's wife, Woodegar, and her friend, Wurry, approaching the camp where Redfern, covered with a blanket, lay still sleeping on the dirt track. The camp was silent, the horses grazing quietly nearby, the embers of the camp fire fading in the sunrise.

As the two women drew closer, however, it was clear that something was wrong. Woodegar moved cautiously nearer to the motionless teamster, who hadn't been roused by their voices. The reason was soon evident. In the half-light of dawn, she could see that Redfern's head was almost severed from his body.

Tracks in the dust around the corpse led the two women to a gully, where they came across a bloodied axe, a blanket, a revolver and some damper. From here, Woodegar and Wurry had no trouble following the footprints until, later in the day, they came upon Wangabiddy asleep in the sandhills. Nearby lay some damper, meat, tea, sugar, another blanket, a handkerchief and some beads.

According to the women, the Aboriginal man made no bones about his role in Redfern's death. While Kaluman was away, he said, the two men had argued over Wangabiddy's refusal to find a grassier place for the horses to feed that night. In the heat of the moment, Redfern had tossed off the fatal insult: 'You're a bloody fool.' Shortly afterwards the two men had prepared to sleep, Redfern pulling out his swag and laying a revolver close by. Wangabiddy, still simmering with anger over the affront and already disapproving of the white man's relationship with Kaluman, lay in the darkness plotting his revenge. Some time in the night he crept quietly over to Redfern and, with one blow, buried Redfern's own axe in the sleeping man's neck.

The trio sitting in the sandhills fell silent, each contemplating their next moves. By now the sun was high in the sky and something would have to be done. Wangabiddy and the two women returned to the gully, where they buried the axe, a blanket, a handkerchief and some foodstuffs. Back at the scene of the crime they took the other blanket and some more beads from the cart, and walked slowly away into the quiet landscape, hiding Redfern's possessions as they went. They made no attempt to hide Redfern's body or the manner of his death.

It would be eight days before another local settler, John Edgar Sewell, stumbled on the gruesome scene. Sewell gazed with horror at Redfern's swollen body, broken jawbone and bloodstained skull. He saw that his neck had been severed with what seemed to be a sharp instrument. Sewell left the grim tableau as he found it and rode off to alert Redfern's erstwhile employer, Mackintosh.

By the time Sewell raised the alarm at the station it had been thirteen days since Redfern's departure. On hearing of his fate Mackintosh set off immediately in search of his employee's remains, and within a few days came across the now badly decomposed body of Charlie Redfern, still lying on his mattress with his head on a folded jacket, as if he had simply gone to sleep.

The station-owner buried the body near where it lay and tended to the horses, which were still hobbled in the bush nearby. The cart was empty but for a blanket and a bag with a few beads in it. Redfern's rifle, axe and stores were gone but his revolver was found lying beneath the blanket that he had pulled over himself some time before he died. Before leaving the scene Mackintosh took mental notes of the barefoot prints in the dust, then set off to share the news with Carnarvon police.

It was Constable Richard Troy who, led by Woodegar, arrived at Willy Willy to investigate. He soon found the axe where it had been buried with other possessions belonging to Redfern, including a pair of spectacles, a mirror, a box of cartridges and a pair of scissors. Not far away Troy found the gully where a towel, an old felt hat and a white handkerchief lay. Woodegar then led him a few kilometres further where, hidden in the crevice of a rock, the policeman located the last of Redfern's goods: a blanket containing two coloured handkerchiefs, two neck comforters, a velvet smoking cap and some bead necklaces.[36] With the witness accounts of Woodegar and Wurry and the locations of Redfern's secreted belongings, he now had all the evidence he needed to place Wangabiddy squarely in the frame.

That August, some three months after the alleged murder, Police Sergeant Patrick Troy arrived with Commissioner Fairbairn and Mackintosh to exhume the body.

'THE POOR WRETCH CONDEMNED'

The Crown, having established its case against Wangabiddy in close detail and supported by testimony from a number of witnesses, handed the courtroom to the accused's defender, Frank Stone. In contrast to the prosecution's case, the remainder of the trial would be brief.

Notwithstanding Stone's formidable reputation and pedigree, his defence was short, almost perfunctory. There was evidence, he stated, that the two men had quarrelled, probably about the feeding of the horses and, therefore, this served as provocation for the attack. Stone argued that such provocation should lead the court towards a finding of manslaughter rather than of murder. The judge disagreed, the jury quickly returned a verdict of guilty as charged of wilful murder and Wangabiddy was sentenced to death by hanging at Rottnest Island Prison.

News of the sentence was received with satisfaction at the ports of Carnarvon and Geraldton, and soon spread inland.

There was a general feeling at the time that the executions of Aboriginal people convicted of murder would only act as deterrents if they were carried out publicly at the places where the crimes had been committed.[37] This sentiment had existed since the first two executions took place in the nascent Western Australian colony in 1840. Both were of Aboriginal men—Doodjeep and Barrabong—who had been found jointly guilty of spearing a white woman to death and burning her baby alive when they set fire to a homestead south of York. The two condemned men had been transported from their trial in Perth back to York to be hanged from a tree by the blackened remains of the farmhouse. Their bodies, casually desecrated by settlers over the coming weeks,[38] were left there as a grim warning to other Aboriginal people. Western Australia's third execution took place the following year when another Aboriginal man, Mendik, was hanged at the location near the Canning River where he had killed a twelve-year-old settler boy.[39]

For most people on the northern frontier, however, there was a broad feeling that the hanging of Wangabiddy at Rottnest, while not perfect, would still serve as a deterrent. As *The West Australian* newspaper pointed out:

although the effect of the punishment of the poor wretch condemned to death might have been more dramatically telling, and, therefore, more useful, had that punishment taken place at the scene of the murder, where hundreds of blacks could have been collected to witness it, still there happens to be a very large number of Gascoyne natives—supposed to be [the] worst characters in the district—gathered together at Rottnest, who will witness the execution, and who, when eventually released, will report the occurrence to their friends. The compromise, therefore, though it does not show much strength, is open to defence, and is probably as much as can be expected ...[40]

'DEATH IN ACCORDANCE WITH THE LAW'

A month went by and the day of Wangabiddy's scheduled execution arrived, but for a week the wind and rain of winter made crossing the sea from the mainland to Rottnest Island out of the question. The condemned man was held at Fremantle until the third week of June when the storm finally subsided. That Saturday afternoon the colony's sheriff and inspector of prisons J.B. Roe, some local constables and the colony's hangman started out for the island prison some twenty kilometres offshore. With them on the cutter *Will Watch* were Wangabiddy and another Aboriginal prisoner, Guerhilla, who had been sentenced to death for a murder on the Fitzroy River.

On the morning of Monday 18 June 1883, the jury arrived on the steam lighter *Amy*. By two o'clock that day the scaffold was ready and the 175 Aboriginal inmates of Rottnest Island Prison were ranged around the yard with their backs to the walls. Pensioner guards and constables manned the scaffold while the prison's wardens, armed with pistols, stationed themselves around the perimeter.

The small group of officials made their way to Wangabiddy's cell, where they found the prisoner finishing his midday meal, seemingly unaware of his imminent fate. The hangman pinioned him quickly and walked him briskly towards the centre of the yard. It was only when he began fastening the rope around Wangabiddy's neck that the prisoner gave the first sign of understanding what was about to happen. He struggled desperately above the watching eyes of the other prisoners and the guards. But there were none there that could save him.

According to one observer:

[Wangabiddy] looked about him as if seeking some means of escape, and there was a malignity in his furtive glances at those around him that bespoke his fierce hatred of the white men, whom he had threatened, when in his district, to drive into the sea.[41]

At 2.30 pm the lever was pulled and Wangabiddy fell to his death. Guerhilla followed soon after, and two of the other prisoners laid the bodies in rough coffins while a brief inquest returned two verdicts of 'Death in accordance with the law'.[42]

A Perth newspaper hoped that:

> the aborigines living in the far-distant parts of the Colony may learn that the shedding of man's blood will be surely followed by the equally violent death of the murderer.[43]

As subsequent events would prove, it was not a lesson well learned. Within less than a year another Gascoyne settler was dead, and the long arm of the law would stretch once again to the far reaches of the North-West and drag three more alleged murderers to its southern courtrooms.

ANOTHER MURDER

In March of that same year, an ex-convict by the name of Robert Grundy had been making his way eastwards from Carnarvon to look for work as a shepherd on the various sheep stations that had begun to spring up on either side of the Gascoyne River.

Grundy had arrived on a penal transport ship in 1851, having been sentenced to seven years in the far-flung Swan River Colony for larceny. After receiving a conditional pardon in 1854, the former mariner—who was literate but apparently incorrigible—was convicted of forgery and sentenced to another seven years' imprisonment.[44]

Now once again a free man, in his early sixties and sporting grey stubble, the balding Grundy was dressed in his usual white moleskin trousers, cotton shirt, boots and braces.[45] As always, trotting alongside him was his black-and-tan sheepdog.

Not far out of the township he joined a small group of men heading in the same direction, and for six days the little band made its way by cart along the dirt track that skirted the southern bank of the Gascoyne River. They had travelled more than one hundred kilometres when they reached Millie Millie Pool on Captain Alfred Russell's station, near the junction of the Gascoyne and Lyons rivers. It was here that Grundy shouldered his swag once more and, with his dog by his side, set off towards the Kennedy Ranges. No white man would see him alive again.

Five days later, the old man's already badly decomposed body was discovered on the side of the track by Percy Gibbons, manager of the Gascoyne and Lyons Squatting Company, and Beewar, a young Aboriginal man who had been working for Gibbons for about a year. The two men noticed blood on Grundy's face, stomach and chest. By the old man's side, as close in death as in life, lay the body of his dog.

Beewar had known old Grundy for a long time, and had also lived among the people of this land. He peered at Grundy's body. He guessed from the wounds that the old man had died from spear thrusts to the chest and stomach and a *kylie* (boomerang) wound to the head. Someone had also speared the dog.

Beewar's eyes then scanned the broader scene. He looked closely at the telltale footprints that were scattered around the dusty bush track, and recognised at least some of them: three men called Nowaraba,[46] Gnalbee and Geeler and two women, Warribee and Yorilba.

He and Gibbons followed the footprints until, about forty metres away, they came across another pool of blood. Beewar guessed that the old man had been felled in two places before he finally expired. The two men left the body where it was and headed off to inform police in Carnarvon.

It would be May before Magistrate Foss arrived on the scene to conduct a formal inquest into Grundy's death. The lawman's verdict was unambiguous:

> ... the deceased, Robert Grundy, was murdered near Millie Millie on or about the 10th March, 1884, by the Aboriginal natives Nowaraba, alias 'Big-headed Harry', and Gnalbee.[47]

All that remained now was for the alleged murderers to be rounded up and for colonial law to take its course. Lance corporals Keen and Wall, who made up Foss's escort, took care of that by arresting Nowaraba and Gnalbee on their return journey westwards. The two Aboriginal men put up 'considerable resistance'[48] and attempted to escape, but they were no match for the armed policemen. A third man, Geeler, was arrested later.

In December 1884, the three Aboriginal men from the country around the Kennedy Ranges were arraigned before a court in Geraldton, five hundred kilometres to the south.

'A DUSKY VENUS'

In the end it was Beewar's evidence that sealed the fates of the three defendants. Describing himself as Mr Gibbons' servant, Beewar told the court that he believed the men in the dock were the owners of the footprints scattered around the crime scene. Ignoring the protests of Nowaraba, Gnalbee and Geeler, the chief witness continued:

> I don't know where the prisoners lived but I had seen their tracks before; I saw plenty of blackfellows' tracks but I recognised the prisoners.[49]

The question now turned to motive. Why had Grundy been killed?

Warribee and Yorilba, the two Aboriginal women whose tracks Beewar had also identified at the crime scene, now filled in the missing details about Grundy's final moments. Their tales were convoluted, sometimes contradictory, and involved an intricate web of relationships that sometimes confounded the court. What gradually became clear to the judge and jury, however, was that at some point Warribee had made the fateful decision to join Grundy along the track. This had provoked several of the men of her tribe to anger, particularly Nowaraba.

One morning the shepherd, accompanied by Warribee, had found himself surrounded by a group of men, led by Nowaraba, who had appeared silently out of the bush armed with spears and kylies. Grundy must have sensed the danger. According to Warribee, she had cautioned the old man to be careful as there was resentment brewing among her people. Even so, standing there vulnerable on the open track, Grundy didn't reach for his loaded revolver—perhaps he hadn't understood the Aboriginal woman's warning, or maybe events had just moved too quickly. Whatever his reasons, Grundy now had no choice but to face the small group of armed men. He turned to Nowaraba. 'Why do you look so angry?' he asked.

Warribee told the court what happened next. Nowaraba stared at the defenceless man before him. 'Did you take my woman?' Grundy replied simply: 'Yes, me take her.' Those were his final words. Without further warning Nowaraba speared him, with Gnalbee and Geeler quickly joining in the assault. The wounded man, bleeding from the face, neck, back and stomach, staggered away before collapsing in the dust. Then Geeler speared his dog. It was over. Within minutes the killers were once more swallowed up by the silent bush that was their home.

CHAPTER 1: DEATH AND THE 'DUSKY VENUS'

In the hushed Geraldton courtroom, defence counsel James Barratt made no attempt to argue the fact of murder, but said he was not convinced that the murderers were in the dock. Surely, he argued, the chief witness alone could not be believed without corroboration—particularly given her own questionable character and possible ulterior motives:

> It appears to me that Warribee was a dusky Venus, and a bone of contention amongst the natives, and possibly she was interested in getting Harry [Nowaraba] out of the way, whose woman she was.[50]

In Barratt's mind there could be no certainty that the court had heard the whole truth of the matter just because a single witness had had her day in court. The prisoners themselves claimed innocence, and Barratt reminded the jury that:

> [just] because a murder was committed by a native it does not follow that we are to catch hold of the first native we came across and hang him. They are subject to our laws and cannot be treated as a hostile race. But although they are subject to our laws they do not know how to defend themselves when brought before a Court of Justice and, therefore, as far as possible these laws should be allowed to operate in favour of them.[51]

The judge was unmoved by this argument. He explained to the jury that, while Warribee's evidence could not be corroborated, neither could it be dismissed. Her eyewitness account combined with the identification of the accused by Beewar made a telling case for the prosecution.

The jury duly retired to consider their verdict. That consideration proved brief: in just forty-five minutes the fate of the three prisoners was sealed when the jury returned with a finding of guilty.

Nowaraba, Gnalbee and Geeler listened silently as three sentences of death were passed down. It was only when their sentences were explained to them by interpreter Henry Pass that all three vigorously protested their innocence. But by then, as every white man in the room knew, it was far too late.

'STORIES OF A REVOLTING NATURE'

When the sentences of death were passed down on the killers of Robert Grundy, one newspaper made the prescient observation that, 'in the majority of the murders which have been committed at the Nor-West, native women have been at the bottom of them.'[52] This was certainly true of the deaths of both Redfern and Grundy.

Commissioner Fairbairn, on his earlier fact-finding mission to the Gascoyne, had himself noted allegations of sexual mistreatment of Aboriginal girls and women, and a general atmosphere of lawlessness on the part of the settlers. During his visit to the region, he'd said, 'stories were told to me of a revolting nature, by some of the principal settlers, touching on the treatment of girls of tender age by [white] men on the stations'.[53]

Back in Perth, the Gascoyne's parliamentary member Maitland Brown had used parliament to scoff at Fairbairn's findings. It seemed to him, he said:

> that the settlers on the Gascoyne and the Upper Murchison are no exception, as regards their moral relations with the native women, to other people who resided in the very centres of civilisation, not only within our own Colony, but in every part of the world where the two races are brought in contact with each other.[54]

The government, he proclaimed, could not condone the 'outrages committed by these natives' by virtue of 'the simple allegation that some of the white shepherds and some of the white settlers had voluntary intercourse with the native women'.[55]

Brown's point was clear: white men of the northern frontier could not be subjected to real or threatened violence just because black men didn't like their women entering into sexual relationships with white station hands, drovers and teamsters.

According to the Honourable Mr Brown, the interests of both the settlers and the Aboriginal people would be served by the establishment of a permanent police force in the region. That police force had soon arrived, and at its head was the town's first resident magistrate, Charles Foss. But if the arrival of the law was intended to bring about the end of 'voluntary intercourse' between white men and Aboriginal women, the evidence suggests that it affected matters differently.

In and around the Gascoyne, the situation of Aboriginal women now became even more precarious. With the arrival of Magistrate Foss, their men were being arrested wholesale and they found themselves and their children vulnerable in the face of this strident application of the law that sided overwhelmingly with the growing numbers of white landowners and itinerant workers. The impact on Aboriginal social and family life was stark; in 1900 a government inspector wrote with dismay of the sight that met him on the eastern outskirts of Carnarvon:

> The women, in almost every case, are less fitted for work than the men, and I hardly think make much, if anything, by prostitution ... There are a great many children about the natives' camps of all ages, amongst them being three or four half-castes. It is a great pity to see these children, black and half-caste, growing up amongst such surroundings. I fear they will become utterly useless and a curse to the country unless something is done to remove them and teach them to earn their own living.[56]

A decade after the inspector's report, and twenty years after the deaths of Redfern and Grundy, the relations that occurred between some white men and Aboriginal women were, while not approved of, still widely accepted, even in more genteel quarters. Such common knowledge were they that the average Carnarvon reader was expected to easily understand what was implied in this verse by a wag from Yanyeareddy Station, printed in Carnarvon's local newspaper in 1910:

> It's grand to be a publican
> In bright Carnarvon town
> When there's lots of 'lambs' to slaughter
> And a lot of thirst to drown
> It's grand to camp at Yankee Town
> And act the heavy swell
> And then go 'bardie'[57] hunting
> With a dusky little nell.[58]

But it wasn't a joking matter to everyone. Seasoned police sergeant Thomas Houlihan, who had been on the job in Carnarvon for nearly five years, dismally described to the Roth royal commission on 'the condition of the natives' in 1905 his frustration in trying to protect Aboriginal women:

> Another instance I know of is that of a man taking a native woman away by force. About twelve months ago a woman was taken away, and, on her man following and demanding her, the white man produced a revolver and

threatened to shoot the native. Information was laid and the white man was arrested and charged with pointing firearms. If the white man had not pointed the firearms we could not have arrested him or prevented his action in any way. Cases have come to my knowledge for years and years past where men have taken women around the country with them, and I have not power to prevent it, even when I have been complained to on the subject.[59]

Houlihan's evidence was in stark contrast to that of his own resident magistrate at the same hearing. When asked whether he knew of any cases of cruelty or ill-treatment of Aboriginal people in the Gascoyne, Charles Foss merely replied: 'I consider the natives in this district are well treated, and I speak from twenty-two years' experience.'[60]

A VEXED RELATIONSHIP

In January of 1885, a Geraldton newspaper reported, with palpable disappointment, that:

The three natives condemned to death for the murder of Grundy at the Gascoyne were sent to Rottnest by the last steamer. We have received no definite intelligence, but we understand that their sentences have been commuted to penal servitude for life.[61]

It was true enough. The fate of Nowaraba, Gnalbee and Geeler mirrored that of most of their countrymen convicted of capital crimes since the beginning of white settlement in Western Australia—Wangabiddy and Guerhilla being among the exceptions. Until the abolition of the death penalty in 1984, Aboriginal people made up around sixty percent of those sentenced to death, but four out of five subsequently had their sentences commuted to life imprisonment.[62]

So there would be no noose for the killers of Robert Grundy. Instead, the three men would disappear from history's view into the hellhole of Rottnest Island Prison, where dysentery, influenza, measles, hard labour and floggings awaited. They made up just one more consignment to the notorious island prison that would, over time, eventually house some 3,670 Aboriginal men. Three hundred and sixty-five of them would never leave.[63]

Along the length of the Gascoyne River, the investigations of Commissioner Fairbairn and the cases of Redfern and Grundy had shone a light on the vexed relationship between white settlers and the Aboriginal people who were forced to watch as their ancient connection to country slipped away. As the next thirty years would show, the arrival of Magistrate Foss, under the guise of protecting both the landowners and the Indigenous people, would only hasten the ascendency of one race and the destruction of another.

CHAPTER 2
THE LONESOME DEATH
OF THACKABIDDY

> From the earliest days of white settlement in Australia the unfortunate aborigines have been sadly misunderstood and ill-used. Many have been the wrongs inflicted upon them, and in some instances most shocking have been the cruelties to which they have been subjected, bringing to one's remembrance the terrible atrocities of African slavery. But nothing, I suppose, in the shape of human cruelty could be more revolting, whether perpetrated in Africa or any other part of the world, than the case of poor Thackabiddy, a savage of Minilya River, in Western Australia.
> —*The Christian Colonist* (Adelaide, SA), Friday 25 January 1889

WHITE MEN ON THE MINILYA

In the winter of 1880, George Joseph Gooch and his younger partner, Charles Thomas (Charlie) Wheelock, travelled nearly two hundred kilometres north from the fledgling port at the mouth of the Gascoyne River to set up a sheep station.

Ignoring warnings that the land beyond Minilya Pool was waterless, the pair set out for their destination taking with them a 'civilised native'[1] named Jacob, three horses, and enough flour to survive the journey.

When they reached the western banks of the Minilya River, they were fairly sure they were the first white men to have set foot there; to mark the occasion they carved their initials into a large tree.[2] Gooch then rode around six hundred kilometres south to Geraldton to stake their claim,[3] and within four months the pair was droving more than two thousand sheep from the Irwin River to the new property, which they called Wandagee.[4]

Twenty-two-year-old Wheelock, always cheerful and ready with a joke, was no stranger to long overland treks into the unknown country of the north. While still a teenager he had helped George Brockman to drive sheep from Mingenew to the Gascoyne, where Brockman subsequently turned forty thousand acres of bushland into Boolathana Station.[5] A year before hitching his fate to that of Gooch, Wheelock had driven another mob of sheep across several hundred kilometres of bush and plains to where Doorawarrah Station newly sprawled along both sides of the Gascoyne River.[6]

Gooch was only two years older than Wheelock, but he too carried the lessons of a life lived hard in a hard land. Growing up with his mother and stepfather in Greenough, Gooch would later recall:

> I was educated by an English gentleman named Edward Hayes Laurence, who was Resident Magistrate of Greenough. The tuition was given at night after a day which started with milking eight cows and heavy farm work all the hours of light.[7]

The boy was further schooled in Perth, but by the age of fourteen he was minding lambs at Mingenew. He returned briefly to school but, as he grew older, stories of expeditions to the far north began to fire his imagination. One day he told his stepfather that he was determined to try his luck there.[8]

'WE CARRIED OUR LIVES IN OUR HANDS'

For the two young pioneers, establishing Wandagee would require every ounce of their energy, courage and persistence. One of the biggest challenges was droving stock from the green pastures in the south to the drier, harsher foothold they had carved out for themselves in the northern wilderness. They were not alone: at the time there were many head of stock being driven north to newly established stations, and drovers had learned to travel in company and at times when there was likely to be less heat and more water. Even so, it was a treacherous undertaking across an unforgiving landscape.

But distance, heat and loneliness were not the only hardships—as Gooch would learn when, in 1881, he found himself camped one night by the Gascoyne River with a team of horses and several hundred sheep bound for Wandagee. Fifty years later, another surviving member of that expedition would recall the party's narrow escape from death:

> The Aborigines were treacherous and we carried our lives in our hands. When we laid down at night we were never sure whether we were going to see the sun rise next day.[9]

On this particular night the moon appeared intermittently through the clouds to create below an eerie bush pantomime of light and dark. According to Gooch's travelling companion:

> On June 21, 1881, about 400 niggers [sic] came down at night and, making a yard of themselves, drove off all Gooch's horses. The natives were not able to get the hobbled horses away quickly so they left these behind after going some distance. Gooch recovered these and then went on following the natives through the night. They drove two young fat horses 14 miles to a natural enclosure which was about a mile and a half long and about 12 feet wide and was called Shipka Pass. By the time Mr. George Gooch overtook them he found that they had speared the animals.[10]

Such events soon became folklore shared around the camp fires, shearing sheds and homestead kitchens of the men and women who made the first tentative inroads into the tribal lands of the Gascoyne and Murchison.

Although it was clear that the Aboriginal people were more interested in the stock than the men who drove them, it was because of experiences such as this that Gooch never travelled far without his pistol, and slept with it under his makeshift pillow every night. It was a sound practice. Less than a year after his own escape Gooch found himself burying the murdered Charlie Brackell in the bush in 1882. 'I read the burial service over him but when burying the poor chap, his head nearly fell off in my hands,' he would later recall.[11]

The murder had occurred in the dead of night only a few kilometres from Gooch and Wheelock's newly established station. Brackell had been employed there as a cook for the lambing season. An Aboriginal man called Nanacaroo and his wife were also helping out at the station, their camp fire glowing just a few hundred metres from where Brackell was removing his boots before lying down to sleep by his fire. It was a cool night and the cook left his shirt, trousers and socks on as he folded his jacket into a rough but serviceable pillow. By his side rested a pistol, a rifle and a knife. As he drifted into what would be his final sleep, he had probably forgotten the angry words he'd had with Nanacaroo earlier that day. 'If you lose a lamb again,' he'd told the Aboriginal man, 'I'll shoot you.'[12]

By his own fire, Nanacaroo was still awake, the echoes of the white man's threat running through his head. Some time before midnight, when Brackell was asleep, Nanacaroo crept up and struck him twice in the neck with an axe. Then he and his wife slipped away into the moonlit bush.

Nanacaroo was soon captured by Gooch and Wheelock—who wrote to Commissioner Fairbairn reporting that they had shot the Aboriginal man during their attempt to arrest him—and, following a brief trial, was hanged at Rottnest on a wintry Friday in July 1883.[13] An influenza epidemic was sweeping through the prison at the time, and only those few prisoners who were not sick or dying witnessed his final moments.[14]

The murder of Brackell and the ongoing clashes between drovers and Aboriginal people of the Gascoyne–Murchison left a residue of apprehension and mistrust that lay heavily on the minds of the new settlers along the Minilya River. It was in this setting that the tragedy of Thackabiddy would unfold.

'THERE IS NOTHING UNUSUAL IN ESCORTING A NATIVE CHAINED ROUND THE NECK'

One day in the autumn of the year after Brackell met his violent death, evening was settling over Gooch and Wheelock's property on the Minilya River. Resting after another hard day's work, Gooch was roused by the news that there might be trouble brewing not far from the homestead where a shepherd called Charles (Charlie) Clifford was minding a flock of sheep. One of the station workers, Keane, had spotted a local Aboriginal man, Thackabiddy—long suspected of stealing stock—nearby. Gooch dressed hurriedly and rode off with Keane to investigate.

This was a chance for which Gooch had long been waiting. If the man seen near the sheep really was Thackabiddy, Gooch was keen to capture him as soon as possible. He was convinced that the local Aboriginal people were becoming used to living off his sheep, and he was tired of the continual theft. He was also certain that Thackabiddy was the ringleader.

The sheep were less than two kilometres away from the homestead and it wasn't long before Gooch and Keane came across Thackabiddy, armed with a spear, a woomera and several boomerangs, a few hundred metres from the flock. Gooch handed a revolver to Keane and told him to watch the suspect while he went to check the sheep. The landowner hadn't gone far when he heard a desperate shout and three gunshots rend the evening stillness.

Riding back to where he had left the two men, the station-owner found himself confronted by a dazed Thackabiddy, still clutching his weapons but now bleeding from bullet wounds to the neck, chin and arm. Keane, still mounted on his horse, was pointing his revolver at the Aboriginal man standing before him. According to Keane, he had been attempting to disarm his captive when Thackabiddy made several thrusts at him with the spear, the point passing through his shirt, under the left arm.[15] 'He was going to throw it at me!' Keane exclaimed.

Although wounded, outnumbered and outgunned, Thackabiddy made no attempt to flee. His eyes darted from one man to the other, then he made his decision to stay and fight. As a boomerang flew by his head, Gooch yelled at Thackabiddy to drop his spear, but the Aboriginal man simply reached quickly for another weapon. The station-owner leapt to the ground, closing fast on Thackabiddy and only just avoiding being struck by the woomera. Before he could raise his spear again, Gooch had overpowered him and the alleged sheep stealer was quickly bound and led back to Wandagee Station.

When dawn arrived, Gooch saddled two horses for himself and Clifford in readiness for the ride south to Carnarvon, where they intended to hand Thackabiddy over to the police. With the memory of Brackell still fresh in their minds they were taking no chances, and the prisoner was chained by the neck to the shepherd's horse. The group travelled like this for three days and, according to the two white men, their prisoner showed no discomfort or weakness from his wounds as he walked steadily behind them.

By the fourth day the trio had travelled some 160 kilometres when, at around noon, two riders also heading southwards caught up with them on the track. They were Richard Gale J.P., a prominent sheep farmer from the South-West, and his sixteen-year-old travelling companion Ted Roach. Gale and Roach would later testify that Thackabiddy seemed to be suffering no distress at that time. Gooch and Clifford told them that their prisoner was eating his meals without complaint and having no problem keeping up with the horses. He had caused no trouble, they said, only once picking up a branch of a tree which was quickly wrested from him by Clifford. Even so, they added, it was best to watch him closely.

After the two parties had shared a midday meal, Gooch and Gale decided to ride on ahead of the others, leaving Thackabiddy with Clifford and Roach. Later, young Roach wandered off to look for some of the horses that had strayed from the camp while the men were resting. He had been gone for about thirty minutes when he suddenly heard Clifford calling his name in panic.

The boy rushed back to the camp site where he found the two men struggling on the ground, Thackabiddy on top and still chained to a horse. He saw too that the Aboriginal man had an iron stirrup in his hand. Roach lifted his revolver and fired it into the air above the fighting men, but Thackabiddy had the better of the shepherd and barely paused in his desperate attempt to overcome his captor. The teenager lifted the gun again and, this time aiming for the prisoner's leg from about eight metres away, fired once more. The bullet struck Thackabiddy in the ankle and he clutched his foot in agony while Clifford, seizing the opportunity to quickly regain his feet, cried out, 'He knocked me off my horse! He tried to do me!'

It was now clear that Thackabiddy could no longer walk, and Carnarvon was still some sixty kilometres away. The deeply shaken Clifford was in a quandary, but he was also in no mood for niceties. He decided to take matters into his own hands and, attaching the prisoner's chain to his horse, dragged the wounded man by his neck through the scrub for more than a kilometre. Thackabiddy somehow got a hand on the chain and fought desperately, sometimes on his back, at other times on his stomach or side, to keep from choking.

Clifford stopped and tied the naked and bloodied man's arms behind his back and chained him to a tree. Roach offered to ride ahead to Carnarvon to fetch the police but Clifford, obviously shaken by his near miss, said he didn't feel safe spending time alone with Thackabiddy. Instead, he passed his revolver to the teenage boy and told him to go and find the horses, which had wandered away while Thackabiddy was being secured to the tree, and then wait with the prisoner until he returned. Then he rode off through a gently falling rain towards the Gascoyne port settlement.

Roach set off to look for the horses. As he glanced back he could see the prisoner slumped against the tree, unable to stand upright because the chain was too short. The boy was gone all night in search of the horses, and in the morning returned to the tree where he found Thackabiddy in the same position as he had left him the day before. Nervously he threw the shackled man a piece of damper but, although he could pick the food up, the wounded man's arms, tightly pinioned at the elbows, could not bring it to his mouth. Unsure of what to do next, Roach then galloped away towards the township of Carnarvon. There was a chill in the air and more rain on the horizon.

It would be another full day before Constable William (Bill) Turner of the Carnarvon police arrived in the area. With him were Clifford and a group of other men. The small contingent arrived at nightfall and waited until morning to locate the scene. Turner easily found where the helpless man had been dragged through the bush and, following the trail through the dust, it wasn't long before he came across the lifeless body of Thackabiddy. The dead man was still slumped against the tree where he had been chained for two days.

Turner couldn't help but notice that Thackabiddy had been dragged past many trees before Clifford had brought his horse to a standstill. The officer also found a large stick by the track, the end of it clotted with blood, sand and hair. By the dead man's body lay two pieces of untouched damper.

The policeman unchained the corpse from the tree. Then, as he would later recall, 'We carried the body into Carnarvon slung on horseback, and a considerable quantity of blood flowed out of the native's mouth on the way.'[16]

Statements were made to Magistrate Foss in Carnarvon, and an inquest was duly called into the fate of Thackabiddy. While there was no formal post-mortem, Constable Turner expressed little doubt about the cause of death. He pointed the blame squarely at the bullet fired by Keane, which had travelled downwards into the victim's neck leaving a hole about the size of man's little finger. As to how the events that followed the shooting might have contributed to the wounded man's death, Turner was dismissive:

> I don't attribute it [Thackabiddy's death] to the prisoner's treatment. There is nothing unusual in escorting a native chained round the neck to a horse: that is how the police escort them.[17]

It would be another month before Charlie Clifford was arrested for manslaughter for his role in Thackabiddy's demise. As one of the few times a white man faced the courts over the death of an Aboriginal person on the Gascoyne–Murchison frontier, the settlers and pastoralists on the long river watched the trial with great interest.

Clifford was charged with manslaughter before Magistrate Foss at Carnarvon, and the trial was referred to the Geraldton quarter sessions.

Local magistrate George Eliot quickly remitted the case to Perth, however, 'in consequence of the serious nature of the charge'.[18]

Legal proceedings finally commenced in the Western Australian Supreme Court in Perth on 10 January 1884, some eight months after the bloody events had taken place.

THE STAGE IS SET

Appearing for the Crown was the dignified but sometimes haughty[19] Attorney-General Alfred Peach Hensman. Stephen Henry Parker appeared for the defence.

If posthumous justice was to be served, then Thackabiddy could have had few better advocates than the liberal-minded Hensman. Equipped with a dry sense of humour, he was a keen supporter of social reform and an early advocate for women's rights to vote and to access higher education.[20] Keenly intelligent, Hensman would have been well aware of the larger issues at stake as he took the floor to prosecute the case of manslaughter against Clifford. He would need every ounce of his skill if he was to have the jury return a verdict of guilty.

His adversary for the defence was an equally formidable legal intellect, 'a dashing young reformer, orator and horseman'[21] who worked tirelessly for the wresting of responsible government from England to the colony. Parker would go on to serve as Chief Justice of the Supreme Court of Western Australia, and was said to have possessed 'the gift of sifting the essential points of a case and explaining them in the clearest language'.[22] Both men were respected stalwarts of the colony's legal establishment but, on this day, only one would walk from the court a victor.

Arbitrating between them was the handsome, dignified and moderate Chief Justice Edward Stone, elder brother of Frank Mends Stone who had served as Wangabiddy's defence counsel the previous year. Well known and popular in the Perth settlement for his common sense and fairness, Chief Justice Stone had once told a defendant, 'You may be poor, but you are still entitled to justice.'[23]

So the scene was set and these illustrious actors took the stage. Between them they would seek to establish who was responsible for the lonesome death of a little-known Aboriginal man in the heart of his homeland on the northern frontier.

Hensman began by outlining the events that took place from the shooting of Thackabiddy to the discovery of his body chained to a tree. Then he addressed the jury:

> The charge against the prisoner is that of manslaughter, and what is alleged against him is this: that by his gross (I would not call it negligence), by his brutal treatment of this native, Clifford contributed towards his death. It is not necessary for the prosecution to prove that it was the act of the prisoner alone that caused his death. If the prisoner and others contributed to the man's death, and the prisoner took his share in it, he was equally guilty. Nor is it necessary that his death should have been entirely caused by the prisoner; if his death was accelerated by even a short time by the conduct of the prisoner, the prisoner would be equally guilty of manslaughter.[24]

Then, one by one, each of the witnesses took their place on the stand, swore the oath and recounted the events as they recalled them.

When key witness Ted Roach stood and faced the courtroom, the evidence he gave differed slightly from that he had given earlier to the inquest held by Magistrate Foss. As he explained to the court:

> My story to-day and the story I told before the magistrate at Carnarvon only varies in one particular. I there said that Clifford was leading his horse, and not riding it, while the native was being dragged along. I said so because Clifford asked me to do so.[25]

Parker, sensing the damage this remark could do to his client's case, was quick to cross-examine Roach and did so for more than an hour. It was clear that the teenager's current account was materially different from his earlier version of events, and thus important for Parker to cast doubt on its veracity. The defending counsel would not have appreciated Roach's own assertion that there was another reason for the changes to his story: 'The police went with me through the depositions at Geraldton,' the boy explained, 'and made some suggestions to me as to the evidence.'[26]

If the chief justice was concerned at these imputations of duress by the police, he didn't show it. Instead, he invited Parker to begin his case for the defence.

'A CONSIDERABLE AMOUNT OF SELF-RESTRAINT'

The defending counsel took to his feet and spoke calmly and clearly:

> Before addressing the jury, I should like to place Dr Scott in the witness box. That gentleman has been good enough to remain in court, at considerable inconvenience to himself, to listen to the evidence, so as to be able to pronounce an opinion as to the probable cause of death.[27]

At this, prominent Perth surgeon Dr Edward Scott approached the witness box and turned to face the court. While the medical man had not been present when the events in question unfolded, nor been privy to the examination of the body that followed, he had been listening attentively to the evidence presented in court. Now he gave his professional opinion:

> I should say—of course, I can only surmise—but I should suppose death was caused by secondary haemorrhage, the result of injuries previously received in the track of the ball which penetrated the neck. I cannot say that the dragging had any material effect in producing death; it certainly was not the immediate cause, otherwise the haemorrhage would have produced more immediate results.[28]

Surely, cross-examined the attorney-general, such an injury could only have been aggravated by Thackabiddy's subsequent treatment? The doctor replied coolly:

> I should say that a person suffering from a gunshot wound should be kept as quiet as possible. Dragging him along the ground for about a mile, with a chain round his neck, would not accelerate his recovery, nor could it be regarded as judicious treatment. It is not the course of treatment I myself should recommend. The probability is that it may have done him some harm.[29]

Hensman could scarcely disguise his contempt for the apparent attempt at humour with which Scott had delivered his conclusion.

When Parker resumed the floor, he sought to turn Hensman's contempt to his own advantage, addressing the court:

> The attorney-general seems to ridicule the idea of Dr Scott, a professional man, being able to form an opinion as to what caused this native's death, although the doctor has heard all the evidence. And yet the learned counsel would ask the jury, in the absence of any medical testimony to that effect, to come to the conclusion that death had resulted from the treatment which the man had received at the hands of the defendant. If a medical man is not in a position to form an opinion upon the evidence, is it not gross presumption on the part of the Crown to ask a body of non-professional men[30] to form an opinion, and to say that it was the prisoner who caused the native's death?[31]

The real culprit, asserted Parker, was the man who had fired the shot into Thackabiddy's neck. Then he proceeded to pour scorn on the notion that a few hours without food, shelter or clothing might have contributed to an Aboriginal man's death. Lest Hensman or the court miss his point, Parker drove it home with heavy sarcasm:

> The learned counsel is probably not aware that this would be no hardship whatever in the case of a Gascoyne native. The learned counsel is perhaps unaware that these natives seldom or ever indulge in such superfluities as clothing, and that they certainly would not consider themselves the objects of much sympathy, outside of Exeter Hall, if they did not get their meals regularly.

As for Clifford's dragging of the wounded and helpless Thackabiddy for more than a kilometre through the scrub, the defence lawyer merely asked the jury to accept that the shepherd, in a difficult predicament, had done 'what he thought was best to be done under the circumstances—conveyed him where he could be secured in safety, and then [ridden] in for the police'.

Warming to his theme, Parker even went so far as to praise the virtue of the man in the dock:

> It appears to me that, under all the circumstances, Mr Clifford exercised a considerable amount of self-restraint. He certainly was more humanely disposed than either Keane who shot the native in the neck, or Roach who shot him in the ankle.

Surely, concluded the defence counsel, in no other of Her Majesty's dominions could such a man be arraigned for manslaughter without a shred of evidence, medical or otherwise, to suggest his guilt. He was sure that the jury would share his view.

'DONE TO DEATH'

Now it only remained for the attorney-general to sum up for the prosecution. Hensman gazed with his usual air of disdain around the courtroom. He began by singling out Parker's attempts at humour throughout the trial.

> The prisoner's counsel has from time to time in the course of the trial raised a laugh by treating the case as if there was something rather funny

> and comical about it. For my own part, I can say I do not regard it in any such light. I think it is a very serious case and I am not ashamed to say so.[32]

Next he turned to the jury.

> Whatever you might think of it, no-one could doubt that this native was, so to speak, done to death, after he was arrested at the Minilya [River]. No-one could possibly entertain any doubt that his death was caused by human agency, and that he was treated with a considerable degree of brutality.[33]

He paused, allowing his words to punctuate the silence that had descended on the courtroom.

Hensman was no fool. He knew that, once again, it was the northern frontier that was on trial as much as the hapless Clifford. Within the past two years alone two Aboriginal men had been executed for the murders of white men, and several others were languishing in prisons for the same reason. The attorney-general would have been well aware that from Geraldton to Minilya, eager settlers and pastoralists would be watching to see how the actions of one of their own would be judged in the colony's highest court. He now broached the subject delicately but openly.

> I am not here to attempt to say it was not right for the settlers to protect their flocks, by all reasonable measures, from natives who may wish to kill or to steal them, but this I do say: that, in doing so, it was their duty, and the duty of those who like the prisoner were called to assist them, to carry out their task in a humane manner.

Hensman reminded the court that there had been no warrant out for Thackabiddy's arrest, nor had he been apprehended in the actual commission of a crime. 'As a matter of fact,' he added, 'Mr Gooch himself was acting illegally in arresting him.'

Few comments could have done more to incite an angry reaction from the northern frontier. Here, yet again, was another well-heeled city-dweller applying arcane legalism to a population that feared for its life and property far from the safety of the comfortable southern suburbs.

The attorney-general would have been sensible to this but it was not in his nature to back away from a fight. He looked across at the faces of the twelve white men sitting in judgment of Clifford. If he was to have any chance of winning the day, he knew he would have to move the discussion from the abstract to the personal. He looked at the men before him, and asked them pointedly and gently, 'Can any of you say upon your conscience that this native was treated in a humane manner?'

He paused. Twelve sets of eyes gazed back at him.

'Can you say that he was not treated in a most brutal manner, was not in fact killed by someone or other in the course of those few days of which we have had the history?'

Silence filled the warm summer air and eddied awkwardly around the courtroom.

And so the prosecutor made his final case: no-one could say for certain what had actually led to Thackabiddy's death, but surely no-one could argue that the shooting, the long trek, the chain around his neck and the dragging of his wounded body through the bush had not contributed to it. As for the doctor's opinion, the attorney-general was derisive: 'Dr Scott's evidence incriminates the prisoner as much as it seeks to exonerate him,' he claimed.

In Hensman's eyes, the roles of other people and other factors in the Aboriginal man's death were immaterial to the guilt of Clifford. 'The fact of others having contributed to his death, if the prisoner also contributed to it, does not absolve him from responsibility,' the lawman asserted. Then he took his seat and waited for the judge to give final instructions to the jury.

His Honour outlined the legal principles that must guide the jury's deliberations and the nature of the evidence that had been presented to the court. Then he concluded:

> Whatever your verdict might be, I am sure you will not allow your feelings to be prejudiced because the subject of this inquiry was a native, nor, on the other hand, would you allow your minds to be warped by the fact that he was most brutally ill-treated. If you are able to come to the conclusion that this brutal treatment accelerated his death, if you think it may have been possible the native would have lived longer, although for only half an hour, but for this brutal treatment, you must find the prisoner guilty. But if you thought the evidence was not sufficiently strong to convince you that it did contribute to his death, then you will give the prisoner the benefit of any doubt you might have in your minds on that point.[34]

The jury then adjourned to consider their verdict. It didn't take long. After ten minutes the twelve men returned to their places in the courtroom. The foreman stood and, in answer to the judge's fateful question, answered, 'We find the prisoner not guilty.'

Clifford was a free man but, before discharging him, Justice Stone offered him one last piece of advice:

> Although I agreed with the verdict of the jury, Mr Clifford, I deem it my duty to caution you against pursuing the same line of conduct again, otherwise you might find yourself in a very different position.

IN THE SHADOWS OF GHOSTS

The verdict sped northwards along the telegraph lines and was received with knowing nods in the hotel bars, dining rooms and camp sites along both sides of the Gascoyne River. Settlers on Western Australia's northern frontier who had followed with interest the trials of Wangabiddy, Nanacaroo and Clifford could now see for themselves what their counterparts in the colonies of the east coast had long proclaimed: that the law, deftly applied, was a useful tool in the management of the Aboriginal people.[35]

Wholesale arrests combined with the threat of legally sanctioned death proved a potent pacifying force: from the beginning of the Western Australian colony in 1829 until the abolition of capital punishment some 150 years later, Aboriginal people would come to account for six out of every ten prisoners condemned to death in the colony. While only twenty percent of those convicted were actually executed, the reasons were less to do with mercy than with the fact that commutation was generally applied in cases of murder between Aboriginal people rather than of settlers.[36]

In the fifty years leading up to the death of Thackabiddy, a total of twenty-nine Western Australian settlers had been tried for offences against Aboriginal people. Of these, twenty had been found guilty and just one, Richard Bibbey, had been executed—for the murder of an Aboriginal man called Billamarra at Upper Irwin in 1859.[37] In the same period, twenty-five Aboriginal people had been executed for the murders of white settlers. Few accusations made against alleged white offenders made it beyond local magisterial investigation.[38]

However, while Western Australia's northern pioneers may have been satisfied, even gleeful, at the outcome of the trial of Clifford, the verdict drew responses of anger and disgust from the southern public and from newspapers nationwide. The Melbourne *Age* observed acerbically:

The fact is, that a man who ill-uses or kills 'niggers' [sic] has no more chance of being brought to justice in Western Australia or North Queensland than a thief would have of being convicted by a jury recruited from Little Bourke Street.[39]

In Brisbane, one newspaper cautioned that:

when we are disposed, as we sometimes are, to plume ourselves on possessing more humanity and philanthropy than other races, it will be well to remember the cruel doing to death of this miserable black fellow in an English colony, and of the issue of the judicial proceedings which arose from the case.[40]

A letter-writer to a Fremantle newspaper proclaimed with dismay:

Refined cold-blooded cruelty to blacks shall not meet with our disapprobation. We have taken away their country, we shall take their lives also if they stand in our way.[41]

Not everyone outside the Gascoyne shared these views, however. Several settlers of other wild country areas—where skirmishes with Aboriginal people were more common than they were in the major settlements—wrote letters supporting the finding of the jury. One Geraldton commentator pointedly reminded the reading public that:

It is a very simple matter for individuals to sit down in their comfortable offices and pen high flown articles about the wrongs the natives experience at the hands of the settlers, without any practical knowledge or accurate information as to facts. A little personal experience would, however, convince them that in no part of the world are the aboriginal inhabitants of a country better treated than they are in this colony by the settlers.[42]

In 1884, it seemed that there would remain a world of misunderstanding between those who lived on the northern frontier and those who critiqued it from afar. It was clear, however, that the cases of Redfern, Grundy and Thackabiddy had taught the northern settlers a valuable lesson. The arrival of a resident magistrate in Carnarvon in 1882, combined with the capacity of established pastoralists to act with quasi-legal authority, gave to the white settlers of the Gascoyne the necessary tools by which the subjugation of the Aboriginal people could now be meted out with all the power and apparent objectivity of the law.

The ghosts of the dead men would cast long shadows over the fate of the tribes of the long river for decades to come. And the man who stood in those shadows, wielding justice like a weapon, was Magistrate Charles Denroche Vaughan Foss.

CHAPTER 3
A BUSH BEATING

> Some years ago, when Parson Gribble wrote his blood curdling pamphlet, entitled 'Dark Deeds in a Sunny Land,' he was ferociously denounced as a liar of the first water. His booklet principally referred to the Carnarvon district, and that what he alleged was in all probability true and that matters are not in any way better today is shown by what follows. Attached hereto are the depositions taken in a case heard before the Carnarvon Bench, and forwarded to the SUNDAY TIMES by our Carnarvon correspondent. We recommend our readers to peruse this as an example of the shocking barbarities and immoralities practised in the Black North.
> —*The West Australian Sunday Times* (Perth, WA), Sunday 12 February 1899

'OUR ENERGETIC ITINERANT, MR FOSS'

When Charles Foss had arrived at the mouth of the Gascoyne River in 1882, relations between the northern settlers and the local Aboriginal people had reached crisis point. Rumours of the stealing of stock, the occasional murder of shepherds and harsh retribution by squatters circulated throughout the length and breadth of the Western Australian colony.

The magistrate's arrival was met with relief and high expectations by those on the frontier, a sentiment summed up by one Geraldton newspaper, which supported the need for 'vigorous steps to put a stop to the ever recurring audacity of aboriginal depredators'.[1] Hopes were high that the lawman's appointment would end the years of escalating violence, the fault for which was laid squarely at the feet of the local tribespeople:

> Mr Foss, in command of thirteen constables will shortly be in the heart of the native-harassed districts, and will doubtless have the satisfaction of sentencing many of the sable raiders.[2]

Nothing less, declared the editor of Geraldton's *Victorian Express*, was needed for the 'pacification' of these 'semi-savage pilferers'.[3]

Foss himself would have been in no doubt as to the expectations of him in his new role, and briskly rose to the task. He quickly established himself in the fledgling port, and from there set off to administer justice across the vast expanses of the northern interior. He proved himself a tough and dogged operator in an enterprise that was not without risks. He travelled vast distances with his escort of five itinerant constables, consisting of two white men experienced with the bush and three Aboriginal assistants. In addition to this mobile entourage, also under his command were four policemen stationed at Port Gascoyne (as Carnarvon was still officially known) and four more at Mount Wittenoom, half of each of these teams comprising Aboriginal constables.

While Foss showed himself to be more than equal to the task of 'pacification', his enthusiastic and rigorous efforts soon struck their first hurdle. Due to an administrative error in describing him as a justice of the peace rather than an itinerant stipendiary magistrate, his first convictions were deemed to exceed his authority. In addition, his first act of imprisonment—the sentencing of an Aboriginal man called Bungegoora to three years' hard labour for sheep stealing—was overturned by the colony's executive council on the basis that it was illegally excessive with respect to the crime committed. Indeed, given the prisoner's health, it was tantamount to a death sentence.

Undeterred, Foss continued his zealous reign, and by the end of his first year the new magistrate had sentenced sixty-three offenders, forty-three of whom were sent several hundred kilometres south to Rottnest Island Prison, offshore from Fremantle. The Fremantle *Herald* noted of one of the first arrivals of prisoners from the Gascoyne:

> They were all tried by the new Itinerant Magistrate, Mr. C.V. [sic] Foss. They were taken over to Rottnest on Saturday morning. As a rule they were a miserable looking lot of men, and seemed totally averse or unaccustomed to any sort of covering whatever.[4]

Chief Justice Henry Wrensfordsley was unimpressed by the summary justice meted out by the Gascoyne magistrate and made several attempts to rein in the roving lawman's behaviour. For its part, the colony's executive council took a more pragmatic approach, simply making Foss's illegitimate convictions legal by passing ex post facto legislation.[5] The Natives Convictions Validity Bill of 1883 was designed as a retrospective means of legalising unlawfully excessive sentences already passed relating to the convictions of Aboriginal people in the Gascoyne–Murchison.[6] It was, admitted the colonial secretary in parliament, quite specifically intended to 'affirm the convictions made by Mr Foss at the Gascoyne'.[7]

Wrensfordsley remained dissatisfied, but it was to no avail. His concerns about the Gascoyne magistrate's zeal were brushed aside by Sir John Bramston at the colonial office in England, who asserted:

> If this process will teach the natives to leave the sheep alone I see no objection to it—it is better than the collision between white and black that will otherwise be inevitable.[8]

Bramston's colleague Sir Robert Herbert agreed:

> Having regard to the wretched condition of these natives and the readiness of the northern settlers to shoot them as the easiest mode of administering justice, no practical hardship has resulted from this error.[9]

In this way the colonial office accepted Foss's transgressions as the lesser of two evils that might befall the Aboriginal people of the northern frontier.

The Gascoyne's travelling magistrate needed no further encouragement. The following year, eighty-two of the 113 Aboriginal people from across Western Australia who were sent to Rottnest Island Prison were from the Gascoyne–Murchison.[10]

Geraldton's *Victorian Express* could not help but express its satisfaction that the settlers' man had prevailed over the do-gooders of the south:

> The steamer takes down forty native prisoners for Rottnest, sentenced by our energetic itinerant, Mr. Foss, to various terms of imprisonment for thieving and settler-harassing. Probably Mr. F. will get a gentle hint from Perth, directly, to 'go slow'—for Rottnest isn't made of India-rubber, and in this respect is unlike a lawyer's conscience, which, they say, will stretch a mile, before it tears an inch.[11]

Just one year into his job, Foss himself seemed to believe that his vigorous sentencing regime was a temporary measure that would quickly result in a steep decline in Aboriginal arrests. Soon after his arrival he reported optimistically that there was no need to consider employing prisoners in the region, since:

> the expense of supervision would be very great, and the natives could only be worked in chains. I do not think that for the future very many natives will be convicted from this district, as they are now aware that if they commit crimes they will be punished.[12]

CROSSING A LINE IN THE SAND

For the first seven years of his appointment, Magistrate Foss maintained his relentless and exhausting regime of expeditionary justice. Then, in July 1889, the energetic lawman came face to face with the precarious and highly charged nature of the position he held in the relationship between the traditional owners of the land and those who had usurped it.

That year was particularly noteworthy for the heavy rains that swept the district. Many creeks and rivers were flowing, and boggy roads made overland travel slow. As the itinerant magistrate followed his circuit inland he found twenty Aboriginal men in the lock-up at The Junction, on the upper reaches of the Gascoyne River. Some still bore wounds from the resistance they had put up when local constables Walker and Bird had arrested them for sheep stealing.[13] Foss found the group guilty and sentenced them to two years' imprisonment at Rottnest Island Prison.[14]

This was not an unusual outcome for groups of Aboriginal people who came before Magistrate Foss and, despite frequent queries raised by successive Western Australian attorneys-general about the nature of evidence used to convict such offenders en masse, little was done to curb the practice.[15] In 1887 Attorney-General Charles Nicholas Warton had been so concerned by the prevalence of group sentencing that he had issued a reminder that:

> when two or more prisoners are before a magistrate each should be separately asked if he pleads guilty or not guilty and each prisoner's words in answer should be taken down. Prisoners (in the plural) can't make an admission.[16]

Warton's reminder was prompted in part by the fact that, two years earlier, the colony's governor had been forced to remit the sentences of some fifty Aboriginal people whose convictions—many made by Foss—had led to serious overcrowding of the prison on Rottnest Island. Even so, Foss and his fellow frontier magistrates were generally given considerable leeway in matters relating to the charging and punishing of Aboriginal people.[17]

Having dealt with the sheep-stealing allegations at The Junction, Foss now proceeded to Mount Gould, where Scottish brothers Arthur and Gordon Shaw and their foreman Thomas Mead were accused of a range of offences against Aboriginal people on the Shaws' pastoral property, Erivella. Stories of cruelty on the station had first reached Geraldton police some months earlier, through a white worker on the property. They included allegations of setting dogs onto an Aboriginal woman and of beating to death an Aboriginal man, among other misdeeds. Constables Smith and Houlihan from the Carnarvon station investigated, and local justice of the peace Everard Firebrace Darlot, owner of Beringarra Station, was asked to take up the case. Darlot declined, however, explaining that:

> the accused were [his] neighbours, and were very unpopular, and therefore, if he found them guilty on the prima facie charge, it would be put down to ill feeling, whereas if he acquitted them, a section of the public would accuse him of sympathy with the offenders.[18]

It was more likely that the experienced Darlot, known for his own zealous sentencing of Aboriginal people,[19] was concerned about how the arrest of fellow pastoralists would look to his white countrymen. In any case, as a result, Foss was ordered to travel from Carnarvon to Erivella Station to investigate the matter.

The allegations against the men were as serious as they were numerous, and Foss dealt with them decisively. He began with the less grave of the crimes. Arthur Miller Shaw and his foreman Thomas Mead were charged with assaulting an Aboriginal man named Youngyu, for which they were each fined three pounds and costs. Arthur Shaw was also charged with assaulting an Aboriginal woman named Jenny, for which he was fined a further five pounds and costs, and Mead was fined an additional five pounds and costs for assaulting an Aboriginal woman named Judy. Gordon Douglas Shaw was found guilty of assaulting an Aboriginal man named Jenuethenbean, for which he was fined three pounds and costs.

Now Foss turned his attention to the most serious of the charges. The lawman wrote his deposition as follows:

> [Aboriginal man] Bungurdie had been in the service of the Shaw Bros, and had run away, but when not far away from the station he picked up 230 sheep which were going astray. He took them in. On arriving at the station with them Gordon Shaw placed handcuffs upon him and fastened him to a post. He was afterwards kicked and beaten by Arthur Shaw[20] while in that position. He was left there all night without food or fire. On the following morning he was removed from the shed to the store and during the ensuing night died there.[21]

Foss charged the three men with murder: the brothers Shaw with the killing of Bungurdie, and Thomas Mead with the death of another Aboriginal man, Coonthenmungajarra, in another incident on the property. The prisoners were then committed for trial in Perth.[22]

Whether he knew it or not, Magistrate Foss had just crossed an invisible line in the sand: for the first time, white landowners were in the dock for the treatment of their Aboriginal workers.

'BE VERY CAREFUL HOW YOU CONDUCT YOURSELF WITH REGARD TO THE NATIVES'

The trial of the Shaw brothers, which began in October, was watched closely by pastoralists throughout the colony. For many it must have felt as if the power and protections offered by the law, until then squarely in their favour, were now in the balance.

The early signs were ominous. On the face of it there seemed little doubt that Bungurdie had been 'very roughly, if not brutally used', as one newspaper reported.[23] Story after story from some nine witnesses, Aboriginal and white, alleged a litany of abuse and callousness. And yet it was not enough to secure a conviction.

On the second day of the trial, despite the damning evidence of witnesses already heard, Attorney-General Charles Warton, acting for the prosecution, made the surprise announcement that:

> after carefully considering the evidence which had been taken from the witnesses for the Crown the previous day, he had come to the conclusion that the weight of evidence was insufficient to convict the prisoners.[24]

The prosecutor concluded: 'I intend, therefore, with the leave of Your Honour, to withdraw the case.'[25]

The murder trial of the Shaws' foreman, Mead, had been held over until after the appearance of the brothers themselves. Along with the Shaws' release, Attorney-General Warton also sought the release, without trial, of the foreman, arguing that, since the witnesses were largely the same, the outcome would be similar.[26] To both requests, Acting Chief Justice Septimus Burt, albeit somewhat reluctantly, acceded. But he was far from happy. As he dismissed the jury, the judge went as far as he could within the technical finding of not guilty to highlight the culpability of at least one of the brothers:

> As for you, Arthur Shaw, I cannot allow you to quit that box without impressing upon you that you must take more care in your conduct towards the aboriginal races amongst which you are placed ... I cannot conceive how any person with the spirit of a man could be guilty of such conduct as that with which you have been charged. I hope, and I am entitled to say it, the jury having acquitted you, that you are not guilty of this offence ... I am now only endeavouring to impress upon you, and through you upon the other settlers in this colony, to be very careful how you conduct yourself with regard to the natives.[27]

The newspapers and the general public were largely sympathetic to the plight of the 'two respectable looking young men'[28] who had been put through such anxiety and hardship for a case that was ultimately dismissed. Only Geraldton's *Victorian Express* saw fit to ask some questions about the attorney-general's management of the case:

> The Attorney General in his opening said there were two counts on which the prisoner [the first of the Shaw brothers] was charged, murder and manslaughter. And yet, though the evidence went strongly to show that one at least of the prisoners would be declared to come under the latter of these heads, the learned attorney took the decision out of the hands of the jury and decided the case himself.[29]

If Foss had entered the region acutely aware of the hopes invested in him by the settler population, he could have been in little doubt about the hostile reaction his actions at Mount Gould had provoked. At a public meeting in Carnarvon shortly after the aborted trial of the Shaw brothers, the meeting's foreman Gilbert Rotton, erstwhile grazier, horseracer and town councillor, proposed a motion that was no doubt pointedly directed at the magistrate responsible for the arrests:

> That in connection with the case recently preferred against the Shaw Brothers, and Thomas Mead, wherein they were charged at the Supreme Court of the murder of an aboriginal native, this meeting tenders to whom its sincere sympathy in the unwarrantable manner in which they have been dealt with, the ruinous expense they have been put to, and in the degrading indignity that has been thrust upon them, without justifiable cause.[30]

While some of the men left the room as the vote was taken, perhaps out of tacit support for Foss, the resolution was carried. The magistrate might well have felt that he was now held, by at least some of the landowners, to be on notice.

Ten years would pass before Magistrate Foss would once again find himself tested by allegations of assault by a station-owner of an Aboriginal worker.

A CASE OF 'BLACKBIRDING'

Few Western Australian settlers were known to be tougher or more resilient in the face of hardship than George Julius Brockman. Born in 1850 in Guildford, around fifteen kilometres north-east of Perth on the Swan River, Brockman was one of seven brothers, and was only sixteen when he loaded all his worldly possessions onto his horse and rode southwards to make his fortune. In the years that followed he lived and worked in various parts of the colony, proving himself a hard worker and a formidable adventurer. He was eventually lured northwards by the promise of a new pearling industry in Shark Bay. When that didn't work out he continued up the coast until he arrived in the township of Roebourne, in 1875. It was just south of here that same year that one of the defining events of the young adventurer's life occurred.

Aged just twenty-five, Brockman found himself managing the isolated De Grey Station some 120 kilometres south of Roebourne when two white pearlers, John Shea and Fred Cooper, were murdered by four local Aboriginal men. It was Brockman who rode to Roebourne to sound the alarm. He arrived exhausted, having covered almost seventy kilometres on the second day alone. Even so, when a police party set out to capture the offenders, Brockman had recovered enough to join them. The party soon found the bodies of the two murdered men and, with the help of an Aboriginal tracker,[31] began the laborious task of tracking and capturing their killers. It was an arduous trek during which rations ran so low that the searchers had to fall back on eating wild figs and locusts, but the wanted men were eventually captured and taken back to Roebourne, from where they were transported to Perth for trial.

Only during the trial did it emerge that Shea and Cooper had tricked the four men into signing papers purportedly for work on a station, when in reality they intended to use the men as pearl divers. This nefarious practice, known as blackbirding, was common along the coast at the time. When, on learning their fate, the four men escaped, they were recaptured by Shea and Cooper who attempted to force them back to the coast. En route, Shea, allegedly known for his callousness towards Aboriginal people, severely beat one of the captive men.[32] This led to a desperate melee in which both white men were killed.

On hearing this testimony, the judge ordered the jury to find the four accused not guilty. The city press was equally unsympathetic to the dead men:

> we must ask ourselves what lawful excuse can be set up for one who designedly sets out up country well-armed to catch and drive in niggers [sic] for any purpose. If they won't come, but rise and slay their captors, what call is there on the community to hang these blacks? We are inclined to think that these men who go out 'nigger hunting' [sic] do so at their own risk.[33]

For Brockman, however, the memory of the two white men's violent death likely left a lasting and disturbing impression. But the experience of managing De Grey station was also life-changing in more positive ways. It ignited in him a passion for pastoral exploration and enterprise that would ultimately see him face drought, floods, shipwrecks and near-death skirmishes with hostile tribesmen.

By 1899 the irrepressible pastoralist was the owner of Minilya Station, north of Carnarvon. He had bought the station from his older brother Charles, but early promise had turned to several years of harsh drought. Then a fire had raced through the property, killing most of the stock. A lesser man than Brockman might have been broken, especially when further drought arrived in 1896–97. But the tenacious bushman hung on and, in time, his fortunes turned around, mainly through his own skilled management and dogged determination. So respected was he in the district that he served as a justice of the peace for several years. But all that was to change as the old century drew to a close.

'I AM SO FAR AWAY'

On 5 December 1899, Corporal Bill Turner of the Carnarvon police, on a regular patrol of the area north of the town, was riding his horse towards Point Cloates. He was making camp for the night when an Aboriginal man named Coordie walked in from the surrounding bush and told the policeman that he had been beaten with a bullock-hide whip by George Brockman, placed in stocks and left without food or water.

Turner already knew the Brockman brothers well. As far back as 1885 he had brought in two Aboriginal prisoners following John Brockman's sentencing of them to a year's imprisonment for stealing sheep.[34] The policeman was also aware of stories about the mistreatment of Aboriginal people on Minilya Station, having heard them from stockmen and travellers as he patrolled that desolate stretch of western coastline. Even back in Carnarvon, Sergeant Woods had received reports alleging questionable practices on the distant station.

Corporal Turner took down Coordie's statement and, ten days later, rode out to Minilya Station to put the allegations to Brockman himself. To the policeman's surprise, the station-owner did not try to deny the incident. Instead he merely quibbled about some of the detail—he had certainly thrashed Coordie and put him in the stocks, but it was not true that he had beaten him with a bullock-hide whip. Brockman pulled out two leather valise straps. 'This is what I used to beat him,' he explained to Turner.

To Brockman, the case for administering such punishments to Aboriginal people was clear and defensible. 'I am so far away,' he told the policeman by way of elucidation. 'I must have some control over them.'

Perhaps his mistrust was born of experience—that of his older brother. Back in 1882, before George Brockman had bought the station from his brother Charles, the elder Brockman had returned from a near-fatal northern exploratory trek, the last 160 kilometres without water, to find that his stone house at Minilya had been ransacked in his absence. By his reckoning, some local Aboriginal people had made off with 'nearly £200 worth of goods … consisting of flour, sugar, rice, butter, Crimean [flannel] shirts, trousers, blankets, axes, guns, revolvers, ammunition, boots'.[35] No record remains of Charles Brockman's response to this event.

A month after George Brockman made his admission to Corporal Turner, the policeman returned to Minilya Station to serve a summons on the station-owner. Turner spent the night on the property and, in the morning, was taken by the station's Japanese cook, Cawabila, to the fowl shed. There, in the corner, the cook pointed to the stocks described by Coordie. They were made of crude bush timber less than two metres tall, fastened with bolts and weighing about fifteen kilograms in total.

'A MOST UNUSUAL CASE'

The accusations against George Brockman were heard in the Carnarvon courthouse on 24 February 1900. Sitting in judgement were Magistrate C.D.V. Foss and three local justices of the peace: Matheson, Butcher and Hickenbotham.

Sergeant Woods opened proceedings on behalf of the Crown. It was, he acknowledged from the first, 'a most unusual case'. It is unlikely that anyone present needed to be alerted to the fact: here in the court sat the defendant, himself a justice of the peace, facing a panel of his peers. The sergeant also noted the seriousness of the situation: 'This case is one of much importance as affecting the natives and their treatment, as well as the defendant, he being a justice of the peace.'

It was an awkward moment, and the policeman paused. He was careful to explain that the summons obtained for Brockman had only been initiated after consultation with Magistrate Foss and the Protector of Aborigines. 'I can assure the Bench,' he added, 'that, in bringing this matter forward, the police are only actuated by the best motives, no matter what might be said to the contrary.'

As if to quickly reassure the sergeant, George Brockman sought leave to respond to the policeman's opening remarks. 'I have always been satisfied and pleased with the manner in which the police under Sergeant Woods have performed their duties,' he said. 'In fact, I admit the offence.' The remainder of his statement, however, pleaded justification, and implied that the Aboriginal people under his employ had been bribed to give evidence against him. In particular, Brockman was, he said, keen to bring out the evidence, especially that of the witness Jackie.

His wish was soon granted. Magistrate Foss called as the first three witnesses Coordie and two other Aboriginal workers named Jackie and Billie. The Japanese cook, Cawabila, who had worked on the property for six months, also told the court what he had seen and heard on the night of the beating.

THE ACCUSERS TELL THEIR STORY

First to take the stand was Coordie, who had worked for George Brockman since he was a child. He recalled the afternoon his boss had returned by carriage from the well. Coordie and Jackie were unharnessing the carriage horses to put them in the stable when Coordie heard Brockman call to him from the fowl shed.

Entering the shed and adjusting his eyes to the shade, he noticed the station-owner standing motionless before him. Something glinted and Coordie looked down to see that his boss was holding handcuffs by his side. 'Sit down,' Brockman told him and, when he did so, the station-owner attached the handcuffs to the Aboriginal man's legs. Brockman then walked off to have lunch.

A short time later Brockman returned with Jackie and, removing the handcuffs, directed the apprehensive Coordie to the roughly hewn wooden stocks in the corner. Here he was forced into the apparatus where he remained without lunch or supper, all that afternoon and into the night.

Some time after midnight, as the pain in his legs increased, Coordie became increasingly desperate to free himself. Gradually he found a way to rock the stocks and eventually kick down the wire door of the fowl house. In the darkness he cast his eyes quickly around the yard, hoping to see a piece of iron with which to knock off the nuts holding him fast in the stocks.

But he had made too much noise. The Japanese cook, woken by the sound, woke Brockman, who immediately knew what was going on. 'That's Coordie!' he cried as he pulled on his boots. 'Get me a light!'

Brockman then ran out into the night. 'What the bloody hell are you doing there?' he yelled.

The station-owner strode across the yard and shook his prisoner until the stocks and their victim fell to the ground. Then he kicked the helpless man in the head. His boots opened a wound in the scalp of Coordie, who now found himself on his hands and knees with his legs still attached to the stocks by the handcuffs.

As he tried to find his way to his feet, Coordie now became aware of a light approaching him through the streaming blood and the darkness. It was the cook, Cawabila, walking across the yard with a lantern. Quickly taking in the scene revealed by its dim glow, the cook ran back to the kitchen and, returning with a wet cloth, leaned down to wash the blood from Coordie's face. Brockman stopped his ministrations abruptly and instead forced the bleeding man, still confined by the stocks, back into the fowl house. There he did some rough repairs to the wire fencing of the building and, satisfied it would hold until morning, he went back to bed.

Coordie was left there until dawn.

But if the Aboriginal man thought his ordeal would end with the sunrise, he was wrong. Brockman's anger had not abated with sleep. When he returned to the fowl house in the morning, Coordie caught a glimpse of a whip made of four strips of bullock hide attached to a handle. It was this instrument that Brockman now began to swing through the air and bring down on the man at his feet, who helplessly attempted to dodge and duck to escape the blows. Then, as quickly as it had started, the flogging stopped, and a dazed Coordie felt Brockman unsuccessfully trying to remove him from the stocks.

Eventually, breathing heavily from his exertions, the Minilya Station owner turned to the nearby Jackie and, pointing to the broken wooden frame of the stocks, said, 'Saw them off.' When the stocks were finally removed and the prisoner freed, Brockman ordered the cook to give the exhausted Coordie damper for breakfast, and then ordered Coordie to leave for nearby Wadarra with some newspapers for the men there.

Those gathered in Carnavon to observe the trial soon heard Coordie's story corroborated by Jackie, Billie and Cawabila. Only the question of motive now remained. What possible reason could Coordie give to explain the events of that night? What had driven his employer to such a violent and sustained attack on a defenceless man?

Coordie looked at the bench. 'Mr Brockman flogged me because I had his woman, Maggie,' he said. 'She is a young [Aboriginal] woman and Mr Brockman keeps her and two other [Aboriginal] girls, Katie and Kitty, at the house.' Coordie paused. 'He keeps them until they grow up,' he went on. 'That's what he did to Maggie too.'

There was silence as those gathered in the courthouse digested the story related by the witness in front of them.

BROCKMAN TAKES THE STAND

When George Julius Brockman J.P. stepped up to the witness box to defend himself, he recalled the night in question somewhat differently. For a start, he said, while it was true that he had put Coordie in the stocks, it was incorrect to say that Coordie had been given no dinner. In fact, Brockman claimed, he himself had given the station hand supper and a pannikin of water.

Nor was it the case, asserted Brockman, that he had struck the Aboriginal man with a bullock-hide whip. The pastoralist explained that he had used two leather saddle straps from a valise to measure out around two dozen strokes to Coordie. The accusation that he had kicked his prisoner in the head with his boots was also emphatically denied. At the time, stated the justice of the peace, he was not even wearing boots.

Then the station-owner turned to the question of his motive for administering such treatment. The court, he said, was not to view his behaviour that night as some random act of cruelty. Brockman informed the assembled lawmen and spectators that he was merely meting out punishment for Coordie's earlier theft of a pair of shoes, trespass into the station storehouse and attempted assault of an old blind woman.

Corporal Turner interrupted: this latter allegation was news to him. Brockman had certainly advised him that Coordie had stolen shoes and broken into the storehouse, but he was sure he would have remembered if a cowardly assault on a defenceless woman had also been mentioned.

Then local contractor Sam Hough took the stand. He had been erecting a windmill on Minilya Station at the time of the incident, and he remembered Brockman telling him that he had handed out a whipping to Coordie after putting him into the stocks. He didn't remember being told the reason for this but, in the five years that he had been working on Minilya, he had never known the owner to ill-treat the Aboriginal people who worked for him.

Another Aboriginal worker, a man called Sunday, also gave evidence. He too knew of Coordie's thrashing and of his being put in the stocks. He also thought Coordie's punishment was due to some incident involving an old woman, but he didn't know what it was. Sunday told the court that he too had been put in the stocks in the past.

SOME KIND OF JUSTICE IS SERVED

The arguments against and for Mr Brockman were complete, and it was time for Magistrate Foss and his justices of the peace to retire and consider their verdict. About the facts of the case there appeared to be few material disparities between the recollections of the witnesses and those of the defendant himself: Brockman had most certainly placed Coordie in stocks for some twelve hours, and had beaten him with some kind of straps. Only the issue of mitigation remained to be resolved by the small bench gathered in Carnarvon that day. To what extent did Brockman's belief that his employee had been guilty of stealing and assault provide reasonable cause for the punishment administered?

The court understood clearly that Coordie had not been found guilty of any wrongdoing by legal process. Even if he had, Foss would have known that there was nothing in the legal statutes of Western Australia that would grant a justice of the peace the power to administer punishments that even the most hardened murderer in Fremantle Prison would fear.

On the face of it, George Julius Brockman appeared to have been a law unto himself on Minilya Station: he was his own judge, jury and warder. The case appeared, even by Brockman's own admission, fairly clear-cut.

But Magistrate Foss had a dilemma. As Sergeant Woods had intimated earlier that morning, this was no ordinary defendant: the pastoralist awaiting the court's verdict was a fellow justice of the peace. He was well known in the area and respected for his tenacity and toughness. What message would it send to all the other pastoralists of the district if the court appeared to compromise their right to take retaliatory measures against the Aboriginal population that surrounded and outnumbered them?

As if that weren't enough, Charles Foss also had another problem to consider as he pondered the weight of the law that might be brought down on the head of the station-owner. Whether the court knew it or not, he and Brockman shared a distant but critical piece of history: twenty-eight years previously, in 1871, the Carnarvon magistrate's first wife had died. Her name was Joanna Elizabeth Brockman, and she was the sister of George Julius Brockman.[36] In that small frontier-town courtroom, Magistrate C.D.V. Foss knew that in the next few minutes he must pass judgement on the man who had once been his brother-in-law.

The court fell silent as the lawmen returned to the bench. A verdict of guilty was read, and punishment pronounced: George Julius Brockman was fined five pounds, and costs of nine pounds and eight shillings were awarded against him. As for Coordie, the young station hand was, decided the court, to be released from his indenture to Minilya Station.

And so the matter appeared to come to a close. Some kind of justice had been seen to be served, and the witnesses dispersed as the next case was called.

The newly sentenced George Julius Brockman J.P. then joined his fellow lawmen on the bench to hear the evidence against a Japanese man alleged to have provided liquor to an Aboriginal man named Willie. It was a quick trial: the accused admitted to the charge and was promptly fined twenty pounds; however, as he couldn't pay, he elected to go to prison for two months instead.

Few in the courtroom that day could have helped but note that it was safer to beat an Aboriginal man in the open than to sell him grog on the sly.

His work in town now finished, Brockman, having been defendant and judge in the same few hours, made ready to ride home to Minilya.

A LAWLESS AND CRUEL FRONTIER

The matter might well have ended there but, on the ride back to his station, Brockman, still smarting from the court's verdict against him, had many solitary hours to dwell on his grievances. When some time later he found that several of the colony's major newspapers had portrayed him as cruel and vicious, his smouldering resentment turned white-hot. In May 1899 the angry J.P. fired off his side of the story in a letter to Kalgoorlie's *Western Argus*:

> SIR, I must ask you in common justice to myself to kindly publish this letter referring [to] a case heard against me some time ago at the Carnarvon Police Court for the alleged ill-treatment of a native named Coordie, and on which several of the newspapers thought fit to make untruthful and libellous comments. Several of the papers have only been lately received else I would have replied sooner. On December 4th last P.C. [*sic*] Turner called at my place en route to Point Cloates and on his return said to me, 'I say old man, what's this your people have got about your putting Coordie in the stocks and flogging him with a bullock-whip?' To which I replied that there was not such a thing as a whip on the station. I admitted that I had put him in the stocks and given him two dozen lashes with a pair of saddle straps, which I showed him, and he remarked 'That would not hurt him.' I may remark here that the fact of placing a native in the stocks is not a cruel punishment. He suffers in no way beyond the confinement. Should it be otherwise it was surely P.C. Turner's duty to have produced the stocks in court.[37]

In fact, the irate pastoralist continued, had he been less lenient and allowed the legal system to adjudicate the matter, Coordie could have expected at least twelve months in chains for his crimes.

Brockman then relayed his account of begging Corporal Turner not to require him to come straight to Carnarvon for the trial as he was in the middle of erecting a series of windmills that were a matter of life or death to his sheep. The policeman rejected the plea, he continued, and:

> [o]n arrival in Carnarvon, I immediately reported the matter to the Resident Magistrate, who said, 'There was no necessity to hurry you in, and I did not expect you before the 9th of February.' Having to leave my sheep unprovided for with regard to water, I lost 700 sheep, there being only one white man left on the station to work the whole place in the middle of one of the worst droughts ever known in the district.

It was clear that the pastoralist held the policeman, Turner, solely responsible for the position in which he now found himself. The story of the kicking and starving of Coordie, Brockman now maintained, was simply a fabrication worked up between the constable, the cook and the two other Aboriginal men en route to Carnarvon. Not only had the three witnesses been coached by the policeman but, Brockman claimed, they had been rewarded by him with blankets and shirts. He did not offer any reason for the policeman to do this other than that it would 'give pleasure to certain friends of the police, by whom the case was got up'.

Then he addressed the insinuation of his accusers, not tested at the trial, relating to the keeping of young girls. Turner, he wrote,

> acted altogether outside the case by asking Coordie what two little native girls were doing on the station. Coordie replied that these girls were kept by me until they grew up for immoral purposes. There are, in all, 35 women and girls on the station, born and reared on it. Twelve of these are young girls from two to eight years of age. Their parents are all on the place, and are kept constantly employed. Because I feed and protect these children, and at the express desire of their parents, does it, of necessity, follow that I keep harems of children for immoral purposes? But would it be a Christian act to drive these children off the station to starve to death because I feared public scandal? I have always made it a rule to protect the natives of both sexes, and am independent of what people think or say on the matter. There are considerably more than sixty natives on the station to-day. When I settled here fourteen years ago there were but twelve. Had I been guilty of the ill-treatment I am accused of towards them, they most certainly would not have remained here to be persecuted by me.

This might well have been true: there is no evidence that contradicts Brockman's assertion of his motives or of his behaviour towards Aboriginal women or girls on Minilya. There is considerable evidence, however, that the kind of sexual predation and exploitation alleged by Coordie was experienced by many Aboriginal women across Australia at that time. In the same year that Brockman faced his accusers in Carnarvon, a South Australian royal commission was told by a pastoralist that there were stations where 'every hand on the place had a gin [sic], even down to boys of 15 years of age'.[38] And in Western Australia just five years after the Minilya affair, the colony's own royal commission heard from one witness that on many pastoral leases 'the Aboriginal women are usually at the mercy of anybody, from the proprietor or manager, to the stockmen, cook, rouseabout'.[39]

Brockman, having repudiated any such claims made against himself, now moved on to make a number of serious allegations—including of murder, cover-up and conspiracy—against his fellow pastoralists in the region. His letter continued:

> On the day of the hearing, G.J. Gooch, of Wandagee, told me that he and Snook, his brother-in-law, intended to publish the case, and that they intended to do me all the injury they could, and would use every means in their power to do so, because I had reported to the Aborigines' Protection Board that a native boy of mine, whom I had lent to Snook whilst driving the mail, had been killed in a mysterious manner, and asked the board to hold an inquiry. This I did after repeated reports had been made to me both by natives and whites. At the time this boy was killed it was stated that there were no white people on the station but W.S. Snook and Mrs. C. Wheelock. Prior to reporting this matter, I was told personally by an onlooker that the boy was struck on the head with a piece of wood, which had some nails in it.

Brockman now struck home by once more putting Corporal Turner squarely in the frame. The policeman, he alleged, had failed to properly investigate the matter of the Aboriginal boy's death and had allowed his friendship with the owner of Wandagee Station to seriously compromise his enquiries. 'The very ones who could have thrown light on the matter were never questioned, and the whole matter seems to have been hushed up from the first,' the indignant letter-writer claimed.

But Brockman didn't stop there. He seemed unaware that his claims, coming as they did on top of the facts of his own brutality towards Coordie, only added to the general perception in the south that the North-West was a lawless and cruel frontier. In an effort to justify his own behaviour and to place it within the context of greater injustices, Minilya's owner was unwittingly laying the foundation for increasing public disquiet about life on Western Australia's remote pastoral leases. This would culminate in an inquiry in 1904 that would lift the lid on the often brutal interactions between whites and blacks since the establishment of the Swan River settlement in 1829.

In May 1899, though, George Julius Brockman had not finished publicly venting his spleen against those he believed had conspired against him. In particular, he was keen to relate further examples that would 'show the intimate terms that P.C. [sic] Turner is on with some of the settlers here'. He followed through by regaling newspaper readers with an account of the time he had reported to Corporal Turner a case of animal cruelty alleged to have happened on nearby Williambury Station. Brockman had told both Turner and Sergeant Wood that the Williambury teamster, Blackall, was using three-wire whips on his working bullocks and flailing them until they were skinned and bloody and subject to flies and infection. According to Brockman, the police constable had claimed to find no evidence of such maltreatment, a fact that Brockman put down to his understanding that Turner owed seventeen pounds to the owner of Williambury from a previous game of euchre. He went on:

> If the police are to be allowed to take up private disputes between the settlers, and to persecute certain persons to please those who fear and pander to them, by collecting false evidence from natives by bribery or intimidation, then who is safe?[40]

In fact, if further proof of his unjust treatment was needed, Brockman quoted a remark made to him by Magistrate Foss just a week previously. The town's leading lawman, while privy to several reports about Brockman's behaviour, was of the view that, unless these allegations were put in writing, he could only conclude that '[i]t is nothing less than a systematic persecution, and I don't believe one word of the reports'.[41]

Finally, Brockman asked readers to accept that he had been unfairly libelled and that, while he was a strict disciplinarian who lived by the motto 'Be just and fear no-one', he defied anyone, including the police, to find any evidence of his ill-treatment towards Aboriginal people or that he had 'in any other way behaved towards them unbecoming a gentleman and a Christian'. He concluded by offering a reward of one thousand pounds to anyone who could provide such proof.[42]

'HUMAN BRUTES IN THE NORTH'

If Brockman had already forgotten that such proof had just weeks earlier been well established in the form of his conviction at the Carnarvon courthouse, the editors of the southern newspapers had not. Brockman's challenge only reignited the press's condemnation of the outlaw behaviour on the north-western frontier that the trial and now Brockman's subsequent revelations appeared to confirm.

The West Australian Sunday Times, especially incensed, published the stockman's letter verbatim, emblazoned with the headline 'More Light on the Black Slavery Question' and interposed with commentary by the editor railing against the culture of subservience, violence and neglect that he believed the missive revealed about the treatment of Aboriginal people on pastoral leases in the Gascoyne:

> Mr. Brockman's offer to donate £1,000 if it can be proved that he has ever ill-treated a native is sheer BOMBAST AND HUMBUG. A man who cannot see that two floggings and a night in the stocks is cruelty has probably never been cruel, according to his barbarous notions. The rest of his letter may be summed up in the classic phrase, 'YOU'RE ANOTHER,' but the charges he makes are so sweeping and so terrible that the credit of the colony, as well as common humanity, calls loudly and imperatively for investigation.
>
> Does not this letter bear out what the SUNDAY TIMES has long ago contended, namely, that these human brutes in the North are pretty well all TARRED WITH THE SAME BRUSH?
>
> What about 'isolated instances' of cruelty now? Here is a squatter who denounces his neighbours as worse than savages; his neighbours apparently say much the same of him. On no account would we doubt the veracity of either.[43]

The newspaper called for nothing less than a royal commission into the accusations that Brockman's letter contained.

Even after this call was answered with such an inquiry in 1904, the shadow of the Minilya Station affair lingered bitterly in the form of continuing criticism directed mainly at Magistrate Foss by *The Sunday Times* (as *The West Australian Sunday Times* was renamed in 1902) over the coming years. In 1906, for example, the newspaper would ask:

'How long are the liberty and property of the residents in the Carnarvon Magisterial District to remain at the mercy of a shocking old incapable like Foss?'[44] This was only one of many salvos that came the magistrate's way over the next ten years, with the newspaper never tired of highlighting the vagaries of 'fossil Foss',[45] a man so out of touch with the modern world that the paper doubted he had ever seen a train.[46]

For Brockman himself, the newspaper's reaction to his letter must have been galling. But matters became worse when, on hearing of the station-owner's conviction, Western Australian Attorney-General R.W. Pennefather sought the removal of Brockman from the state's list of honorary justices of the peace. In June of the year after Brockman's conviction, questions were still being asked in parliament but it was made clear by the colonial treasurer that no further action would be taken in regard to the treatment of Coordie.

The matter was over.

'THEY RECEIVE KINDNESS AND JUSTICE'

Soon after these events, Brockman sold up his pastoral lease in the Gascoyne and eventually found himself living again in Guildford near Perth. In 1912 he was making his way north to Broome, in the hope that the tropical air might improve his ailing health, when he fell ill in Geraldton. There he died of pneumonia, aged just sixty-three.

By the time of his death, at least one local newspaper could generously recall that George Julius Brockman:

> was an intrepid explorer and a pioneer of the dauntless type which seems to find difficulty an incentive and an encouragement. He did much good service to Western Australia in an unostentatious way, and was widely known from end to end of the State.[47]

To another he remained a semi-heroic figure from an era already past, a 'genuine battler and worker, and of a most energetic nature'.[48]

Minilya Station itself had undergone a transformation at the hands of its new owners, Donald and Charlotte McCloud. When Western Australia's Chief Protector of Aborigines Henry Charles (Harry) Prinsep came through the station in 1901, he remarked on the large number of Aboriginal people now living on the pastoral property. Prinsep had no doubt as to the reason for this:

> And no wonder, for they have found out that under the new management they receive kindness and justice, with liberality. The children are clothed, and all the natives are compelled to wash themselves and their clothes, and to keep their hair short, and to appear weekly in a clean condition. Their appreciation of this—quite a new sensation I should fancy—appears quite evident. The children are taught every day not only their letters and sums, but in everything which tends to civilise and Christianise them, and the parents seem very grateful for the kindness shown to their children.[49]

It was clear that the humanitarian McClouds practised a different way of living alongside the country's first people in remote parts of Western Australia. While their efforts 'to civilise and Christianise' them would have their own unforeseen tragic impacts on the Aboriginal people, the McClouds—and others like them—demonstrated at least that the relationship between blacks and whites need not be characterised by fear and physical violence.

CHAPTER 4
THE SHARK BAY STAND-OFF

> It is a moral certainty that where Chinese gather in numbers there will be difficulties. America, Queensland, New South Wales, Victoria and South Australia have all had their share of troubles on account of the swarms of Chinese which have landed upon their shores, and the only wonder is that West Australia has so long escaped. Why difficulties should be the consequence of an influx of Chinese is a debatable question, but so patent is the fact that the Chinese are a nuisance that most of the eastern colonies have set in motion machinery, for at least limiting their influx. The first difficulty of any importance which Western Australia has experienced, is that at Sharks Bay [sic].
> —*The West Australian* (Perth, WA), Monday 22 November 1886

'A MOCKERY, A SNARE, AND A DELUSION'

Back in 1873, a small community of colonial pearlers was struggling to make its fortune on the shores of the remote expanse of coastline that formed Shark Bay,[1] some eight hundred kilometres north of Perth. The small fleet had found permanent shelter in Useless Harbour,[2] inauspiciously named some seventy years earlier by French explorer Louis-Henri de Saulces de Freycinet, who had mistakenly thought the potential shipping haven to be entirely blocked by a sandbar.[3] Far from useless, the sheltered little inlet proved a boon to many of the boats that had begun exploiting the pearl beds of Shark Bay from 1850.

Ramshackle camps of tents and huts littered the edges of Shark Bay, with Useless Harbour and Freshwater Camp (now Denham) being two of the largest and Wilyah Miah another. Some of the men and women who lived in these camps made their fortunes, but most did not. It was hard work, with only about three pearls found for every hundred shells opened. The living was harsh and illness, drownings, cyclones and heat took their toll. In summer, the smell of rotting shellfish filled the air.

By 1873 there were, according to a visiting magistrate, some fifty Europeans, eighty Aboriginal people and 110 Malays working the deposits of pearl shell that stretched away from the coast.[4] The dangerous work of diving was done mainly by the Aboriginal and Malay men, while the Aboriginal women gathered in groups on the beach and opened the shells.

It was clear to the magistrate that there was need for some police presence in the bay.

> Men of bad character find their way to a place which affords great facility for theft and other offences, and the presence of a police officer would act as a check … Should it be decided to locate police at Shark's Bay, I think it would be well to give the officer instructions to regulate the camps, in the interest of health and decency. At present the pits of rotten oysters are mingled with the tents, while other offensive matter accumulates around. I urged the pearlers to establish some sort of order and decent arrangement for their own sakes; and a constable might with advantage be directed to insist upon a proper arrangement of the camps, which are all on Crown land.[5]

Over the years these small pearling ventures seemed to fluctuate between optimism and disillusionment. One correspondent to the Fremantle *Herald* summed up the prevailing atmosphere with sardonic humour:

> Alas! that I should write it, the anticipated glories and profits of Shark's Bay are a mockery, a snare, and a delusion; Canvastown, like the 'baseless fabric of a vision' is rapidly vanishing, and the fair bosom of Useless Inlet[6] will soon have respite from the breast-harrowing treatment it has for so long received, and all will once again be a howling wilderness (the latter adjective is not metaphorical; dingoes abound). In a word, Shark's Bay is worked out, the shells remaining turning out about an ounce of inferior pearls per 100 bags of shells, and unless new and richer banks be discovered very shortly, Wilyah Miah will be totally abandoned in a month or two; or, as a friend expressed to me, the 'Tag, rag and bobtail' have gone, the rest will soon follow.[7]

Sickness, in particular, dogged the lives of those in Useless Harbour, adding to the general sense of isolation a daily reminder of life's fragility. One local correspondent to the Perth newspapers in 1874 sounded a note of despair:

> What with our worst season's [sic] (the summer southerly gales), the fever, dysentery, short salt rations, and the worst seasons [sic] periodical cry of the Harbour ('Useless') being worked out is quite enough to start any but a stout heart home again. Many return from the best goldfields, and say it is no use staying; so do some pearlers.[8]

Into this dispirited atmosphere was added the simmering racial tension brought about by the European pearlers' reaction to the growing community of Chinese and Malays. The Western Australian colony—which, especially since the cessation of convict transports, needed the cheap labour offered by Asian immigration—found itself in a fix. On the one hand it abhorred the vices it believed grew among men forced to live without women; on the other, it feared that introducing Asian women into the colony would lead to Chinese and Malays outnumbering the white population.[9]

This anxiety ensured that the overwhelming number of Chinese and Malay migrants would continue to be men. In 1891, for example, the census revealed that of the 917 Chinese people in Western Australia, only three were women.[10] As a result, loneliness was a fact of life for most Asian workers in Shark Bay, as it was in most parts of the western colony. Many of them, far from home and deprived of relationships with women of their own culture, took solace in gambling and opium. This, combined with their tough living conditions and exclusion from mainstream colonial life, meant that violence and suicide were not uncommon.

A YEAR OF BLOODSHED AND UPHEAVAL

It came as some relief when, in 1874, the Shark Bay settlements at last witnessed the arrival of the first policeman to be permanently stationed there. Lance Corporal Mainland, 'a very civil, attentive and obliging official',[11] was delivered ashore with his family by the packet *Clarence* early that year. The new officer's presence was felt almost immediately: he promptly located a stolen pearl, arrested the alleged offenders and dispatched them on Her Majesty's schooner *Beagle* to Geraldton's Champion Bay for trial.[12]

Mainland would be kept busy over the next few years. The isolation and hardship combined with the distrust between the various races meant that Shark Bay was a tinderbox of tensions. Over the decade following his arrival the small settlements along the bay grew raggedly and slowly, and with them the barely supressed antagonism between their European and Asian inhabitants. One visitor conveyed the brooding atmosphere thus:

> The population of Sharks Bay consists of about 350 people, the majority of whom are Chinamen, Malays, and Manilamen, who are a great source of trouble and anxiety to the Government and to the pearlers. Under the least provocation they will draw their knives, which they always wear, and stab you if they get the chance. There have lately been several serious riots between Malays, Chinamen, Manilamen, and whites. The Manilamen are a very hot blooded race, and very daring. The Magistrate and police are doing all they can, within their power, to suppress these riots.[13]

In 1884 these rising racial tensions would come to a head in a year of bloodshed and upheaval. That fateful year, to the many hardships already piled one upon the other was added one of the district's worst ever outbreaks of dysentery[14] and measles. It struck the Aboriginal community especially hard, with one newspaper of the time warning that:

> The prevalence of measles among the aboriginals at the North-west if, unfortunately, they should travel so far, would have a very depressing effect upon the pearl-shelling and squatting industries in that neighbourhood.[15]

Disease was not the only threat to the original people of Shark Bay. Prostitution of Aboriginal women, often in return for alcohol, had also become rife.[16] Meanwhile the attitudes of the white settlers of Shark Bay towards the region's Asian workers, generally characterised by fear and suspicion, were met with offhand dismissiveness when matters reached the court in Carnarvon. This is evidenced by Magistrate Foss's judgment that year against Shark Bay pearler George Fry, whom he fined a mere two pounds, three shillings and sixpence for 'non-registration of the death of a Chinaman who was in his employ'. Foss also fined Fry almost double that for the apparently greater crime of 'non-registration of two dogs'.[17]

Crime had become so common in the distant bay by 1884 that *The Daily News* reported on the violent death that year of a Chinese man in almost jocular fashion:

> Murder at Sharks Bay appears to be more popular among some of the residents than pearl-fishing. We learn that during the present week a Chinaman took the life of his mate by striking him on the head with an oar.[18]

In this case, an argument between Sing Hay and Ah Hor,[19] two men aboard the pearler *Matchless*, had resulted in Sing Hay forcibly striking his colleague overboard and then hitting him in the head with a wooden oar as the dazed man had tried to climb back on deck. Ah Hor's defeated body sank beneath the bloodied waters of the bay before the crew of the nearby *Milly* could reach him.[20]

The dead man's body was never recovered, the general conclusion being that it had either been 'eaten by the sharks or been carried away by the tide'.[21]

Sing Hay appeared before Magistrate Foss's Carnarvon court before being committed to trial in Geraldton. While awaiting trial, the desperate prisoner tried several times to commit suicide, including by attempting to 'hang himself with the band of his trousers' and to 'cut his throat with a piece of glass', and by swallowing 'a quantity of glass which brought on violent internal haemorrhage'.[22] Then, one morning in November 1884, he was found hanged in his cell, his body still warm but lifeless.

These first two violent deaths of the year would prove fateful portents of what was to follow. A third death soon ensued, and once again it was a Chinese man who committed the deed and another who became his victim. But this time the law would not be cheated.

The saga unfolded in May of that year, when a fight broke out between two men, Sing Ong and Ah Foo, over Ah Foo's employment of a man whom Sing Ong considered his servant. What happened next formed the testimony of Yu Chi, one of the witnesses to the fatal events:

> I am a pearler and work at Sharks Bay. I know the prisoner Sing Hong [*sic*]; he is a pearler at Cape Lesueur. I knew Ah Foo; he is dead now; the prisoner shot him. I know he did so because I was in Ah Foo's tent at the time. The prisoner called him outside and said he wanted to fight him; Ah Foo went to the door and picked up a piece of wood and the prisoner shot him. Ah Foo fell down and tried to get up again, and the prisoner shot him again. He was about four yards off and stood in the same place when he fired the second shot. After he had fired the second shot the prisoner went to his tent; he took the pistol from his trousers pocket … The first shot hit

the deceased in the back of the hips, and the second in the chest; I saw the bullet mark in his chest. It was a round hole, and there was some blood round it but not much. I did not hear any quarrel between the prisoner and deceased that day.[23]

Sing Ong was soon sentenced to death, his defence being barely more than perfunctory. His lawyer, a Mr Arthur Houssemayne du Boulay, while eminently capable and highly respected, was brought into the court by the presiding judge just moments before the case began, and was totally unprepared. He himself would assert this as he addressed the jury towards the trial's conclusion, as Geraldton's *Victorian Express* later explained to its readers:

> Mr. du Boulay, addressing the Court for the defence, said he regretted that the prisoner was so badly represented, for he had merely the same knowledge of the case that was possessed by the jury themselves, having been even unable to converse with the prisoner. He would in the first place submit that the Crown might have prepared the prosecution in a better manner, and obtained more complete evidence.[24]

Du Boulay was not alone in his misgivings. The sentence also caused some discomfort among other Geraldton residents, who felt that the case had been badly handled. They petitioned the governor to intercede but his response through the local resident magistrate was as short as it was final:

> His Excellency the Governor wishes you to inform the petitioners in the case of Sing Ong that … the statement of this witness fails to establish any palliating circumstances, and that the facts of the case are so clear that His Excellency does not feel justified in interfering.[25]

Any slim hope that Sing Ong's life might be spared was now gone, and his fate sealed.

> The first execution that has been held at Geraldton took place on Wednesday morning last, when a Chinaman named Sing Ong suffered the extreme penalty of the law for the murder of a brother celestial at Sharks Bay. The gallows was erected in a temporary enclosure in the gaol yard and the execution took place at 8 a.m. Mr. Inspector Rowe acted as Deputy Sheriff.[26]

The terrible deaths of Ah Hor and Ah Foo and the gruesome ends of their killers were not the only violent deaths of Chinese people at Shark Bay in 1884. But the fifth, at the hands of a white man, would take much longer to come to the surface. When it did, its consequences would lay bare the deep inequities that existed between the respective legal treatments of the two communities.

THE YOUNG ADVENTURER

In December of the same year that Ah Hor was beaten and drowned and Ah Foo fatally shot, a more mysterious death was to occur in Shark Bay. Once more the victim would be Chinese, but this time the accused murderer would be his European master.

In 1884, twenty-five-year-old Leopold von Bibra was no stranger to the highs and lows of living between the makeshift camps that abutted the pearl beds of Shark Bay and the budding settlement of Carnarvon further up the coast. In fact, just a decade earlier he had been in charge of the cutter *Hampton*, one of the first boats to deliver cargo to the white pioneers at the mouth of the Gascoyne River.[27] Some fourteen metres long and weighing around fourteen tons,[28] the vessel was at the time a familiar sight along the Gascoyne coast as it made its way south with consignments of pearl shell or northwards to the small communities and stations along the loneliest reaches of the colony. It would eventually founder off North West Cape in 1908, in an unsuccessful attempt to salvage the wreck of the *Mildura*.[29] In the early days of white settlement around the Gascoyne, however, the *Hampton*'s skipper, young Leopold von Bibra, was as well known as the vessel itself.

Like his father, Francis von Bibra, the young adventurer was never idle. The two of them, while living on Dirk Hartog Island just off Shark Bay in the 1860s, had been quicker than most to see the potential of pearling in the region long before the rush precipitated in 1872 when settlers Howlett and Cadell brought the first Malays to work the waters.[30]

For the older von Bibra, pearling and other fishing interests at Shark Bay were just some of his many endeavours. He also held the lease on Wooramel Station, just inland from the bay, and during the 1870s he had become known as 'Dugong von Bibra' thanks to the large amounts of money and effort he had expended in trying to introduce dugong oil to the Australian and European markets. The would-be entrepreneur had been convinced that his product would eventually rival cod liver oil as a remedy for tuberculosis and other ailments; unfortunately, no-one else agreed and he soon lost most of the money he had pumped into the venture.[31]

Undeterred by this setback, Francis von Bibra had continued to work his lease of Wooramel Station, named for the nearby and usually dry river 120 kilometres south of Carnarvon. Like many landowners in the area, his pastoral and pearling interests soon became entwined, as pearling luggers were often put into service carrying wool clips southwards to other parts of the colony.[32]

Leopold von Bibra proved as much of an entrepreneur as his father, embarking on a range of enterprises of his own. For a period he operated a sandalwood business out of Wooramel Station, and soon afterwards established his own store to service the area. He also became one of the first people to deliver camels to the region when he landed sixteen of the creatures on his father's pastoral lease.[33] The animals had little trouble adapting and quickly became at home among the saltbush and acacia of the remote Wooramel plains.

A MYSTERIOUS DEATH

On a December afternoon in 1884, Leopold von Bibra and Jack Shea had been supervising three of von Bibra's Chinese workers—Ah Tong, Jim Chu and Yu Quong—in the digging of a well at Wooramel Station. Shea had been living with the young pearler for about a year, working on a number of his projects. The trio of Chinese workers had sailed out from Singapore together under a contract to work for von Bibra for three years—just a few of some one thousand indentured Chinese brought to the colony from Singapore as pastoral and agricultural workers, boat crew and domestic labour between 1847 and 1897.[34]

The digging of the well hadn't got far. Ah Tong was hip-deep in the hole while Jim Chu, aged in his mid-twenties, was standing above him smoothing the earth away from the edges as he dug it out. Yu Quong was drawing water from an existing well nearby. According to von Bibra, some time in the afternoon, without a word, Jim Chu simply lay down on the sand and quietly passed away.

Von Bibra, Shea and the remaining two Chinese men buried Jim Chu's body the next day, placing some wood from an old cask over it before covering it with sand.

It was von Bibra himself who first reported the incident to Constable Enoch Odling, on von Bibra's arrival by boat in Carnarvon that same month. The young pearler then went straight to Magistrate Foss to let him know what had happened. The lawman wasted no time in dispatching Constables Odling and Skinner to Shark Bay to investigate the circumstances of the Chinaman's death.[35]

'ALTOGETHER CHINESE'

The two policemen duly arrived at Wooramel on 18 December and, after taking a statement from Shea, proceeded to exhume Jim Chu's remains the following day. Constable Odling would recall that 'the body was much decomposed and crushed by the weight of earth on the boards placed above it. I did not take it out as it would have been impossible for me to have seen the traces of any blows'.[36]

Odling made a reconnaissance of the area around the well and then returned to Carnarvon, where he handed his report to Magistrate Foss. Despite this, and the gathering speculation and gossip that surrounded the circumstances of the death, a year would pass before any further action was taken.

It wasn't until Christmas 1885, as Leopold von Bibra disembarked in Carnarvon with one of his workers, an Aboriginal named Georgie, that Constable Odling next acted. Taking Georgie aside, Odling obtained a formal statement from him through an Aboriginal interpreter named Billy.

A few days later the policeman returned to Shark Bay and, for the first time, interviewed the two Chinese men who had been present at the well when their companion had passed away. Ah Tong and Yu Quong were still working for von Bibra, and Constable Odling was able to obtain statements from the men through an interpreter called Dunn, who explained that the two men were speaking Malay, not Chinese. This would be the first indication that the issue of language and interpretation would add a layer of ambiguity and uncertainty to the events of that day.

Just before Easter of 1886 the police believed they had enough evidence to charge Leopold von Bibra with manslaughter and, on Ash Wednesday, he was arrested and brought up to Carnarvon. The pearler was remanded in custody for eight days, but not before he had time to telegraph James Barratt, a solicitor based in Geraldton some five hundred kilometres to the south, requesting representation.

Despite the distance and the short notice, the colourful Mr Barratt[37] arrived to represent his client within a week.[38] Even so, Barratt was too late to be present at the committal hearing held by Magistrate Foss, at which evidence was heard from Ah Tong and Yu Quong, this time through interpreter Robert Fry,[39] another Shark Bay pearler.

Once again, Fry told the hearing that the language in which the two men gave their evidence was Malay, not Chinese. In any case, what they said was sufficient in Foss's mind for von Bibra to be committed to the next criminal sittings at Geraldton. He was released on bail but, as *The West Australian* reported, his family was not about to 'entertain fears about the final outcome'—after all, the newspaper reminded its readers, the evidence was 'altogether Chinese'.[40]

A MATTER OF INTERPRETATION

The violent deaths of five Chinese men in 1884 still cast long shadows over Shark Bay by the time Leopold von Bibra faced court in Geraldton on 22 June 1886. His trial also coincided with a general mood of anxiety spreading across the Western Australian colony about the growing numbers of Chinese making a living there. This tension was mirrored in a nationwide suspicion that Asian immigrants threatened the economic and cultural interests of the European colonists. Even Geraldton's *Victorian Express* made frequent sallies into this issue.

> The Chinese are on the upward grade in these parts. Until recently their energies were directed to such pursuits as gardening, in which their competition had not such a baneful effect. But now the innocent celestial is seen soaring higher and entering more congenial callings such as storekeeping, several small shops having been opened by Chinamen lately … it is an unmistakable fact that the British employees and labourers cannot compete with the barbaric hordes from the East and maintain even the present status of civilisation enjoyed by British workers. This means that unless our great and glorious competitive system is overhauled, the British labourer must sink to the level of a Chinaman or black fellow.[41]

It was within this climate of anti-Asian sentiment that von Bibra's fate would be decided. While this must have given rise to the hope of a sympathetic hearing, the accused man took care to ensure that he was well represented: in addition to Mr Barratt, his legal team included another local solicitor, Mr Alfred Farrelly.

The case for the prosecution would be delivered by no less a man than the distinguished policeman in charge of the Geraldton Region, Inspector Thomas Rowe. Having commenced his career as a detective sergeant back in England in the 1860s, on arrival in the colony in 1873 Rowe had been instrumental in setting up Western Australia's Central

Intelligence Bureau.⁴² As later events would prove, this would not be the last time the inspector would be dragged into the affairs of the Chinese at Shark Bay.

Arbitrating between Inspector Rowe and Mr Barratt as chairman of proceedings was Mr Arthur du Boulay, who two years earlier had been appointed to defend—albeit without opportunity for due preparation—Sing Ong at his trial for the murder of Ah Foo. Du Boulay was a formidable lawman in his own right, widely known and well respected since his arrival at Champion Bay as a sheep farmer in the 1860s. Drought and poor wool prices had put paid to that dream, and in 1868 he and his wife had returned to England, where du Boulay became a barrister. In December 1874 the couple returned to Geraldton, where he began a long and distinguished legal career.

At the commencement of the manslaughter proceedings, Leopold von Bibra formally pleaded not guilty to the charge that he had, on or around 6 December 1884, feloniously killed Jim Chu, at Wooramel Station, Shark Bay.⁴³ The trial was to last two days, often descending into farce as the issue of translation became increasingly fraught and tempers frayed.

Having submitted his plea, von Bibra sought leave to sit in the dock as he was feeling unwell, and this was granted by Chairman du Boulay. Inspector Rowe was then invited to make the Crown's case. Almost immediately there arose a technical difficulty. Barratt asked for a copy of the original report on Jim Chu's death, as provided by von Bibra to the police at Shark Bay and subsequently sent to Foss in Carnarvon. The court was cleared while arguments about this request were heard but, in the end, for reasons that no-one could explain, the document was determined to have been lost.

The trial resumed, and Inspector Rowe stood to commence his case by calling a Chinese interpreter to assist with the cross-examination of the first witness, Ah Tong. Once more Barratt interrupted, informing the court that, as luck would have it, the person who had interpreted the two Chinese witnesses' first statements in Carnarvon, Robert Fry, was in the vicinity. Surely, he declared, it made sense to again hear the witnesses' evidence in Malay—a language Inspector Rowe's Chinese interpreter would be unable to translate—the way Magistrate Foss had first heard it through Fry. He added that 'Chinese interpreters were decidedly open to suspicion', and objected to a 'Chinese banker or lodging house-keeper'⁴⁴ playing such an important role. Inspector Rowe, taken aback by this happy coincidence for the defence, complained to the chairman that

Fry's 'adjacency seemed suspicious'.⁴⁵ Barratt then admitted that he had, in fact, arranged for Fry to be there.

In the end, du Boulay allowed the Malay-speaking Fry to be brought into the court and, at last, the first witness was called. Addressing Ah Tong, Mr du Boulay asked, 'Can you speak Malay?' When the Chinese man replied that he could speak only a few words of that language, Mr Barratt assured the court that he would prove differently.

'HE WAS A GOOD MASTER TO ME'

For the first time since Jim Chu's mysterious death, a picture began to form—in a mosaic of fractured Malay, Chinese and English—of the events of that December afternoon in 1884. Ah Tong was the first to tell of how, as he was digging the well and Jim Chu was at the top shovelling the excavated sand away, von Bibra urged Jim Chu to work more quickly. The pearler allegedly kicked the Chinese man five or six times, angrily muttering with each kick, 'Work quickly!'

Finally, as Jim Chu knelt at the top of the well desperately scraping the mounting sand away from the hole, his master gave him two more kicks, one to the back and one to the side. According to Ah Tong, his companion did not speak a word throughout the assault but simply groaned and slipped slowly prostrate to the ground. At this point Ah Tong leapt out of the well but von Bibra turned on him, yelling, 'What? What?' until the frightened man returned to the hole and continued digging.

Nearby, Yu Quong and Jack Shea were at the station's existing well drawing water, but neither intervened. Shea returned to the house and, while Jim Chu lay motionless in the sun, Ah Tong and von Bibra continued to work on the new well.

Half an hour went by and von Bibra, presumably still angry at Jim Chu's now complete inactivity, picked up a stick lying near the well and, lifting the barely conscious man by his pigtail, began beating him around the shoulders. Jim Chu moaned, but remained limp.

At that moment, a wind sprang up and blew von Bibra's hat off and across the yard towards Yu Quong, who picked it up and returned it to his boss. Perhaps it was now dawning on von Bibra that the man lying unmoving on the sand was genuinely ill. He took the hat from Yu Quong and told him, 'Take him home to his bed.' Yu Quong knelt down and called Jim Chu's name, gently shaking him as he did so. But it was clear to all three men that life had left Jim Chu.

Von Bibra stood there watching and saying nothing. Then he turned on his heel and walked quickly back to the house. He re-emerged with Jack Shea, and both men looked down at the prostrate man. Von Bibra turned to Ah Tong: 'Give him some water.' Ah Tong tried to force water into his friend's mouth but it ran over his lips and disappeared into the parched sand.

The two Chinese men then carried their companion to the house, Ah Tong told the court through the interpreter, adding:

> He had only a shirt and trousers on. I never opened his shirt or felt his body because I was frightened lest my master should kill me. I thought I could see a swelling on his back. I rubbed my hand down outside his shirt and felt this swelling. I have seen him with his shirt off washing and there was no swelling there before or I should have seen it.[46]

Ah Tong then explained how, the next day, the body of Jim Chu was buried in the sand. The dead man still wore his working clothes, and some bags were placed loosely over his corpse. Present at the sombre scene were von Bibra, Jack Shea, the two remaining Chinese workers and some Aboriginal men.

Several days later, Ah Tong continued, von Bibra approached him when he was out in the bush and urged him not to mention to 'Chinamen, whites, or anyone else'[47] that he had beaten the unfortunate Jim Chu before he died.

As those present in the courtroom digested this unpalatable tale, James Barratt stood up to begin cross-examining the Chinese witness. He began by asking Ah Tong to describe some of the ways in which his master had been good to him and his fellow employees prior to the digging of the well. Ah Tong conceded that he had never said that he wanted to leave von Bibra so as to get more pay, nor had he heard anyone else say so. 'He was,' Ah Tong said, 'a good master to me.' He recalled times when von Bibra had gone off in search of a lost Chinese worker, and nursed another until he had recovered from illness. When he himself was sick, his master had given him medicine, he told the court.[48]

Having gone some way towards rehabilitating his client's reputation, Barratt then pointed to discrepancies between Ah Tong's evidence as given earlier in Carnarvon and as presented now in Geraldton. The lawyer reminded the witness that he had previously said that von Bibra had approached him in his house after Jim Chu's death, but now he was saying that conversation took place in the bush. The defender also noted other inconsistencies: the number of sticks around the well, how his friend was buried. In response, Ah Tong simply denied that he had actually said what was related by the same interpreter, Fry, at the earlier hearing with Magistrate Foss in Carnarvon.

Finally, the Chinese witness asserted that the shoes tendered in court as those worn by von Bibra during the attack on Jim Chu were not in fact the pair he wore that day. The pair he wore, he said, were boots that were higher and had steel tips. Ah Tong also stated that the stick presented to the court as the weapon with which von Bibra had struck the dying man was shorter and narrower than the one actually used.

LOST IN TRANSLATION

Now it was time for Yu Quong to take the witness stand. This time, however, Robert Fry could not get the witness to agree that he could speak Malay. Even the interpreter's frustrated threat that his evasiveness would land him in trouble with the court proved ineffective on Yu Quong, who seemed untroubled by a threat he apparently did not comprehend. Mr du Boulay, equally frustrated, then ordered a local Chinese lodging-house keeper called Ah Sin to inform Yu Quong that the court was already aware that he could speak Malay, and that he would be punished if he continued to pretend otherwise.

An animated conversation in Chinese ensued between Ah Sin and the witness, before the landlord relayed to the court that Yu Quong believed that Fry 'told stories', and that he had not understood what the white interpreter had said to him at the Carnarvon hearing. Robert Fry was equally adamant that he had been painstaking in translating the evidence of the two men in Carnarvon from Malay to English.

Du Boulay was suspicious of the Chinese man's claims, but to hold him in contempt of court he would need a witness who could vouch for the fact that Yu Quong could indeed speak and understand Malay. By chance, such a witness was found in the courtroom in the form of a Malay man named William Silver. A servant for the manager of the Australian Mutual Provident Society in Geraldton, Silver was in the courtroom awaiting his own turn at the witness stand on behalf of the defence. He testified to having spoken to Yu Quong in Malay at Wooramel Station, and that he understood the language well. But when the chairman instructed Silver to inform the witness of this and of the trouble he would be in if he did not admit to his fluency in Malay, Yu

Quong revealed sufficient understanding of the judge's own language to reply belligerently in English: 'I don't care.'

Du Boulay recognised that the situation had reached a stalemate, and begrudgingly allowed Yu Quong's evidence to be interpreted by his compatriot, Ah Sin. But this decision saw the trial descend further into farce when the new interpreter realised that he and Yu Quong were from parts of China that spoke different dialects. This time it was Inspector Rowe who came to the rescue, by sending for another Chinese resident of Geraldton, Ah Fah. However, Rowe's solution too seemed in danger of being thwarted when Ah Fah refused the request until he was guaranteed a guinea for his troubles. This was finally provided, and the trial belatedly resumed.

Yu Quong told the same story of the events by the well as Ah Tong had previously outlined to the court. Before he left the stand, obviously still smarting from earlier imputations of duplicity, he reasserted through his interpreter, 'I never told Mr Foss anything about Jim Chu's death. Fry talked to the magistrate, but I did not understand him, as I do not understand Malay.'

The court was adjourned.

'THE PRISONER TOUCHED HIM WITH HIS BOOT'

At 10.30 the next morning the case resumed, and this time it was the defence team's prime witness who took the stand. Jack Shea had been at and around the scene of Jim Chu's death, and his evidence would either corroborate or negate the testimony of the previous day. It didn't take anyone in the court long to realise that his version of what took place would differ markedly from the Chinese witnesses', and not just in terms of the carefully nuanced language he used.

> Jim Chu was standing up, doing nothing, and Mr von Bibra told him to go on with his work. He did not obey, and von Bibra ordered him again to go on with his work. On his not complying, the prisoner touched him with his boot twice on the hip and thigh. Jim Chu sat down and did not say anything. I also saw von Bibra touch [the] deceased twice with a small switch, on the back and the palm of his hand. Shortly after I went to the hut.[49]

It was soon after this, according to Shea, that his boss fetched him from the house—or the hut, as he referred to it—and both men returned to the site of the well where Jim Chu now lay dead.

Inspector Rowe stepped in at this point: 'What do you mean when you say that the prisoner "touched" him with his boot?'

Shea replied, 'By "touched" I mean that von Bibra merely pushed [the] deceased with his boot; he did not kick him violently.' To clarify further he added, 'The blows were not such as could have caused anyone's death, and I don't think they would have injured a child.'

Shea then continued with his evidence, insisting that von Bibra had not lifted the prostrate man by his pigtail, as claimed by Ah Tong and Yu Quong, but merely tried to raise him. By Shea's account, when Jim Chu did not move, his master exclaimed, 'Why, he must be sick!' and then, leaving the dying man at the edge of the hole, pulled off his own shoes and jumped into the well to assist with the digging himself.

The shoes that von Bibra wore on that day would now become another discrepancy between the Chinese men's memory and that of the only white witness. Shea's description could not have been more different from the first two witnesses': he had no recollection matching Ah Tong's of high boots with steel tips, only of 'light elastic shoes, half worn out, which could not inflict a serious wound'. In fact, Shea said, he had never known von Bibra to own such boots in the twelve months he had known him.

Mr Barratt must have been satisfied that his client's reputation was once more intact when his witness concluded:

> I never heard the Chinamen in his employ express any dissatisfaction with the prisoner before Jim Chu's death. Whilst I was with him, von Bibra always treated his Malays and Chinamen with kindness and consideration.[50]

ANOTHER LANGUAGE BARRIER

In a trial where absurdity was only ever just beneath the surface, a new witness now stepped into the court. By the end of his evidence, however, neither Rowe nor Barratt could have felt their versions of events vindicated.

Both Ah Tong and Yu Quong had declared that they and their master were the sole witnesses to the death of Jim Chu. Shea, on the other hand, had categorically asserted that one more man had been present: von Bibra's Aboriginal worker Georgie. It was Georgie who now took the stand.

At first, his evidence—given in English—seemed to support the testimony of the two Chinese men. He had, he said, been by the well and seen von Bibra take Jim Chu by the hair, kick him with 'big boots' and strike him with a stick. At this point Barratt's offsider Farrelly interrupted, taking to his feet and reading out the Aboriginal man's earlier deposition given in Carnarvon, in which he had told Magistrate Foss that he had not seen von Bibra kick Jim Chu hard or strike him with a stick. That earlier evidence had been interpreted to Foss by an Aboriginal man named Billy, a fact that suggests Georgie's English was not fluent.

Once again, the issue of language and translation was becoming a problem for the court. The flustered Georgie now agreed with this earlier testimony and quickly retracted his latest statement, even adding, 'I have worked for von Bibra for one year; he was a good master to his servants.'

Before he left the stand, however, he confounded his own evidence yet again by declaring, 'It is a summer and [a] winter since Mr von Bibra told me to say he had little boots on. Jack [Shea] told me to say so at the Gascoyne just before I came on the steamer.'

In this way, Georgie corroborated his earlier evidence, in which he had hinted that both his master and Shea had coached him in preparation for his appearance before Foss. It was not the first time, nor would it be the last, that each side attempted to portray the other as having concocted its story prior to trial.

'THEY CAN TALK MALAY AS WELL AS I CAN'

Carnarvon's Constable Enoch Odling was now called to give evidence on behalf of the defence, which had paid him fifteen pounds to cover his expenses. He added little more to the information already presented to the court, other than to say that he believed, from his observations at the time of his investigation, that neither the Chinese men nor Georgie had appeared to be troubled by the interpretation of their evidence to Foss in Carnarvon. Then, hinting at broader problems with the local Asian community, he added, 'I have been acquainted with Shark Bay for eighteen months, during which time there has been plenty of trouble with Chinese servants, through their endeavouring to break their engagements.'

Odling's comments would indirectly support the claims of subsequent witnesses that Jim Chu, in keeping with the supposed habits of his countrymen, had been avoiding work by shamming illness on the day of his death.

The next witness for the defence—Thomas Brown, a labourer who had previously lived with von Bibra on the same property for ten months—lent credence to this claim, telling the court, 'I have heard Chinamen complain about their wages, and I've known them to sham sick; they often did it whilst I was at von Bibra's.' Then he, too, reasserted Shea's earlier claim that the pearler only wore elastic-sided boots with non-steel tips. And finally, in case anyone had missed the point, Brown also observed that von Bibra had always treated his Chinese workers well.

Now it was time for fellow Shark Bay pearler Robert Fry—the man who had translated Ah Tong's and Quong Yu's testimony from the Malay in Carnarvon—to give his evidence. Fry began by repeating the now-familiar refrains about the idleness of Chinese workers and the kindness of Leopold von Bibra:

> I have had eight years' experience among Chinese. They are not good workers, grumble about their wages, and refuse duty. They also complain of being ill if they are given hard work, and knock off. I have worked with Mr von Bibra, and whilst I was with him he treated the Chinese well.[51]

As for language problems, Fry was adamant that he 'did not have much trouble' translating between Malay and English for both Ah Tong and Quong Yu at Mr Foss's inquiry. No-one asked whether the Chinese men had much trouble understanding Mr Fry's translation.

Instead, the defence called William Silver, the 'bright, intelligent-looking Malay' servant of the Australian Mutual Provident Society boss. His evidence was unambiguous, and might well have put paid to the Chinese men's claims to have been misrepresented by Fry in Carnarvon:

> I know Ah Tong and Yu Quong. I was at Sharks' Bay about twelve months ago and conversed with them both at Mr [von] Bibra's station in Malay; they can talk Malay as well as I can. I spoke to Yu Quong a little while ago, and he answered me back in Malay.[52]

The final witness for the defence—Dr Edmund Raghib, a member of the Royal College of Surgeons, England—now took the stand. Dr Raghib strongly doubted that the assault as described by the Chinese men would, in itself, have been fatal. It was possible, he explained to the court, that the victim had a previously undiagnosed ailment that led to his untimely death, one of which even Jim Chu and his friends were unaware. He conceded, however, that:

> It is perfectly possible, supposing a man to be suffering from heart disease, for such a kicking as has been described to cause death; a man suffering

from heart disease might be killed by a sudden fright without any violence being offered.[53]

'MODERATE AND JUSTIFIABLE CORRECTION'

With the doctor's departure from the witness stand, Mr Barratt and his team summarised their case for the defence of Leopold von Bibra. The lawyer noted the discrepancies between the depositions given at Carnarvon and Geraldton, the Chinese men's fallacious assertion that Georgie had not been present when Jim Chu died, the contradiction by Shea of Ah Tong's evidence that there was a lump on his friend's body, and the medical evidence that dispelled any strong likelihood of von Bibra's actions having caused the death of the deceased.

Mr Barratt then turned to the issue of interpretation. He was damning of the 'demeanour of these Chinamen, their disinclination to be interpreted in Malay, and their denial that they understood that language'. As for the charge of manslaughter, he said, there was no evidence that Jim Chu had had a pre-existing medical condition and even less evidence that his client's actions had exacerbated such a condition. Even had the charge been one of common assault, Barratt said, he doubted that the law would hold the Shark Bay pearler to account. After all, he explained, precedent held that 'if a disobedient servant was unfortunate enough to die through the moderate and justifiable correction of his master no guilt can be attached to the latter'.[54]

The jury retired to consider their verdict, and returned soon afterwards. 'Not guilty,' declared the chairperson. Leopold von Bibra was a free man again—a result that saw a local newspaper trumpeting that it was:

> difficult to imagine a case in which the representatives of the Crown could exhibit more vindictiveness ... Of course Mr von Bibra was acquitted and left the Court with the honourable name that his family have always held in this colony. But who and what will repay him for his grave anxiety, and heavy loss of time and money![55]

'TREACHEROUS ASIATICS'

The von Bibra case and the other murders and violence that surrounded it were outward symptoms of a much deeper racial malaise that was gripping Shark Bay and other parts of the colony at the time. Just a month before von Bibra's trial, *The Daily News* in Perth was reporting on growing tensions in Useless Harbour and was quick to point the finger of blame:

> ... the treacherous Asiatics prove only too successful in persuading the divers in European employ to rob their masters, going shares with them in the stolen spoil. It is almost impossible for the white men to put a stop to this nefarious practice, as their coloured employees protest that the pearls found in their possession were given to them by the Asiatic pearlers, a statement which the latter are always ready and willing to corroborate in the most emphatic manner. From these causes a very hostile feeling has arisen between the Europeans and Asiatics at Sharks' Bay ...[56]

The troubles would finally come to a head that same year as the Chinese pearlers of the region set out to establish their own fleet and operate in direct competition with the Europeans. This was deemed a highly provocative move, especially when several imported Chinese labourers indentured to white pearlers broke their agreements to join their compatriots. One newspaper put it this way:

> ... upon their arrival at Sharks Bay they find their fellow countrymen getting far better wages than they do. In consequence they use any means to get out of their original agreement, putting their employers to no end of trouble and expense.[57]

The grievances of the white pearlers of Shark Bay soon coalesced into a clarion call for action against the Chinese and other Asians across the colony of Western Australian more generally, as echoed in this editorial by *The Daily News*:

> ... the legislature will have to deal with the same question of excluding Chinese from our goldfields, and it is to be hoped that, in each case, the majority of our legislators will be strongly in favour of adopting every legitimate means calculated to prove effectual in protecting both our pearl beds and goldfields from an invasion of Asiatic adventurers.[58]

In late 1885, Governor Frederick Napier Broome, responding to constant petitioning by a committee of European pearlers from Shark Bay, had begun to sound out the British government on the possibility of seeking remedy through legislation. He was given some comfort from advice received in January 1886 from the British secretary of state for the colonies, who sympathised with Broome's fear that the livelihood of Shark Bay's European pearlers was in jeopardy because of apparent attempts by the Chinese to monopolise the industry.⁵⁹ This was despite the fact that the Chinese owned only seven of the sixty-eight pearling boats then operating in the bay.⁶⁰

Her Majesty's secretary also saw no problem with the idea, popular among the white population of Shark Bay, of leasing the pearl beds to an association of Europeans. As a result, the legislative wheels were soon set in motion to achieve that end.

Meanwhile, the pressure was continuing to build. In May, the Chinese pearlers, reacting angrily to news of the attempts to block their business interests, shifted their houses further from the European settlement and declared their intention to openly work the pearl banks. The white pearlers immediately called on Police Constable Samuel Tribe to intervene. This proved fruitless when the scrupulous local policemen found that there was nothing in the law to prevent the Chinese from carrying out their intentions. Despite pressure to do otherwise, he would, he declared, 'do his duty impartially, without regard to caste or creed'.⁶¹

The frustrated European petitioners now convened a heated meeting to plan their next move. The result was a telegram to the colonial secretary, signed by pre-eminent Shark Bay landowner Aubrey Brown, asking the colonial secretary to exert his influence on Governor Broome. The message was marked urgent.

> Sir. I beg to bring to your notice that the Chinese intend starting at work on the pearling banks that have formed the subject of the late correspondence between the white pearlers and the Government on Monday next. My opinion is, that if they are not prevented by the Government there will be a very serious outbreak leading to consequences it is not safe to speculate upon. I therefore trust that His Excellency the Governor will see fit to order the police here to keep them out until the future mode of working the banks is finally settled. I would also suggest that they be gazetted closed.⁶²

Brown would have been quietly confident of his telegram's having the desired effect. His own brother, the larger-than-life Member for the Gascoyne Maitland Brown,⁶³ had been actively agitating for the same end on the floor of parliament.

While Aubrey Brown's telegram was being considered in Perth, the diligent PC Tribe set about to defuse a volatile situation before it exploded beyond his control. On hearing of the telegram's contents, he hastily met with the Chinese pearlers and convinced them to postpone their actions until a reply was received from the colony's capital. The Chinese—who when combined with their Malay colleagues totalled 170 Asian pearlers, outnumbering their white counterparts by around three to one—reluctantly agreed.[64]

Soon afterwards, the government cutter *Genesta* arrived in Shark Bay with four additional policemen from Carnarvon to help maintain order and dampen the simmering threat of violence. The uniformed men—Corporal Taylor, Lance Corporal Wall, Lance Corporal Smith and Police Constable Odling—also brought an order from the government declaring that the disputed pearl banks were closed until further notice. The order was posted in each of the camps and explained verbally to those who could not read English. For a time, and largely thanks to the efforts of Constable Tribe, an uneasy but welcome calm descended on the bay.

'UNREASONABLE FEARS'

In July 1886, the *Sharks Bay Pearl Shell Fishery Act* was finally passed. The new law required anyone wishing to fish the area for pearl shell to obtain one of a limited number of annual leases from the government. While it had all the appearances of a fair and just solution, there was a significant catch: despite Chinese pearlers also applying for these leases, they were only ever granted to European pearlers.

The true implications of the new Act appeared to dawn slowly on the Asian people of Shark Bay, and Constable Tribe's peace seemed to hold while they busied themselves with combining their resources to apply for leases. But few observers predicted that this calm would last. One visitor to the area shortly after the passing of the new legislation observed:

> It is expected by several that the Chinese will give some trouble when they find themselves refused the right of pearling but, from what I can gather, this is only fanciful. It may happen that they will be obstinate, and need a little coercion, but as for their showing a hostile and dangerous front I am not the least bit afraid. Even if it did happen so, there are white men down there sufficient to annihilate twice as many Chinamen. But I think the pearlers give way to unreasonable fears, and I am sure that the Bill [*sic*] lately introduced, will make their future way a way of roses, a way of prosperity.[65]

This would prove optimistic. The Chinese had no intention of bowing quietly to the exclusive nature of the new laws governing the harvesting of pearls at Shark Bay.

In November, as tensions began to rise again, Magistrate Foss arrived from Carnarvon to assess the situation. He soon came to the conclusion that the matter could be quickly and effectively resolved if the government were to simply buy up the Chinese fleet and pearling plants. With that in mind, he set about organising a meeting with the Chinese to discuss possible terms. It was not a great success.

> There must have been somewhere about fifty Chinamen at the first interview. None being blessed with beauty, they looked a motley crowd, equal to anything, and one could see, though not a student of physiognomy, that below the yellow skin there lay a heart filled with blackest treachery. They informed the Resident that if the Government bought their property they would all clear out.[66]

The magistrate's early optimism soon turned to dust as the Chinese held out for a price of 1,526 pounds—almost three times what Foss was prepared to offer. The lawman eventually agreed to compromise but, when his revised offer of 973 pounds was declined, he returned to Carnarvon and reported the deteriorating situation to the government.

A RESOLUTION IS REACHED

The final confrontation took place at the Notch Point pearling camp on Dirk Hartog Island on Saturday 20 November. A correspondent from *The Victorian Express* described the scene:

> … on our right were the houses of the European pearlers, in the centre of which Inspector Rowe had pitched his tent. Noble and impressively from the top of this tent floated the ever dreaded British ensign, a flag as dear to the heart of a friend as it is dreadful to that of a foe. On our left, some half mile from the European camp, was the Chinese quarter. The two mimic fleets lay in the Bay, separated by the police cutter Jessie. The line of separation was most marked. From the mast heads of the Chinese boats flew flags various in size and colour—the 'ebony to sepia' of Warangesda was nothing to it.[67] Yellow, however, predominated—the tint of jealousy—and heaven knows there was jealousy enough in the breasts of the Chinese. The Chinese fleet numbered some 21 boats, whilst the English fleet at this particular point were about 30 in number. H.M. cutter *Genesta*, with the Resident Magistrate on board, took up a position between the two fleets, and from her mast head waved proudly the blue ensign.[68]

In the end, the whole affair ended with barely a murmur. Magistrate Foss went ashore, where he was met on the beach by Inspector Rowe and his heavily armed contingent of police. After the magistrate had formally inspected the officers, he and Rowe adjourned to discuss their tactics. The two men then walked over to the Chinese camp, nicknamed Canton, where the final price and conditions of the Asian departure were ironed out. The result was that:

> The Mongolian invaders accepted a thousand pounds, gave up their boats, tents and other chattels, and sailed away to seek, figuratively, fresh woods and pastures new.[69]

The press was jubilant, and in no doubt about the reasons behind the Chinese capitulation:

> The chief cause of the settlement was the appearance of the armed force. The men under Inspector Rowe were creditable alike to the department and the country. Their business-like appearance with fixed bayonets shining brightly 'neath the sun, terrified beyond measure the sons of the flowery land. Once scare a Chinaman and he cannot be again aroused to valour.[70]

And so ended the Shark Bay stand-off. *The Sharks Bay Pearl Shell Fishery Act* of 1886 had proven to be one more effective tool in preventing Asian residents of the colony from achieving economic success beyond the boundaries of a few narrowly defined activities. Ostensibly, however, the reasons given for the legislation's introduction were quite different. The Act, its proponents claimed, was merely a means of protecting the Shark Bay pearl beds from being decimated by the perceived indiscriminate harvesting practices of the Chinese. As one member of parliament put it:

> The object of these by-laws and of the local committee would be to see that the banks were properly conserved, and to compel the pearlers—I understood it was the wish of most of the pearlers that these by-laws should be framed—when cleaning their shells, to throw the small shells over-board. The Chinese, however, took anything that came to their nets, large or small, and the consequence would be that in a very short time the pearling grounds would be completely worked out.[71]

With the Chinese now gone, ninety-two European boats were soon working those fragile pearl beds, uninhibited by any competition. This would prove a disaster, with the new level of unfettered exploitation almost bringing the industry to its knees by the early 1890s. In 1892, urgent legislation would be introduced to overturn the 1886 Act that had ushered the Chinese pearlers out but precipitated the beginning of the end of the pearling heyday of Shark Bay.[72]

THE ADVENTURER DEPARTS

And so the dust settled. White men who could afford a licence were now free to exploit the remaining pearl shell from Shark Bay at will. But the ramifications of the dispute would have far-reaching consequences for the Chinese people of Western Australia. For the next thirty years, legislation would ensure that non-indentured Chinese migrants would be restricted to enterprises that placed them in the least competition with their European counterparts, such as market gardening and some retail and laundry work.[73]

As for Leopold von Bibra, 1886 had been a tumultuous year. On being found not guilty of manslaughter he had returned to Shark Bay with the Chinese in retreat and fresh opportunities for wealth in the offing. The young adventurer bought out his father's share in their pearling business and continued to eke out a living that way for the next decade.

The ensuing years were for Leopold a rich mosaic of new ventures and growing respectability. In 1902, now married and with a ten-year-old daughter, he sold his Shark Bay pearling business. It was time to try his hand at a new enterprise, and the young family made its way north to take up part-ownership of Mardathuna Station. It didn't last long, however, and in 1905 Leopold, his wife Elizabeth and their daughter Bertha settled in Carnarvon, where the erstwhile skipper, sandalwooder, pastoralist and pearler became the owner of his own soft-drink factory.

The new proprietor became one of the town's leading citizens. He was vice-president of the football club and in 1913 became mayor. He oversaw the town's first electric light concession and chaired the public meeting that marked the small community's patriotic response to the outbreak of war in 1914.

At the age of 57, Leopold von Bibra was, to all outward appearances, a successful, popular and prominent member of the small Carnarvon establishment, a player in its dramas and a part of many a curtain-raiser to its steady progress. And then, one Monday in late August 1915, he simply walked off the stage and disappeared.

It was the town's police sergeant who began the search for the missing man. He headed out along the foreshore while, on the Tuesday, one of his constables and two Aboriginal trackers pushed out through the mangrove creeks and sandhills looking for any trace of von Bibra. When no sign of him was found, the small party expanded their hunt over to Babbage Island to the west and northwards across the river.

By Wednesday the search had intensified. Two men set off in a boat to scour the numerous creeks and beaches to either side of the town, while volunteers on horseback fanned out in all directions. By Thursday even the deeper waterholes of the river had been dragged, but no trace had been found of the ex-mayor.

By now the police had every reason to suspect the worst. Several witnesses had reported seeing an apparently despondent von Bibra post a letter in the main street shortly before his disappearance. The police applied successfully for permission to open the letter and a cursory scan of the words inside made it clear that the man they were looking for had decided to end his life. A search of von Bibra's belongings offered one further clue: on the butt of a cheque drawn on the previous Saturday, the missing man had written, 'Last I shall draw myself.'

Three weeks later, on 10 September, the police constable and one of the Aboriginal trackers were yet again combing the coastline as they had done many times in recent weeks when, sixteen kilometres north of Carnarvon, the ocean finally gave up its mystery. There, washed ashore with the drifts of broken shells and tangles of seaweed and lapped by the surf of a lonely beach, lay the body of a man.

Leopold von Bibra, the hitherto dauntless pioneer with equal stores of tenacity and bravado, beset by financial worries, had walked out into the Indian Ocean and swallowed a lethal dose of sulphuric acid.

The constable pulled the body from the surf, and the two men hitched it carefully over a horse for the journey home. One of the last players in the turbulent events of Shark Bay some thirty years before was gone.

CHAPTER 5
THE YANKEE TOWN MURDERS

> When the criminal history of Western Australia is written, it will be found that the police records of the crimes in the vast Nor'-West territory will fill many a page, and that some of the darkest deeds ever chronicled will be recorded on those pages. Though the population of the Nor'-West is but a mere handful, compared to that of the rest of the State, it seems to include more desperate characters to the hundred, than any community of lawless livers anywhere else in Australia. The reason is not difficult to find. It lies in the extraordinary congregation of colored [sic] aliens who have found their way to the pearl coast. These men, Japanese, Malays, Filipinos, Chinese, and others, who have left their countries for their countries' good, herd together in colonies, and there they live a wild, reckless life, even for colored [sic] men.
>
> —*The Daily News* (Perth, WA), Monday 11 January 1904

AT THE GALLOWS

One Monday morning in January 1904, a slightly built Chinese man, around thirty years of age, walked steadily up the few steps leading to the gallows of Fremantle Prison. With a faint smile that showed no outward sign of fear, he glanced briefly at the rope above his head and then at the small and solemn crowd below.[1]

Earlier that morning the Reverend Marshall had arrived for the occasion from nearby Beaconsfield, and it was his voice that the condemned man, Ah Hook, could now hear intoning from John 11:25: 'Jesus said unto her, I am the resurrection and the life.' The prisoner

CHAPTER 5: THE YANKEE TOWN MURDERS

recognised the words from his time at an Anglican mission in China, and from more recently when he had mixed among the churchgoers of Melbourne.

Ah Hook stepped unaided onto the trapdoor and waited calmly. The colony's usual executioner, a Mr Burrows, had died two months earlier and there had been a scramble to find a replacement. The present stand-in, a young man clearly overcome by the gravity of his role, placed a hood over Ah Hook's head and adjusted the knot in the rope.[2]

The bright sunlight of a Western Australian summer blazed its way through the windows of the prison. Nine hundred kilometres to the north that same light burned on the turned earth that marked three new graves in the Asian section of the cemetery of Carnarvon.

It was just before eight o'clock. Ah Hook waited.

'I WON'T SEE YOU TOMORROW'

Five months earlier, on 26 August 1903, the day had begun much the same as any other weekday for Vaughan Foss. The young man, son of Magistrate Charles Foss, worked behind the counter of Dalgety and Company's store in Carnarvon's main street. The respected establishment sold a wide range of goods to service the needs of 'shipping, customs, and squatters' agents' throughout the Gascoyne region.[3]

At four o'clock on that Wednesday afternoon, Vaughan Foss was approached by a young Chinese man wanting to buy a revolver. He didn't think much of it, nor did he recognise the man. Later he would recall that the customer had seemed sober, and that there was nothing about his demeanour that had suggested trouble.[4]

The sales assistant produced two guns for the customer's consideration, and it was the second of these, a Colt .32, that the Chinese man chose. He also bought fifty cartridges. Foss wrapped the goods into a tidy parcel to make them easier to carry. It was just one more dull transaction in another dull day. The young storeman had no way of knowing that one of the bullets he had just sold was meant for his own father.

Ah Hook turned insouciantly away from the counter, giving no outward appearance that he was desperately fighting phantoms that only he could see. Maybe he kept those battles well hidden, or maybe the bored storeman just didn't notice.

The Chinese man emerged onto the sunny street, gazing about him as if slightly bemused to find himself on this distant frontier of a vast land where, since arriving in Melbourne from Hong Kong some years ago, a slow but steady tide of hardship, loneliness and crime was casting him irresistibly onto the shores of one final, tragic tempest.

His early dreams of making his way in this promising new land as a cook or gardener had soon faltered, and he'd found himself increasingly living at the edges of the law. His first brush with the police came in 1899 when, under the name of Ah Ling, he was sentenced to two consecutive six-month terms for larceny and possession. The crime was as much farce as felony: he had stolen a sleeping man's trousers for the sake of a few coins. He was caught almost immediately and soon found himself in Fremantle Prison, where he was described by Superintendent George as 'bad tempered and cheeky'.[5]

In the three years that had passed since then, Ah Hook had made his way north to Carnarvon where he'd found work in the market gardens of Yankee Town, the untidy community of camps inhabited by Chinese vegetable growers, Afghan camel drivers, itinerant drovers, 'natives and undesirable whites'[6] that sprawled haphazardly along the eastern outskirts of the town. But trouble had quickly followed him and, on the day he bought the gun, he was due to face Magistrate Foss's court the following morning, this time over a financial dispute with a compatriot named Ah Tue. His chances of winning the case were slim, and the shadow of more jail time now hung heavily over him as he carried his package along the dusty streets of the port town.

To make matters worse, he had also found himself on the losing side of a battle with another market gardener, Ah Kee, for the heart of a young Japanese woman called Tunnie. His brooding resentment about this rejection wasn't helped when Tunnie, who was also involved in the current case against him, had told him to simply pay Magistrate Foss and Sergeant Thomas Houlihan—the head of Carnarvon police station—fifty pounds each and maybe he wouldn't need to go to court. This advice was 'no good—made me sulky inside', he would later tell police.

Ah Hook now nursed his multiple grievances slowly down Robinson Street, the wide, straight and dusty expanse that formed the main street of the town. One of his countrymen, Ah Saw, was also in Carnarvon that day, delivering vegetables from Yankee Town, and upon running into each other the two men agreed to have a whisky together at the Settler's Hotel.[7]

Nursing his whisky, Ah Hook gazed forlornly at his companion and told him: 'Goodbye. I won't see you tomorrow.'[8]

'Why?' asked Ah Saw. 'Are you going away on the steamer?'

Ah Hook shook his head and then, without warning, yelled at a passing white man, 'I am done tonight!'

His alarmed friend looked at him closely. 'Why do you talk like that?' he asked.

But Ah Hook, sunk deep in some private melancholy, only replied, 'It's alright. Don't talk to anybody.'

After finishing their drinks the two men climbed onto Ah Saw's cart and headed home to Yankee Town. They had travelled only a short distance when, without explanation, the increasingly distracted Ah Hook leapt down from the cart and retrieved a loaf of bread from behind a tree. In answer to Ah Saw's questioning look, he said, 'I bought it at Newman's this morning.'

The pair rode on, arriving at the shack where Ah Hook lived with another Chinese man named Ah Lee. By now, the wattles, tamarisks and eucalypts were fading in the dying light of one more unremarkable sundown.

TRAGEDY LOOMS

The smells of cooking and smoke tinged the air of Yankee Town, its unruly array of shacks, camps and market gardens crisscrossed by a series of dirt tracks that cut through the low scrub. It was dusty in summer and muddy in winter, the red dirt riddled with doublegees, ants and snakes. There was no school, and the single store—operated by William (Bill) Newman, who also served as Carnarvon's council secretary, secretary of the racing club and a commission and insurance agent—catered for the needs of the entire ragtag community.

In 1903, Carnarvon's Chinese community made up only a tiny proportion of the two thousand of their countrymen living throughout Western Australia, but its relationship with the local white population was as fraught as it was in most of Australia at that time. At a public meeting in the town just a few years earlier, one political candidate and prominent member of colonial society had been fondly applauded by Carnarvon's citizenry when he proclaimed that, while he had no problem with the importation of the Chinese as cooks and 'houseboys'—in fact, George Yorke Hubble J.P. declared, he thought this especially important if the state's northern parts were to be developed—he strongly protested against 'Asiatics being permitted to compete with the white man in any other pursuits'.[9]

While Chinese women were not banned from entering Australia, they were actively discouraged from doing so, with the result that the lives of Chinese men in the colonies were often lonely.[10] That loneliness took its toll: while hardworking and largely law-abiding, Carnarvon's Chinese community also had its fair share of crime, opium abuse and suicide. As early as 1885 the town's police had asked the advice of Magistrate Foss as to where Chinese prisoners might be located, explaining that there were 'only two cells, one for whites, and one for natives'.[11]

Violence seemed almost inevitable in this marginalised population. In 1896 the state's major newspaper reported that:

> The charge of shooting with intent recently preferred against the Chinese, Ah Chew, at Carnarvon, for shooting a Japanese, was dismissed. The accused, however, was fined £5 and costs on a second charge of pointing fire arms.[12]

This incident was attributed to jealousy arising out of competition for a Japanese woman,[13] a motivation that would echo tragically through Carnarvon's Chinese community some seven years later as Ah Hook returned to Yankee Town that Wednesday evening.

On arriving at the shack that Ah Hook shared with Ah Lee, Ah Saw jumped from the cart and spoke to Ah Lee about getting some help with a verandah he was building. Ah Hook abruptly interrupted the two men and, giving Ah Lee some silver coins, told him to go and buy them a fowl for dinner. 'It's too late for that, Ah Hook!' exclaimed Ah Lee. Ah Hook then wandered off, saying he would see if he could get a bird from over at their neighbour Ah Low's camp.

As soon as he was out of earshot, the two men looked at each other. Ah Saw was the first to speak: 'What's the matter with him? He's been talking strangely in town.'

Ah Lee shrugged but, when told of the purchase of the gun, muttered solemnly, 'I think he's going to shoot himself.'

Darkness was gathering, and Ah Lee went inside to have dinner. But Ah Saw couldn't let the matter rest, and was soon discussing Ah Hook's erratic behaviour with another friend in a neighbouring hut, Ah Sing. No-one doubted that a tragedy was looming, and it was agreed that the three concerned men would meet again later back at Ah Hook and Ah Lee's shack to find a solution. Meanwhile, Ah Hook had returned to where he lived and, producing a bottle of whisky, shared it with Ah Lee, Ah Saw and a local Malay man. Afterwards he wandered disconsolately into the night.

The remaining men, along with Ah Sing and Ah Low, who by now had joined them, discussed what to do about their troubled friend. Ah Saw, growing increasingly agitated, suggested they confine him to a room for the night. But Ah Low had his own view of why Ah Hook was acting strangely and didn't think locking him up was necessary. Alluding to Ah Hook's previous crimes and his looming court case, he told the men gathered in the dim light, 'No, he has been in trouble in Perth—a telegram came to the sergeant.' Even if this rumour was true, Ah Low couldn't explain the connection between the telegram and the gun.

The group broke up with no plan in place, Ah Saw leaving with Ah Sing. On reaching Ah Sing's shack, the two parted ways and Ah Saw continued walking alone towards his own home, making his way along the dirt track by the light of a lantern he held before him. Glancing up, he noticed that a light still shone in the house of his friend Ah Tue—the man with whom Ah Hook was involved in the financial dispute—which Ah Tue shared with the young Japanese woman, Tunnie. Ah Tue was due to appear as a witness for the prosecution against Ah Hook in court the following day. He and Tunnie had just finished a supper of fishballs and rice when Ah Saw appeared at their door. 'Will you have some?' asked the Japanese woman.

As Ah Saw ate, the three friends chatted. The conversation soon turned to work, as Ah Tue, a teamster for Brickhouse Station on the outskirts of Carnarvon, was in town with a load of wool for a steamer waiting at the Carnarvon jetty. His guest, keen to drum up any business he could, asked him to tell the Brickhouse cook to let him know if he needed any vegetables.

Suddenly Ah Saw paused and, listening intently, asked, 'What was that noise?' The conversation suspended, his hosts turned their gaze towards the open door. It was Ah Tue who broke the silence: 'It's only the mice eating rice in the roof.' Satisfied, Ah Saw stood up to leave. He said goodnight to the teamster and then, turning to Tunnie, added, 'Goodnight, little girl.' It would be the last time he saw her alive.

Ah Tue walked his friend to the door. 'Be careful,' he said. 'Don't tumble down.'

'YOU AND ME ARE FINISHED!'

Ah Tue and Tunnie returned to their seats at the table, their own quiet conversation eddying in the night air. Only a few minutes had passed when a faint noise outside caused Ah Tue to ask Tunnie whether she had fed the dog. Tunnie nodded. The teamster called the animal, and was surprised to see it come from a different direction from the sound. He listened, but once more the night was quiet except for the usual hum of soft voices carrying across the scrub. 'Go away,' he said to the dog.

Then the sound came again, and this time Tunnie moved to the open window and strained to see into the darkness. 'Close the window,' said Ah Tue. Tunnie did so and returned to the table, where the two sat quietly listening.

More minutes passed, and then someone coughed. Ah Tue and Tunnie looked towards the door, and there stood Ah Hook wearing a crepe shirt, a Chinese waistband and a small black cap. The waistband had a deep pocket on either side, and from one of these the uninvited guest pulled a bottle of whisky, which he placed on the table.

'Drink,' he said.

Ah Tue shook his head, but Ah Hook ignored him and half-filled two cups that were standing by the dinner plates. 'No good you go to the courthouse,' he told Ah Tue.

The teamster only shook his head again and said, 'I think you should leave.' Then, for a second time, he refused the drink put before him.

Ah Hook swayed unsteadily, then calmly reached again into one of his deep pockets and, lifting his gun at the startled Ah Tue, screamed at the terrified young Japanese woman, 'You and me are finished!'

For a few interminable seconds the Colt .32 waved uncertainly in the air as Ah Hook's mind raced. Before him sat two people who had only ever shown him kindness. A month before, he and Tunnie had been living together as lovers. And in all the time he had known Ah Tue, the two had been friends between whom no bad word had ever passed.

In that moment of hesitation, Ah Tue and Tunnie saw their chance and quickly bolted for the door. But they had not made it far before a bullet fired hurriedly by Ah Hook passed through Ah Tue's elbow. As they reached the door a second shot felled Tunnie, who screamed, 'I am dead!'

Ah Tue, now in a blind panic, ran into the wire fence to the north of the house, fell though it and stumbled desperately into the darkness. He glanced quickly over his shoulder and saw the silhouette of Ah Hook, revolver in hand, standing over the prostrate young woman. Then he saw the flash of the gun and heard the sound of another shot and one final cry from Tunnie as a bullet pierced her heart.

Ah Tue continued crashing wildly through the bush, scrambling and weaving, screaming until he found himself at the door of one of the white families of Yankee Town, the Birds.[14] 'What's the matter?' came a voice from inside the house. But Ah Tue, wounded and in shock, had collapsed into silence on the verandah.

THE PANIC SPREADS

Earlier, when Ah Saw had left Ah Tue and Tunnie's shack, he had walked the short distance back to Ah Lee's shared hut, where he'd hoped to find Ah Hook. To his dismay, he found that his friend had not yet returned. Recalling Ah Lee's earlier prediction, Ah Saw feared the worst, but figured it was now too late in the evening to do much more than cross the dry riverbed and return to his own home by Yanget Pool.

Ah Lee had another suggestion: 'Stay for a smoke of opium,' he said to Ah Saw.[15] But the words had barely passed his lips when the sound of a gunshot split the night air. Both men's heads spun towards the direction of Ah Tue's house. Ah Lee, not waiting to find out what was going on, ran off into the safety of the darkness. Ah Saw grabbed his lantern and began to make his way hurriedly back to where he could hear Tunnie screaming, 'Ah Tue! Ah Tue!' People were now emerging from the shadows, appearing in doorways, peering through windows and fearfully questioning each shadowy passer-by. As Ah Saw drew closer to the source of the cries, a sense of panic swirled up inside him and he, too, turned tail and rushed from the scene.

The market gardener who lived next door to Ah Tue's shack was none other than Ah Kee, the man who had stolen Tunnie's heart from the bereft Ah Hook. He called after Ah Saw: 'What's the matter?' But there was no reply, only the sound of footsteps disappearing into the blackness.

Ah Kee then ran towards his neighbour's house. The sight that confronted him there was of Tunnie's now lifeless body on the floor, an overturned lantern beside her and, in the light of its gathering flames, the outline of a man raising his revolver. The gunman, face to face with his rival in love, pulled the trigger and Ah Kee, mortally wounded, staggered away into the surrounding market gardens. The murderer briefly dashed after him but quickly thought better of it and returned to the burning house.

By this time Ah Saw had arrived back at Ah Lee's shack and, on hearing the final shot, assumed the worst—this time correctly. 'Now he has shot Ah Kee!' he cried. The two men ran to Carnarvon police station to raise the alarm.

At the crime scene, the fire from the lamp was spreading quickly and soon the small shanty was ablaze. As a flurry of upraised voices made their way towards the flames, Ah Hook disappeared into the surrounding darkness and, still carrying his gun, began to walk slowly back towards Carnarvon. When he reached the Settler's Hotel he stepped calmly into the bar and ordered himself a drink.

By the time Sergeant Houlihan arrived on the scene with one of his constables and local doctor James Ryland Hickinbotham, Ah Tue's shack had almost burned to the ground and the air was thick with the smell of smoke and burning flesh. Houlihan and his constable pulled the almost unrecognisable remains of Tunnie from the house and then, leaving her charred body with the doctor, the two policemen set off in search of the killer.

'I DID IT! I DID IT!'

Back in Carnarvon, most townsfolk were unaware of the violent drama that had just played out on their town's outskirts and were turning out their lamps and settling into their beds. Earlier that evening, about an hour before the murders in Yankee Town, Japanese laundryman Kata Tukenei had tried to coax his business partner Yanoo to come out with him for a game of cards. Yanoo had declined and, when Tukenei had left the laundry where the two men lived together, his friend was already in bed.

It was not until around eleven o'clock that night that Tukenei returned to the laundry. The street was quiet, and the house was dark as he reached the short step that led onto the verandah. At that moment, a slight sound coming from in front of him caught his ear. He paused, his eyes straining into the shadows. 'Who is there?' he asked. A voice he didn't recognise replied cryptically, 'Me.'

Tukenei stepped towards the front door and came face to face with a dark figure gazing at him intently. It was Ah Hook.

The startled Tukenei took a step back. 'Who are you?' he asked. In answer, the Chinese man simply raised the Colt .32 and pulled the trigger. But this time there was only the sound of three metallic clicks. The gun had misfired. Tukenei took to his heels, screaming, 'Murder! Police!' as he fled down the empty street.

Constable Edward O'Loughlin, who lived some one hundred metres from the laundry, was just getting ready for bed when he heard thumping and banging, followed by the loud sounds of two men's voices. He stopped and listened, until he heard the screams of Tukenei, at which he ran from his house and towards the commotion. On the street he met the fleeing man and, making what he could of his garbled story, quickly made his way in the direction of the laundry.

By now Ah Hook was walking slowly across a paddock not more than sixty metres from the laundry. The policeman ran towards the figure disappearing into the darkness. As he drew near, Ah Hook turned calmly to face him and, once more, silently raised his gun. O'Loughlin, like those before him that night, found himself looking down the barrel of the Chinese man's revolver. Ah Hook pulled the trigger but, twice more, the gun misfired.

O'Loughlin launched himself at the murderer and the two men fell to the ground as Tukenei, who had followed the policeman back to the laundry, stood helplessly watching. O'Loughlin was now fighting for his life. He grasped desperately at the hand with the gun in it but, as he did so, Ah Hook's other hand lunged at him three times with a sheath knife he had stolen from Tukenei and Yanoo's house. The blade cut once into the policeman's chest. At this point Tukenei, finally pushing aside the fog of shock and terror, joined the fray and, with his help, the bloodied constable managed to disarm his assailant.

By now more footsteps and voices could be heard approaching the scuffling men. At the forefront of these was Sergeant Houlihan, who had come straight from the Yankee Town murder scene. He quickly handcuffed the struggling Ah Hook.

No-one had yet entered the laundry, but Houlihan, fearing the worst, sent Tukenei to fetch Dr Hickinbotham from Yankee Town. Then, with Ah Hook in tow, the two policemen made their way to the door of the laundry. Looking inside, they made out the lifeless body of Yanoo on the floor. He had been shot five times, and one of his ears would later be found on the street outside. The voice of the captive Ah Hook, gazing wildly at the body, cried breathlessly, 'I killed him! I did it! I did it!'

The policemen now made their way back to the station, with the prisoner rambling, 'You are all jealous of me over that woman. I was going to kill all the police and Mr Foss.'

Meanwhile, Yanoo's body was carried to the hospital mortuary where Dr Hickinbotham would later find four bullets still inside the dead man, one of which had proved fatal by severing an artery in the victim's back.

By now the critically injured Ah Kee had also been conveyed to the hospital, where the doctor set about assessing the serious bullet wound to his abdomen. It was almost 1.30 in the morning but the exhausted

Hickinbotham immediately prepared to operate. As he did so, Sergeant Houlihan had time to ask the bleeding man, 'Who shot you, Ah Kee?' The fading man whispered, 'I not know who shot me; it too dark.' Despite the surgeon's efforts, he passed away at three o'clock that afternoon.

Meanwhile, Ah Hook, although complaining of a pain in his chest, was now calmer and listened quietly as a charge of wilful murder was read out to him. As loose change and spare cartridges were removed from his pockets, he became almost contrite. 'I am sorry for the big policeman,' he murmured. 'I didn't know him in the dark. I thought it was the sergeant.'

To his intended victim, Sergeant Houlihan, Ah Hook would later say, 'Me not sorry for myself, me just sorry for my mother.'

'WHOSE LAW IS THIS?'

For Ah Hook, thirty years of a troubled existence was coming steadily to an end. In December 1903, the penultimate drama would play out some nine hundred kilometres south, in the Western Australian Supreme Court.

Only the case of Yanoo was brought before the court. The defence was conducted by former MLA for Perth Mr William Morton Purkiss, while the state's prosecution was brought by the redoubtable Richard Septimus Haynes K.C., renowned for his perky demeanour and pugnacious jaw.[16]

Justice proved to be swift. Mr Purkiss, in the face of overwhelming evidence against his client, could summon no convincing defence other than that of mitigation in the form of insanity. Following the judge's summing up of the case, the jury retired to consider the fate of Ah Hook. Thirty minutes later they returned a verdict of guilty, while seeking that the prisoner's sanity be medically assessed. The judge agreed and, turning to Ah Hook, asked if there was anything the doomed man wanted to say before a sentence of death was passed.

When it became clear that the prisoner had not understood the question, an interpreter was called. Now Ah Hook, for the first time in the trial, took the opportunity to explain that, while he had not known his victim, Yanoo, he knew that the Japanese man had hired several men to kill him. In fact, he explained, four of those men had chased him with tomahawks on the day of the murders. This was why, Ah Hook explained, he had confronted the laundryman that night. Yanoo's response, according to the guilty man, had been to lunge at him with a knife, and Ah Hook had shot him dead in self-defence.

A murmur passed through the court, and the Chief Justice called for silence. The room fell quiet and, without further ado, the judge uttered the fatal words: 'Ah Hook, the sentence is that you be returned to your former custody and that you be taken thence at a time and place appointed where you will be hanged by the neck until you are dead.'

For most of the trial, the accused man's dubious mental state combined with his poor English had left him largely disconnected from the events that flowed around him. Now he broke into voluble remonstrance and demanded, 'Whose law is this? Is this Carnarvon's law?'

But the judge was in no mood for further discussion. 'It is the same law for a white man, black man, or Chinaman,' he replied tersely. 'Remove the prisoner.'

And with that, Ah Hook was taken to the cells, handcuffed to another felon and transported to Fremantle Prison. Only the last act in the drama of his life remained to be played.

'YOUR TIME IS UP'

The last month of Ah Hook's life passed in the heat of a final Australian summer. While the prison authorities were impressed with his conduct, deeming him a 'superior class of Chinese',[17] no matter how often they asked him for details of family who might be informed of his fate, he divulged only that he had a wife and family back in his home country. Who they were and where they lived would remain a mystery known only to the condemned man.

In the first two weeks following the trial, Ah Hook had seemed moodily careless of his fate, but as the time of his execution drew nearer he became more circumspect and apprehensive. He even confided the details of his crime to a priest, trying ineffectually to explain the mental turmoil caused by his dispute with his compatriot and his feelings for the young Japanese woman, Tunnie. He was, he said, much knocked around and, on the night of the crimes, no longer cared what he did. But those bloody events and their muddy motives had already moved into the irredeemable past, and Ah Hook must surely have known that no new explanation could slow his march to the gallows.

So now, as the prison clock approached eight o'clock on that warm Monday morning, he waited.

He had spent a restless final night, and when his jailers had appeared at his cell door around seven o'clock he was already wide awake. 'It's nearly time,' one of them told him. 'I know,' Ah Hook replied and, when asked if he had any last request, shook his head. He also declined breakfast, taking only the traditional brandy offered to every condemned man.

Just after seven o'clock there was a soft knock at the cell door and two priests, the reverends Marshall and O'Halloran, entered the room.[18] Marshall stayed with the prisoner while O'Halloran, the jail chaplain, left the room to lead a brief service for those outside who had gathered to witness the young man's final moments.

When the chaplain returned at about seven thirty, the three men entered into prayer, which the Chinaman appeared to follow devoutly. Somewhere among those sombre whispers the doomed man again shared his sorrow for the lives he had taken.

The murmured conversation was eventually broken by the voice of the sheriff's officer demanding the body of the prisoner, Ah Hook. It was three minutes to eight.

The men looked at each other. 'Your time is up,' O' Halloran said quietly. 'Have you anything you want to say?'

Ah Hook shook his head. 'No.'

O'Halloran persisted gently: 'Anybody you would like me to write to? Your wife, or anyone else?'

Again the answer was simple: 'No.'

Reverend Marshall stood up and began intoning the Psalms. This was the signal for the small procession to make its way to the waiting gallows.

As he stepped out into the room where the official witnesses were waiting, Ah Hook cut a strange, exotic figure in the sober morning light. As one last gesture, the jail authorities had granted him permission to wear traditional clothing from his homeland on his final day on earth. So there he stood for the last time, a small man in flowing trousers and a black embroidered silk shirt, his long dark hair neatly plaited in a circle on his head.

Ah Hook smiled briefly at the rope and stepped onto the platform.

As the hood fell over his face, perhaps he smelt the brandy on his final breath, heard the words of the Psalms become slightly muffled. 'He that believe in me, though he were dead, yet shall he live.'

Unseen hands fumbled with the rope around his neck, and he heard the young executioner's footsteps move quickly away from him. Before the prayer was finished, the lever was pulled, and Ah Hook felt briefly the sensation of his body dropping quickly and silently into the emptiness below.[19]

CHAPTER 6
AFFRAY AT MONKEY'S WELL

Men constantly living with only a few other humans tired of each other and of each other's company, with the result that some became morose; others belligerent and others keen in their desire to live altogether alone. In those vast areas which are known as the Gascoyne country stretching away from Carnarvon for hundreds of miles to the East and North there were scattered station homesteads ... Kangarooers had their camps near wells, and were jealous if others came into the locality. All men living in that vast expanse of the Gascoyne were known to each other, but were not necessarily pining for each other's company. Lonely places bred lonely people. Sometimes there was enmity between men of different camps. That between two kangarooers led to a tragedy late in 1905.

— *The Daily News* (Perth, WA), Saturday 10 November 1934

A MEETING BY THE WELL

It was a hot morning in November 1905, and kangaroo shooter Sam Cocking was camping at a watering hole called Monkey's Well, on Yanyeareddy Station some three hundred kilometres north-east of Carnarvon. The roo shooter's life was a hard one and lonely, but the work was steady and the money good. As the pastoral industry had gradually taken root in Australia's north-west in the late 1800s, kangaroos were increasingly seen as vermin and bounties were introduced to keep their numbers down. It wasn't long before there was a thriving trade in the animals' skins and, between 1935 and 1936, 1.25 million red kangaroo skins from Western Australia would be shipped to the markets in

Sydney.[1] This lucrative trade made roo shooting an attractive livelihood for seasoned bushmen like Sam Cocking.

Cocking had ridden from Yanyeareddy Homestead that morning and, at around eight o'clock, overtook another traveller, a big man called James Lonton who went by the nickname of 'Queenslander'. Cocking wasn't surprised: it was common to meet friends and strangers alike around Monkey's Well, not far from the homestead of Frank Lefroy's Yanyeareddy Station on the banks of the Lyndon River. Various wanderers of the far-flung bush—shearers, shooters, policemen and those looking for work—often congregated around Yanyeareddy, where the Onslow and Minilya mail coaches also met and exchanged goods and messages.[2] The two men rode together towards Monkey's Well.

Cocking cursed silently under his breath. He had no time for Lonton. He would later say in court, 'I had only seen Lonton three times. From what I know of him he was a fighting man'.

There was no doubt that 'Queenslander' had a reputation. As one Carnarvon identity would later write, it was freely admitted even by Lonton's friends that he was 'notorious throughout the North West as a violent and thorough-paced blackguard notorious alike in temper and language.'[3]

Not everyone felt the same way about the burly bushman, however. One drover recalled him simply to be a 'straight-forward man', adding:

> I had some dealings with him when I was supplying the diggers on the Ashburton Goldfields, and if there were only a few more like him in the Nor'-West, it would be better off. He was well-educated and could write in a really good hand.[4]

Sam Cocking much preferred the mateship of his hunting companion, John Fleming, with whom he had been recently camping at Monkey's Well. In contrast to Lonton, Fleming was a quiet man known for his morose disposition and reluctance to show emotion.[5] He was, as one observer would later state with deftly damning praise, 'when away from drink, a[n] honest, hard-working, semi-bucolic sort of individual'.[6]

Fleming may have had good cause to keep his past to himself: the taciturn man had come into contact with the law more than once in his life. In 1873 he had been a seaman on the barque Queensland when he was brought before the courts in Newcastle for desertion.[7] It was soon revealed that the twenty-three-year-old sailor's absence from his post was not intentional: he had been unable to return to the ship because he was in the local lock-up for drunkenness. The judge ordered him put back onboard by the police. Fleming's troubles didn't end there, however: he had also, around 1891, been found guilty of writing two valueless cheques.

But these indiscretions were all well in the past by the time of the events at Monkey's Well. Fleming, now aged fifty-five, had been clear of the law for about fifteen years.[8]

When Cocking and Lonton rode into Monkey's Well that morning they were unaware that Fleming had arrived during the night, having returned from concluding some business in the northern town of Onslow. Cocking was pleasantly surprised to find his friend back in the camp that they had shared for the past seven weeks.

WHISKY FOR BREAKFAST

Despite Lonton's reputation, the three men found enough to talk about amiably. As Cocking set about unloading his pack, Fleming and Lonton were discussing horses, and were in the middle of a five-pound wager about the breeding of one of his colts when Sam Cocking said, 'Don't worry about the bet. Come over and have a drink.' He shared a half-bottle of whisky with his two fellow travellers and then, when that was gone, produced another full bottle. Though the hour was early it was already hot, and the thirsty men finished the contents of both bottles in a mere fifteen minutes.

At first the conversation flowed easily and amicably between the three men but, as the dregs of the second bottle were reached, the language between Fleming and Lonton became increasingly vituperative. Both men harboured a simmering grudge against the other over a disagreement two years earlier at Brickhouse Station. As the old resentment bubbled to the surface between the two kangaroo hunters, Cocking calmly set about making his breakfast.

It was Fleming, with half a bottle of whisky under his belt, who raised the issue first. 'Where's that surcingle you have of mine?' he demanded. Lonton said nothing, but went back to the well and returned with a leather surcingle, throwing it at Fleming, who was now sitting on the ground by his tent with his back against a tree. 'That's not mine,' he told Lonton.

The big man from Queensland, famously volatile under the influence of alcohol, retorted with sarcasm: 'No, you bastard, it's not good enough for you!'

Fleming, in turn, replied dismissively, 'If you can't behave yourself, you had better go back to your own camp.'

This was too much for the mercurial Lonton. With his fists raised and his bare feet shuffling the dry dust, he cried angrily, 'Get up! Let's have a mouthful of you!'

Fleming stayed where he was. 'No,' he said calmly, 'I'm no fighting man.'

But Lonton was beside himself. 'You bastard! If you don't get up I'll hit you where you sit!'

Now it was the usually soft-spoken Fleming's turn to raise his voice. 'If you call me that again,' he exclaimed, 'I'll punch a hole in you!'

James Lonton, sensing that he had finally goaded Fleming into a fight, repeated loudly, 'You bastard!' As he did so he moved towards the man sitting on the ground.

Fleming started quickly to his feet, as he did so grabbing Cocking's Winchester from where it was leaning against the tree. Cocking looked on in horror as the gun went off and Lonton staggered forward in a stooping position.[9]

'My God!' Cocking yelled. 'You've shot him!'

Fleming cried, 'I couldn't help it!' And then he added hastily, 'I didn't know it was loaded!'

Cocking dashed to the aid of the shocked and bloody Lonton, taking him in his arms and easing him gently to the ground. Blood was running from the upper left side of the wounded man's chest and down his back.

'I, JAMES LONTON, CAME TO MY DEATH'

Cocking moved Lonton under the shade of a tree and told the dazed Fleming to fetch one of the horses from the well so that the alarm could be raised at the Yanyeareddy homestead. The shooting had taken place at ten o'clock and within five minutes Cocking, still feeling the effects of the whisky, was riding towards Frank Lefroy's house, leaving the wounded man and his assailant alone together.

The station homestead was a fair ride from Monkey's Well and when the ashen-faced Cocking rode in that morning Lefroy and his foreman, Richard (Dick) Grey,[10] were packing kangaroo skins under a shed with a contractor who lived on the Minilya River, Stephen Brown. It was Grey who looked up first, and said to the station-owner, 'Here comes Cocking. There's something very seriously wrong with him—someone must have shot or poisoned his dogs.'

Later that afternoon, after reporting to Lefroy the morning's events at the watering hole, Sam Cocking and another kangaroo shooter, George Vann, set out to return to Monkey's Well. Like many of the players involved in the affray on that November day, thirty-four-year-old George Vann had his own history of brushes with the law as well as a problem with the booze. Earlier that year he had been fined, in default of a month's imprisonment, by Magistrate Foss in Carnarvon for selling alcohol to an Aboriginal person.[11]

Meanwhile, in the hours that had elapsed while Cocking was alerting those at the homestead to the shooting, back at Monkey's Well, Lonton and Fleming had been joined by yet another kangaroo shooter with a dubious history. David Charles (Dave) Johnson was a West Indian man who had approached Fleming's camp late that morning seeking supplies, his own camp some fourteen kilometres away having burned down the night before. He arrived at the watering hole to find Lonton—whom he initially mistook for Sam Cocking—lying under a tree and Fleming, whom Johnson had only met once previously, sitting some distance away.

Dave Johnson had been in his fair share of trouble in the years leading up to the events of November 1905. He had been convicted four times of a range of offences, including obtaining goods by false pretences by passing valueless cheques. He had pleaded guilty each time and had subsequently been jailed variously in Fremantle, Marble Bar, Roebourne and Cue.[12]

'What happened to Sam?' he asked as he gazed around the scene. Fleming pulled himself to his feet and simply replied, 'It's not Sam. I shot Lonton this morning.' Then he cut short the West Indian's further questions with a terse, 'I'll tell you later on.' Gesturing to the man on the ground, he added, 'You'd better attend to him—he won't let me near him.'

Johnson, who had never before met the infamous Lonton, bent over the wounded man, who stared up at him and asked for water. Then, noticing Fleming standing close by, Lonton muttered, 'Don't let that dog near me. He shot me like a crow when I was sitting down taking my boots off.'

A little later, Fleming asked Johnson to make Lonton a cup of hot cocoa. While the billy boiled Fleming related to Johnson his own account of the argument, including Lonton's threat of violence and the rash shooting under provocation. Two conflicting versions of what had happened at the camp that morning had begun to emerge. Whatever conclusion Johnson reached from the two inconsistent stories, he kept his peace and returned to the man on the ground.

Lonton appeared to have slipped into a deep depression, possibly realising for the first time the seriousness of his wound and his scant chances of survival. 'Fleming wants me to write a statement,' he told Johnson. 'Can you write?'

The West Indian man nodded but, while he quickly located a half-sheet of notepaper, no pencil could be found. Instead he prepared to record the dying man's words with the tip of a .44 bullet. Lonton looked at him darkly and, nodding his head towards Fleming, muttered, 'The dog wants hanging, but it would do me no good … Write as I direct you.'

Then he dictated the brief statement:

I, James Lonton, came to my death by the accidental discharge of a gun.

Johnson then held Lonton steady as he painfully sat up and signed the paper.

About ninety minutes later Fleming, who was illiterate, asked to see the statement. By now Lonton had also dictated his will, which Johnson had written with the bullet on a scrap of an old telegraph form. Lonton again signed the document and this time Fleming also added his mark.

Shortly afterwards Sam Cocking and George Vann arrived from Yanyeareddy. They were followed by Dick Grey. Johnson, his voice lowered, described the situation that had just unfolded, including the two signed pieces of paper that were now safely in his pocket. Lonton, stirred by the sound of voices, looked up and cried out, 'Vann! Vann! He shot me like a kangaroo!'

Vann was an old friend of the wounded shooter's and, until just the day before, the two men had also been business partners. Vann knew his friend as a good-hearted man but prone to be 'a bit of an outlaw' when drunk.[13]

It was Cocking who spoke next. 'Cheer up, old man,' he said to Lonton. 'You are worth two dead men. You're not going to die.'

Vann then crouched by the wounded man and began to tend his gunshot injury. He would later recall that he noticed the bullet hole at the front was higher than that at the back.[14]

Meanwhile, Dave Johnson headed back to his own camp.

As the sun rose further in the sky, Fleming's nerves began to fray and he became increasingly desperate that the authorities be notified of the incident. Unable to do so himself, he implored Vann to draft two telegrams—one to the police in Carnarvon and the other to the doctor there—explaining what had happened. Vann did this and, in the presence of Fleming, Cocking, Brown and Grey,[15] read the telegrams out to Lonton, who gave no indication of having heard or cared either way.

Fleming now mounted his horse and told Vann he would pay him for his trouble if he would stay with the wounded man while he dispatched the telegrams. Then he rode the 110 kilometres to the closest telegraph station at Winning Pool, from where he wired the messages to Carnarvon, a further six hundred kilometres away.[16] In the meantime, Vann decided to ride back to Yanyeareddy to get a cart with which to transport the injured man to the homestead.

When Dave Johnson returned later that evening only Cocking and the wounded man remained. Johnson spent the night close to Lonton, who woke in the morning saying he felt slightly better.

According to Johnson, he returned Lonton's purse and some bills of sale given to him by the wounded man during the night, then left Monkey's Well for the last time. As he made his way down the track he met Vann, Brown and Grey with a spring-cart as they went to collect their stricken friend.

Lonton was able to stand and even have a cigarette as the two men placed him in the buggy. This gave everyone a sense of optimism and they drove the cart slowly back towards the Yanyeareddy homestead, arriving there later that day. A makeshift bed was put together in the woolshed and the injured man was laid gently on his back. He survived another night but by noon the next day he was fading fast. George Vann remained by his side, while Lonton told him of the Brickhouse Station affair, the fight at the watering hole and how Fleming had shot him 'like a dingo'. 'I didn't think he had the pluck to do it,' said Lonton, 'but by God he shot me.'

Twenty minutes later he was dead.

NO CHARGES RECOMMENDED, NO BLAME APPORTIONED

By now the authorities in Carnarvon, alerted by the telegrams sent by Fleming from Winning Pool, had begun to mobilise. Lonton's death was soon confirmed by Justice of the Peace M.C.R. Bunbury, a Busselton-born pioneer of the district who owned Williambury sheep station about 250 kilometres inland from Carnarvon and was a good friend of Charles Foss.[17] Bunbury informed police that he intended to hold an inquest into the bushman's death and had pulled together a jury to assist him. This consisted of George Vann, Dick Grey and Frank Lefroy—the three men who had overseen the burying of Lonton a few days earlier.

In the port town, local opinion had already begun to form that the death was little more than an unfortunate accident or, at worst, justifiable self-defence. Even the newly arrived but already much respected local head of police Sergeant Smyth expressed the view that there was nothing about the case that suggested foul play.[18]

Bunbury's inquest, held at his Williambury homestead just a few days after the events, seemed to settle the matter. He and his jury of three found that James 'Queenslander' Lonton had died as a result of an accident. No charges were recommended, and no blame apportioned.

A MAGISTERIAL INQUIRY

The case might have been closed there had the depositions, when they arrived in Perth, not attracted the attention of the Crown law authorities. Interest was further provoked when an anonymous letter was received by the commissioner of police, alleging irregularities relating to the inquest into Lonton's death and uncertainty about the justice of the outcome.[19]

As a result, a warrant was issued for Fleming's arrest and Magistrate Foss was wired instructions to undertake a magisterial inquiry to determine whether the man should be charged and committed to trial.[20] Police from Carnarvon were dispatched on horseback to bring in the arrested man, round up the witnesses and exhume the body of Lonton. It was a mammoth task; the round trip to Yanyareddy alone would cover some 640 kilometres.

First to return to Carnarvon in early February 1906 was mounted police constable Buck, who brought in the prisoner, John Fleming, now facing the possibility of being committed to stand trial for wilful murder. Two nights later the first witnesses, under the escort of Constable George Saunders, arrived. Also with Saunders was the body of Lonton, sealed in a tin that had been soldered shut before the journey. The next day, Dr Hickinbotham undertook a post-mortem examination of the badly decomposed remains.

Presiding over the inquiry were Magistrate Foss and two justices of the peace: Edward Angelo, manager of Carnarvon's Union Bank; and John Harman Mansfield, owner of Maroonah Station.

Fleming's barrister was a stalwart of the small community who had served intelligently and skilfully as the legal advocate for many a citizen brought before the town's court. He was also paid a retainer as the solicitor to the fledgling town council. He was known to be a good shot with a rifle and was an avid member of the local golfing club, as well as being able to hold his own as a singer at any social gathering. Despite being known for his good humour, he was a formidable and serious man when he took to a courtroom. This inquiry would try his skills to the full. In the meantime, he informed the court that his client proclaimed his innocence.

Cocking appeared as the first witness, and relayed his version of the events that had taken place on that November morning at Monkey's Well. For the first time, the issue of the gun itself was now brought into focus. Given that it was common practice to ensure that any gun brought into a camp was unloaded, the court wanted to know how the Winchester owned by Cocking had come to contain a bullet on that fateful day. It was an important question: had Fleming, when he grabbed the Winchester, been merely bluffing under the misapprehension that the rifle was unloaded?

Cocking had a ready reply. He explained that he had used the rifle that morning on his way from the homestead to the well, after which he had emptied the barrels a few kilometres from the camp. It had then struck him that he might see a turkey, so he had reloaded one cartridge into the rifle, and forgotten to take it out again.

'Why,' asked Mr Ewing, 'did you not tell my client that the gun was loaded when he picked it up?' Cocking could only repeat lamely that he had forgotten about it. A little later, perhaps beginning to realise the importance of this piece of evidence, he added that Fleming would have believed the gun to be empty, having, over the previous seven weeks, repeatedly seen his mate empty the gun on returning to camp.

The rifle was then produced for the court to test Cocking's assertion that the trigger was easy to pull. The witness swore that no alteration had been made to the rifle since the incident, except that the stock had been broken. He had also taken the rifle to pieces about two days after Lonton was shot.

Claude Ewing began to exploit the issue of the gun. He cross-examined Cocking again: 'What condition was the rifle in at the time of the shooting?'

Cocking replied confidently, 'The rifle was perfectly clean, oiled, and in good working order at the time of the occurrence.' Then, perhaps suspecting where Ewing's line of questioning was leading, he added quickly, 'The trigger would go off with less pulling then than now. The rifle had a very easy trigger.'

The barrister listened carefully as the kangaroo shooter continued: 'I cleaned the rifle with a piece of leather and rag, sometimes carrying it wrapped around the rifle above the trigger and sometimes in my pocket. Sometimes I wound the rag around the breach and sometimes on the barrel. But if I thought I was not going to use it I would put it around the barrel near the muzzle.'

Cocking explained that the leather was about a quarter of an inch wide, and was easily stuffed down the barrel. Then, probably sensing that he had said enough, he looked around the court and concluded, 'The morning I put the rifle against the tree the cleaner may have been attached; it was not when I picked it up.'

The imputation was clear: it was possible that Fleming might well have believed the rifle to be unloaded when he pointed it at Lonton. From Ewing's perspective, it was enough to sow the seed of doubt that would be necessary to defend his client.

Lonton's friend George Vann now took the stand. He, too, was soon questioned about the Winchester. Vann, who had sat as part of the exonerating jury at the initial inquest, explained that he was now the owner of the fatal rifle, having bought it from Cocking some two weeks after the affray.

Vann then relayed what the dying Lonton had said to him as he'd tended his wounds. By and large his testimony supported the earlier evidence given by Cocking, with Vann repeating once more Lonton's dying words: 'He shot me like a dingo. I didn't think he had the pluck to do it.'

He also affirmed that Lonton had reported having an argument with Fleming about a surcingle or 'some old sore at Brickhouse about two years ago'.[21] Then he added one more detail, which for the first time saw his evidence differ markedly from Cocking's portrayal of the events: Vann told the court that Lonton had told him he had not been standing when shot by the accused, but squatting on the ground.

When Dick Grey took the oath, he too cast doubt on the circumstances of the shooting. According to Grey's version of events, Lonton had told him that he hadn't seen Fleming pick up the rifle, and had not heard it go off. Even more incriminatingly, Grey asserted that Lonton had said to Cocking in Grey's presence, 'Look here, old man, if I liked to be nasty and make you speak the truth it would go very close to putting a rope round that bastard's neck.'

Vann's and Grey's evidence had moved the inquiry's impression of the affray from one of misadventure towards calculated murder.

Claude Ewing saw this immediately, and raised objections to the magistrate. None of this could be verified, he argued. No-one but Grey had heard such an accusation and, as such, surely it was merely hearsay.

Grey continued his evidence, now adding that Lonton had said bitterly to Fleming, 'I'm a bit crook in the back, and if I have to live on charity and am able to crawl at all I will do for you, you bastard.'

It must have seemed odd to Magistrate Foss and those in the room that Vann and Grey, both jurymen on the inquest that had found Fleming had no case to answer, were now actively undermining that same verdict.

The next witness called to take the stand was the contractor Stephen Brown. It was Brown who had helped Grey and Vann to transport the dying man by spring-cart to the Yanyeareddy homestead. He supported Grey's remarks about Lonton's fear of being permanently disabled by the wound. According to Brown, he had heard Lonton say to Fleming at one point, 'Look out, old man; if my backbone is hurt, look out for yourself. I would not walk the earth a cripple.'

Ewing was untroubled by this evidence. After all, any man in Lonton's situation would have held such fears and made such threats. None of it got at the heart of his client's motive or intent. But Brown's next piece of evidence was a bombshell that took even Mr Ewing by surprise. Stephen Brown now relayed how, just before going in to give evidence at the first inquest, Cocking—the Crown's chief defence witness—had turned to him and said that he was not happy about having to give evidence. 'I don't like it,' Cocking had allegedly told Brown. 'If I spoke the truth I would put a rope round Fleming's neck.'

A buzz rippled through the room, and Ewing quickly objected. Once again, he urged Magistrate Foss to dismiss the allegation, there having been no other witnesses present or within earshot. When this was declined, he turned to the man on the witness stand and said, 'Tell me, Mr Brown, did Lonton ever tell you that Fleming had intended to shoot him?'

'No,' replied Brown. 'He said it was an accident.'

Ewing let the word 'accident' reverberate through the room.

Now it remained only to settle the question of Lonton's position when he was shot. But Ewing need not have been concerned on that count. Dr Hickinbotham gave short shrift to the theory that Lonton had been squatting when shot. The autopsy, he said, suggested that the bullet had been fired from below the level of the wound, not from above or horizontally. Claude Ewing settled quietly back in his chair.

THE DEFENCE MAKES ITS CASE

John Fleming chose not to testify in his own defence. Instead, his counsel again stood to address the three men on the bench.

'The accused is charged [sic] with the crime of murder,' Ewing began, 'and it will be for you to give the evidence, both direct and circumstantial, the most serious and fullest consideration. Before the accused can be committed to take his trial you will have to come to a reasonable conclusion that the murder was committed, and that John Fleming was the murderer.'

The barrister then turned quickly to the issue of his client's intention in the shooting of Lonton. 'On a charge of murder,' he put to the three men presiding over the inquiry, 'it is necessary for the prosecution to give evidence of criminal intent on the part of the accused, and to prove criminal intent the court must look for the motive which urged to [sic] commission of so great a crime.'

Ewing warmed to his topic. Cocking was the only witness to the incident at Monkey's Well, he said. What credence could the court give to the second-hand reports of those who were not present? And what value could be placed on the evidence of known lawbreakers such as those involved in the aftermath of the event? Most importantly, the evidence pointed clearly to the likelihood that Fleming had had no idea that the Winchester was loaded, and, therefore, effectively removed any suggestion of criminal intent to harm or kill.

The defence counsel then reminded the magistrate and justices of the peace that the trigger of the rifle was easily pulled. He took this point further: 'Is it not probable that the leather attached to the rag may have become entangled with the trigger, and that Fleming grasping the rifle hurriedly may have pulled the leather cord, causing the rifle to go off?'

The barrister chose his words carefully as he continued to whittle away at the bench's sense of certainty: 'If Fleming picked up the rifle with the intent of shooting Lonton, why did he not put a bullet clean through the centre of his aggressor, he being only three or four yards distant? The fact of the bullet entering on the left breast suggests an accidental random shot, and not a malicious shot.'

To add authority to his supposition, Ewing then quoted at length from *Roscoe's Criminal Evidence* to remind the bench yet again that there must be strong evidence of criminal intent before a charge of murder can be sustained and the accused committed to stand trial.

The room was silent as the barrister drew his argument to a close: 'In conclusion, I admit that James Lonton was shot by John Fleming, but there is no evidence, direct or circumstantial, for you to reasonably come to the conclusion that the said shooting was done with the criminal intent to take Lonton's life, and on that ground I ask for a dismissal of the charge.'

The accused man and his lawyer did not have to wait long to find out whether Ewing's argument was persuasive. After a brief retirement, Magistrate Foss agreed that the evidence was not sufficiently strong to warrant a committal.

John Fleming, visibly emotional, was immediately discharged from custody. The audience, finally given licence to vent their sympathy, broke into spontaneous applause. To all intents and purposes, the matter was over.

A SECOND MAGISTERIAL INQUIRY

Fleming must have been relieved to have the matter resolved in his favour for a second time. But his relief would be short-lived. By May of that year, none other than the state's attorney-general, Mr Norbert Keenan, was questioning the outcome of the magisterial inquiry. *The Sunday Times*, once more sensing that its old foe Magistrate Foss was applying less than the highest standards of justice on the northern frontier, began to press for a fresh inquiry. The newspaper had received a long letter from Dave Johnson—who, despite his involvement at the scene, had never been asked to give evidence at either the inquest or the magisterial inquiry—in which he recounted a substantially different version of events.

In June, the attorney-general gave orders that the hapless Fleming again be arrested and a second magisterial inquiry be held. On the second day of that month Constable Buck once again arrived in Carnarvon with the prisoner, who was remanded for eight days in the Carnarvon lock-up to await the third official investigation into the affray at Monkey's Well.

The second magisterial inquiry began in July and, once again, Magistrate Foss and justices of the peace Angelo and Mansfield sat in judgement. This time the Crown prosecutor George Tuthill Wood conducted the case against Fleming, while Mr Ewing returned to take the floor for the accused. If he was intimidated by the eminent prosecutor from Perth, Claude Ewing did not show it. He more than held his own as the finer points of the law were thrashed out between the two men.

The evidence of the first witnesses followed a similar pattern to that provided at the previous two hearings. It was only when Dave Johnson, called to give his account for the first time, took to the witness box that things took an ominous turn for Fleming.

Johnson was adamant that Lonton had told him he'd been seated and taking off his boots when he was shot. Even more damning was Johnson's allegation that Fleming had confirmed this aspect of the events shortly afterwards.

Johnson then relayed how the dying man had said to him, 'You can have my saddle and everything. I don't want them anymore.' Lonton had then, according to the witness, directed Johnson to write on a scrap of paper, 'I am on my dying bed, and leave David Johnson my packs, horses, and all that belongs to me.' Lonton had signed this statement with Johnson's assistance, the witness said, and then asked the illiterate Fleming to witness it. Unfortunately for the inquiry, Johnson said he had destroyed the paper some time later. He added that the dying man had also given him a purse with some money in it, as well as some bills of sale for horses, both of which Johnson had returned to Lonton the following morning.

Ewing must have known that this latest account cast serious doubt on Cocking's earlier evidence. Not only had Johnson demonstrated an honest nature by returning the money and documents to Lonton the following day but, as Johnson himself asserted, there was no reason for him to lie. After all, he had only ever met Fleming once before, and Lonton had been completely unknown to him until that day.

To compound Ewing's woes, Johnson then went on to explain that Lonton himself had committed a final act of great decency by choosing to relieve from his murderer's shoulders all responsibility for the crime. He told the court how the wounded kangaroo shooter had said to him, 'Fleming wants me to write out a statement. I may as well do it. The dog wants hanging, but it would do me no good, for I am a done man.' It was then that Lonton had dictated the statement vindicating his killer by describing the shooting as accidental.

This, combined with Johnson's assertion that both the shooter and his victim had told him that Lonton had been sitting and removing his boots when shot, raised again the possibility that the death had been more deliberate than other accounts had suggested. It placed Fleming in a much less sympathetic light, and his lawyer knew it.

Only one course remained open to the defending barrister: Claude Ewing set to task attacking the witness's credibility. Johnson fended off the accusations as best he could. No, he had not been chased off Mr Twitchin's station for interfering with Aboriginal women. Yes, he did know Mr Hearmac, but he had never been cleared out from his station either; he had left of his own accord. He also knew Mr McCarthy but, likewise, he had never been forced to leave his property.

Ewing, having established an image of Johnson as untrustworthy, then moved in for the kill. Johnson was forced to concede that, 'Yes, I have been in jail in Fremantle for something over a cheque. I was convicted at Cue. I don't know how many times I was convicted. I was convicted at Marble Bar for something over a cheque. I will not swear that there are no more convictions.'

Claude Ewing resumed his seat, satisfied that, while he had not been able to erase Johnson's evidence, he had successfully undermined his integrity.

Now it was the state prosecutor's turn to re-examine his star witness. Once more he got Johnson to confirm the account of the shooting of Lonton as he took off his boots. Then he asked the witness to relay what had happened some time after the death of Lonton.

Johnson told the court of a meeting with Fleming about a month after the shooting: 'I came to Mr Lefroy's [property] and I saw Fleming. Fleming said, "It's a month ago since this affair happened and the police have not come up, and I don't think they will bother their heads." I said, "As sure as your name is Fleming the police will come up."'

Johnson then alleged that Fleming asked him, 'Are you still kangarooing afoot?' When Johnson responded that this was the case, Fleming said, 'I will lend you a horse and pack saddle.' Johnson declined the offer.

Wood allowed the imputation to hang ominously in the air. Those presiding over the inquiry were at liberty to believe that Fleming was offering a subtle bribe to the witness to buy his silence.

In response to Wood's gambit, Ewing simply fell back on his previous tactics. He stood and gazed sceptically at the man in the witness box. 'Have you been in jail in Roebourne?' he asked. 'Yes,' Dave Johnson replied.

'A BAD CHARACTER'

Now the Crown prosecutor made his final appeal to the inquiry. In Wood's mind there was surely a prima facie case for Fleming to face trial, and he took head-on Ewing's attempts to discredit his witness. He implored the presiding magistrate and justices of the peace to consider whether a man's previous transgressions precluded him from telling the truth or, worse yet, made inevitable his subsequent telling of untruths that would cost another man his life. The matter must, said Wood, go before a jury where the accounts of all witnesses could be weighed in the balance. The Crown prosecutor resumed his seat.

Claude Ewing had time for one final defence. First he argued with Wood's view that a prima facie case existed and that, as such, the bench had little option but to commit Fleming to trial. Magistrate Foss also challenged this position, clearly frustrated that he was being offered 'little discretion' in the matter. But Wood stood firm in his contention that the matter had proceeded to a point where a trial was legally inevitable.

The defence lawyer once more begged to differ, and moved on to the facts of the case as he saw them. If the dead man had indeed been taking off his boots, he said, why then were they neatly placed some six feet from where the incident had occurred? And what was the bench to make of Dr Hickinbotham's evidence that the shot had passed upwards into Lonton's body? And finally, how was the word of Johnson to be believed?

Mr Ewing looked around the room as he provided a withering assessment of the Crown's main witness: 'Johnson says he had not met Lonton before the morning when he was shot. Why then did Lonton, when he caught sight of Johnson, address him in the following manner: "How are you, Dave? I'm glad to see you." Why did he make a will in his favour when his "pal" Vann was present?'[22]

Ewing let these questions tick away in the minds of his audience. Then he continued, 'Johnson is a bad character. After considerable persuasion he told the court he had been convicted four times, also for obtaining goods by false pretences by passing valueless cheques. I contend a man who will defraud the public once will defraud it again, and will defraud the bench.'

Magistrate Foss listened as each of the two men before him lodged their final arguments. Then he asked Fleming if he had anything to add. The accused man shook his head, and the bench retired once more to consider their verdict.

They were not gone long. Within ten minutes the three lawmen returned to their stations and explained that they were of the opinion that there was more in the accused's favour than against and, as such, that there was, yet again, insufficient evidence to issue a warrant for Fleming's committal to trial.

If there was any doubt about the public sentiment in Carnarvon regarding this matter, it revealed itself at that moment. As Foss told the prisoner that he had no case to answer, the spectators burst into applause, just as they had at the second hearing. Fleming was a free man for a third time.

TRIAL BY JURY

When the attorney-general in Perth, no doubt ably informed by Crown Prosecutor Wood of the dubious judicial process that passed for justice on the northern frontier, learned of the second inquiry's outcome, he acted immediately. A.E. Barker issued an ex officio order for the arrest of Fleming for murder.

For the fourth time, the kangaroo shooter's fate would hang in the balance. But this time it would be decided by a judge and jury many miles from home. In late September 1906, the accused man and all the witnesses boarded the steamers *Bullarra* and *Paroo* and pulled away from the Carnarvon jetty bound for Fremantle.

On Thursday 4 October 1906, almost a year after the initial inquest into the shooting of James Lonton, John Fleming for the first time faced a jury of his peers. There would be no more bush lawyers, no more bush magistrate, no more sympathetic audience assembled in a frontier courtroom. Instead, the full legal apparatus of the young state of Western Australia lined up in Perth's Criminal Court to thoroughly scrutinise, for the last time, those increasingly distant events at Monkey's Well. Fleming would have been keenly aware that he now sat squarely within the shadow of the gallows.

Justice Rooth took his seat at the front of the court as Mr C.R. Penny, defending, sat by the prisoner. Mr A.E. Barker shuffled his papers nearby as he prepared to act for the Crown.

Mr Barker was soon outlining the events of that day to the jury and, as the day went on, the now familiar parade of witnesses came forward to tell their stories. And then, after two days of hearing evidence that rarely deviated materially from that heard at the previous inquiries, it was time for Justice Rooth to give a final summing-up to the jury.

Fleming must have dared to hope for some leniency when the learned judge expressed 'sympathy with the prisoner in having been before three tribunals already'. Rooth went even further and left little doubt about what he perceived to be the reason for such a miscarriage:

> The coroner's inquest was nothing more than a farce. As for the trials [*sic*] at Carnarvon, it is a matter of the utmost astonishment that in this country, or anywhere else, any man vested with the important function of justice of the peace could have found it consistent with his idea of duty to refuse to send this case to trial, and I must say that if the Crown had not taken the course it did, those who advise the Crown would have been grossly

wanting in their duty had they not advised the attorney-general to prefer the indictment on which this man now stands charged.[23]

Fleming would also have taken early comfort from the fact that Justice Rooth had, of his own volition, downgraded the charge against him from murder to manslaughter. He listened intently as the judge continued his summary of the case against him.

His Honour now turned a sympathetic eye to Dave Johnson, the Crown's main witness, whose credibility, rather than testimony, had sustained such damage over the course of justice ostensibly being pursued.

'I don't know,' said His Honour, 'whether, as has been stated, it is a fact that Johnson has not been in trouble since 1891. If it is, then I, for my part, must protest against any man's character being ripped open in the way Johnson's has been for no purpose at all, except for the mere purpose of damning him.'

It was clear that the judge was not swayed by Ewing's or Penny's attempts to deflect Johnson's evidence by attacking his own history.

Justice Rooth now turned his attention to Lonton's final act in exonerating his killer by dictating the note that described the events at Monkey's Well as nothing more than an accident. Whether Lonton believed his fate to be accidental or intentional, his forgiveness represented, according to the judge, perhaps the greatest and most generous act of Lonton's life.

The screw was slowly but perceptibly tightening on Fleming. Rooth turned it further when he asked the jury how they should interpret Lonton's actions after signing the document. Had it truly been an accident, he asked, would not the dying man have completed the act of forgiveness by shaking Fleming's hand? Instead he begged his comrades to keep 'that dog' away from him, not to leave him by himself with the shooter.

'If, members of the jury, you take this point into consideration,' Rooth continued, 'it might prove a very good clue to the ultimate determination of whether or not the death had been brought about by accident.'

His Honour then remarked that at no time had he noted any sign of contrition in the accused man. No-one hearing Mr Rooth's words that day could have misunderstood which way his own judgement was leaning.

Justice Rooth concluded with a final instruction to the jury:

> If you think the prisoner took up that deadly weapon, although provoked by words of a most opprobrious and revolting character, and it went off and killed Lonton, then I direct you to find that it is a case of manslaughter.[24]

THE FINAL VERDICT

For Fleming, there would be little opportunity to contemplate the fate that was being spelled out for him in the nearby jury room; no time to hope for cheering from the gathered spectators. The minutes slipped by quickly and, after only an hour's retirement, the jury filed back into the courtroom. They had agreed on a verdict of guilty, softened only by a recommendation of mercy on the grounds of provocation.

Asked by Justice Rooth whether he had anything to say before sentence was pronounced, Fleming replied, like so many before and after him, and in a voice that audibly trembled, 'Only that I'm not guilty.' Then he stood quietly awaiting the final verdict that had taken so long to arrive.

'John Fleming,' he heard the judge intone, 'you have been found guilty and found guilty, I might say, on evidence that could leave no doubt in the minds of reasonable men.'

The courtroom was hushed as each and every person present waited for the prisoner's sentence to be delivered.

> I have had occasion to express my regret at the way you have been harried in this case, and I have had occasion to regret also that so far as I could see you have not expressed the slightest contrition for what you did. Although everything has been done for you, and said for you, that could be done, and said, I cannot but regard this matter as a very serious one. You are fortunate that you are not standing there to receive a sentence for an offence of a more serious character; for had I not taken it upon myself to reduce the charge, you had been tried for murder, and I think the jury would have been justified in finding you guilty of murder.[25]

All Fleming could hope for now was that the leniency recommended by the jury might somehow find its way into the punishment for which he now waited with equal measures of dread and impatience. As if reading his mind, Justice Rooth addressed Fleming directly:

> I had intended giving you a very severe sentence, one that would have involved your seeing the end of your days in [jail]. But the jury has recommended you mercy on account of the provocation you received … I will, therefore, pass upon you a very much lighter sentence than you would have received but for the jury's recommendation to mercy.

He paused, as Fleming waited for his final words. 'You will be imprisoned with hard labour for a period of seven years.'

For a man nearing sixty years of age, it might just as well have been a death sentence. Eleven months after the shooting at Monkey's Well, John Fleming was led from the court to begin paying for his crime.

'SUCH OLD HUMBUGS'

Reaction to the sentence in Carnarvon's and Geraldton's newspapers was as swift as it was dismayed. Both *The Northern Times* and the *Geraldton Express* published point-by-point rebuttals of the southern court's findings. The *Express* purported also to sum up the general mood of those on the northern frontier:

> We cannot help thinking that most people must come to the conclusion that there is grave reason to fear that an injustice has been done. Anyhow, the 'Express' is of the opinion, and it does not hesitate to express that opinion, without any intention of reflecting on the honour of the parties concerned, that the course of the proceedings, taking them from first to last, coupled with the demeanour of Mr Justice Rooth in his address to the jury, was prejudicial to the prisoner receiving that impartial treatment which every person put on his trial has a right to expect in a British community.[26]

By contrast, *The Sunday Times* in Perth took the opportunity as usual to claim credit for this latest act of justice and to carry on its crusade against Carnarvon's legal establishment. Shortly after the trial's conclusion it proclaimed gleefully:

> We aren't boasting but would like to seize the opportunity to point out the foolishness of having such old humbugs on the bench as Dad Foss of Carnarvon.[27]

This sentiment did not appear to be shared in Carnarvon, where public opinion swung heavily towards the now imprisoned Fleming. Even the town's mayor, Mr Hearn, was soon writing to the newspapers:

> I am sure that I voice the opinion of 99 per cent. [sic] of the intelligent portion of this community when I say that even were Fleming found guilty of manslaughter a short sentence at the most was all that was thought possible. The judge appeared to lay great stress on the fact that Fleming

had not said he was sorry for the deed. Without saying so, I presume most people are sorry (more especially when found out) after having committed any crime, but I have yet to learn what that has to do in a legal sense with any mitigation of any sentence.[28]

The Carnarvon racing carnival was about to commence, and Mayor Hearn took the opportunity to begin gathering petitions for a remission of Fleming's sentence. This act would mark the beginning of a long campaign by those in the North to set the newest inmate of Fremantle Prison free.

In 1907, the first petition—which included the signatures of every member of the jury—was presented to the government, which responded that, should it be resubmitted after another year, due consideration might be given to its petitioners' wishes.

By November 1908 the town of Geraldton had also formally petitioned the government to cut short Fleming's period of incarceration. In addition, the *Geraldton Express* pointed out that the state's main witness was a 'coloured man ... a West Indian native' with a known history of crime. In fact, the paper lamented, it was well understood that, since the events at Monkey's Well, Johnson had been in trouble with the law a further three times.[29]

Finally, on 2 February 1909, following intervention by newly appointed attorney-general Norbert Keenan, Fleming was released from Fremantle Prison. He had served two years and three months of his seven-year sentence.

The fifty-eight-year-old looked older and weaker from his experience. Even so, he was soon on the steamer *Charon* bound northwards to the frontier where he felt most comfortable, and to the community that had not forgotten him. The steamer stopped first in Geraldton and then, in mid-February, John Fleming found himself once more stepping onto the jetty at Carnarvon and gazing fondly at the familiar shimmering summer landscape of the Gascoyne.

A FINAL TWIST

The story of John Fleming might have ended there, but for one final act of deadly irony.

The released man now resumed his old profession and, within a few months of his homecoming, was once again crisscrossing the eastern bushland in pursuit of kangaroo skins. By Sunday 4 July 1909 he had set up camp with his horses on Arthur River Station, some two hundred kilometres east of Carnarvon.

Fleming was just settling down for the night when he noticed that one of his animals, a young foal, had begun pawing at a box on which a loaded Winchester rifle was resting. The roo shooter yelled at the horse, causing it to take fright and rear awkwardly away from the box. As it did so, its hoof struck the hammer of the gun, releasing the spring and causing a shot to ring out into the still bush air. Fleming fell to the ground, the bullet having passed through the fleshy part of his leg.

The wound was serious enough that by Tuesday the worried Arthur River station-owner had decided that the injured man needed to be conveyed by trap to the Gascoyne Junction police station for medical attention. Once there, Constable Spry and his wife took Fleming into their home and made him as comfortable as possible. By morning, however, he appeared to be steadily declining. Spry helped his colleague Constable Gray load the wounded man onto the police buggy, and Gray then set off with his patient for Carnarvon. The two horses made good time across the 170 kilometres of harsh terrain, and by Saturday morning Fleming found himself lying in the small hospital of the remote port town.

John Fleming lingered on for almost three weeks from the day of the shooting, but his strength continued to fail. On Thursday 31 July 1909, he passed away in the Carnarvon hospital, felled by a bullet from a Winchester rifle just like the one he'd used to end the life of James Lonton three years before at Monkey's Well.

CHAPTER 7
IN THE SHADOW OF THE
CLEOPATRA'S PEARL

In the Criminal Court this afternoon Charles Hagen, Pablo Marquez, and Simeon Espada, who were recently found guilty of the wilful murder of Mark Liebglid at Broome on August 30 last, were brought before Mr Justice Burnside to be sentenced. The three prisoners stood firmly on the dock and, with apparent composure, awaited sentence. The Court was crowded.
—*The Evening Journal* (Adelaide, SA), Wednesday 22 November 1905

Justice Burnside, in passing sentence said: 'The law requires me to pass sentence on you ... the sentence which I now pass upon you is that you each and all of you be taken back to the place of your former custody, and there be hanged by the neck until you be dead.'
—*The Coolgardie Miner* (WA), Wednesday 22 November 1905

Hagen received the dread pronouncement with the same unconcern that he exhibited throughout the trial. His face betrayed not the slightest emotion, and his step was firm as he descended from the dock to the cells in the basement of the court. Espada looked more solemn than usual, but otherwise he wore a composed air. Pablo, who is in delicate health, betrayed some emotion as he accompanied his fellow prisoners to the cells, and gave vent to audible sobs as he disappeared from the view of the spectators.
—*The Daily News* (Perth, WA), Tuesday 21 November 1905

Thursday morning saw the closing scene in one of the most terrible tragedies that has been known in any part of Australia—the murder, on August 30 at Broome of a commercial traveller, Mark Liebglid, by Charles Hagen, Pablo Marquez, and Simeon Espada—when the three men paid for the crime with the forfeit of their lives.
— *The Sunday Times* (Perth, WA), Sunday 17 December 1905

When the cap was being adjusted, Hagen expressed a wish to speak and it was removed. The condemned man gazed earnestly for a moment at the group of pressmen in front of him and glanced at the officials on his right and left. Then, addressing those present, he said: 'Gentlemen, I want to say a few words before I go. I have not been believed. I have done almost everything I could to make people believe that I am innocent of this crime. I am ignorant of law and ignorant of court. I am a bushman, and for the last ten years have been in the bush. I am not a schemer of crimes ...'
— *The Western Mail* (Perth, WA), Saturday 23 December 1905

Then with the rope round his neck he talked for a quarter of an hour, speaking coherently and with a good flow of words, and with a conviction that made a great impression on the small band of officials and pressmen ... 'That is all. I am innocent.' The cap was pulled over Hagen's eyes. 'Draw the rope tight. Put it firmly round my neck. Steady, not too tight. Gentlemen, I am going. I am ...' These were the last words uttered by Charles Hagen.
— *The Coolgardie Miner* (WA), Friday 15 December 1905

Shortly after 9 o'clock, Espada and Marquez were led from the cells they occupied to the scaffold. They were accompanied by the Rev. Father Cox O.M.I., who recited prayers, which were repeated in a tremulous voice by Marquez. Espada, however, did not utter a word, but looked straight ahead.
— *The Western Mail* (Perth, WA), Saturday 23 December 1905

Espada and Marquez were brought to the scaffold together. Espada, in reply to the usual question ['Do you have anything to say before judgement is passed?'], said, 'Me kill white man.' After this Espada and Marquez carried on a heated altercation in their own language, and the executioner was unable to check it.
— *The Braidwood Dispatch and Mining Journal* (NSW), Wednesday 20 December 1905

After the cap had been adjusted over Espada's head, the hangman crossed to the lever and was just about to release the bolt when it was observed that Espada had managed to work his pinioned arms in such a position as to enable him to seize the rope in his right hand. Only in time was the order given to stop. Espada's hold on the rope was released, and when the hangman was readjusting the noose, with tears running down his cheek, the condemned man several times asked for water, which, however, was refused. Then the trap-doors were released, and the bodies of the two Manilamen fell into the pit below.
—*The Western Mail* (Perth, WA), Saturday 23 December 1905

After the rope had been taken from Espada's grasp it would appear that he made another attempt to reach it, and on observing this, Chief Warder Webster, who was standing on the platform behind, stepped forward with the intention of preventing his effort from being successful. Just as he had placed his foot on the trap-door the executioner pulled the lever and Webster fell, simultaneously with the condemned men, to the bottom of the pit, which is about 12ft. deep. A scarce repressed ejaculation of horror arose from those present, and Mr. George, Superintendent of the gaol, Dr. Hope, and the Sheriff's officer immediately proceeded to the unfortunate warder's assistance. He was found lying at the bottom of the pit, with blood flowing profusely from a wound on the left side of the head above the forehead. Webster, who is about 60 years of age, was carried to the gaol hospital.
—*The West Australian*, Friday 15 December 1905

The confusion over the execution in Fremantle Gaol of the three men, Charles Hagen, Simeon Espada, and Pablo Marquez, for the murder of Mark Liebglid, at Broome, is accounted for by the nervousness of the hangman, who broke down and cried like a child …
—*Evening News* (Sydney, NSW), Friday 15 December 1905

A PEARLER STEPS ASHORE

Not far off the coast of Corsica, in the warm waters of the Tyrrhenian Sea, the steel hulk of a forgotten ship lies quietly rusting where it was sunk by a German submarine more than one hundred years ago. Mostly unremembered now, in the first decade of the twentieth century the ninety-five-metre steamer SS *Minilya* was a welcome sight as it regularly offloaded people and cargo to the isolated communities on the northern edges of the rugged, barren coast of Western Australia. Able to carry ninety passengers and travel at eleven knots, the single-funnelled vessel started its Australian service in 1901. It would later be renamed the *Rizal*, before being fatally struck by a German torpedo en route from Manila to Barcelona in 1917.

One winter's day in 1907, the southbound *Minilya* berthed at the Carnarvon jetty, having left the pearling port of Broome a few days earlier. Stepping ashore to start a new life at the mouth of the Gascoyne were pearler John Travers, his wife, Georgina, and their new baby, Sheila. No-one knew it yet, but that landfall was to mark the beginning of the final instalment in one of the North-West's most abiding mysteries.

The little family was greeted by the dusty, salty visage of a mangrove-edged town that had clung precariously for more than twenty years to the shores of the Indian Ocean. The Travers family would add to the settlement's official population of around 400 people,[1] their needs serviced by two bakeries and three main stores.[2] When visitors came they stayed with Mrs Bryant who ran the local boarding house, or in one of the fourteen rooms of the new Settler's Hotel. An assortment of other enterprises in the town—two wheelwrights, a solicitor, two milk sellers, a fisherman, a saddler and some tailors—made what money they could from the coming and going of sheep and cattle drovers, teamsters, ships' crews and Afghan cameleers.

While the soft-drink factory of Mr von Bibra kept the town supplied in lemonade, most men found alternative refreshment at the front bars of Carnarvon's three hotels.[3] Those same men could sometimes also be found in weekly gatherings at Carnarvon's makeshift churches. Anglican minister J.W. Sharp held his services in the courthouse, competing for God's attention with the Congregationalists who met each Sunday at the Masonic Hall under Reverend Loughhead. The Catholics had their own chapel where they were ministered to by the good sisters of the nearby convent. A small school, under the stewardship of Mr Paul Sheard, educated the town's white children. When the townsfolk became ill, Dr Hickinbotham and his small staff tended to their care.

As the town's population and business activity grew, so did the number of minor government officials overseeing, supervising and regulating all areas of life and industry. Mr Isles, who took care of communications through the Post and Telegraph Office, also acted as the town's customs officer. The goods shed and jetty were managed by wharfinger Mr Mills and his staff, while Magistrate Foss—supported by a sergeant, three constables, a jailer and a warder—applied the rule of law far and wide.

It was into this growing hamlet at the edge of the northern frontier that the young Travers family stepped in 1907. The sight of the bleak, windswept town might have daunted other families, but John and Georgina had seen wilder places and lived in more dangerous times.

MURDER ON THE *MIST*

Two years earlier, back in January 1905, John Travers had been a single man living in Broome as the proud co-owner of a newly built pearling lugger called the *Cleopatra*. Travers was in partnership with another Broome identity called Tony Ulbrich. Both men had shadowy pasts, and both would ultimately meet untimely deaths cloaked in either mystery or violence, or both.

John Travers' real name was Cecil John Wilks, but some time after arriving alone in Queensland as a sixteen-year-old boy in 1886 he had, for reasons unknown to anyone but himself, left that name and his Oxfordshire origins far behind him. His business partner had been born Gustav Anton Ulbrich in Freiberg, Saxony, and arrived in Sydney in 1890, where he became known as Tony.[4]

The pair's wooden, two-masted pearling vessel had been built in Broome in 1904, measuring some fifteen metres long and weighing around fourteen tons. By the end of the first decade of the twentieth century it would be just one of around four hundred pearling luggers bearing more than 3,500 people fishing for pearl shell in the waters around the remote town of Broome, the world's largest pearling centre. Most of the divers were Japanese or Malay, but there were also Chinese, Filipino, Timorese and Macassan divers, as well as Aboriginal men and those from various European countries.

Travers and Ulbrich's joint venture seemed destined to be a successful one when, on 17 June 1905, while Travers was in London marrying the Scottish-born Georgina Campbell,[5] one of the *Cleopatra*'s divers returned to the surface with a pearl, reported at the time to weigh more than forty-four grains. Some estimated its worth to be around eight hundred pounds,[6] a small fortune in those days. The Swiss diver who discovered it was jubilant, as was Ulbrich, who was skippering the *Cleopatra* at the time.[7]

Word soon spread from boat to boat about the precious find, and it wasn't long before the crew of the *Cleopatra* was joined by fellow pearlers from the lugger *Toniko Toko*, among them Filipino crewman Simeon

Espada and diver Victor Nabor. Drunken celebrations followed, and when they finished and the *Cleopatra*'s guests had returned to their own vessel, the prize pearl was discovered to have gone with them.

It would later transpire that Nabor had substituted some valueless shell for the pearl and slipped the real catch into his pocket. Foolishly, he then entered into a written agreement with two of his fellow crew members to share the proceeds if they kept quiet about the deed. This damning piece of paper was subsequently found and police swooped on the *Toniko Toko* at the beginning of July, searching unsuccessfully for the missing treasure. The hapless Nabor, faced with the written evidence of his crime, could only plead that he had hidden the pearl under a coil of rope but that when he went to recover it, the gem was gone.

Back in Broome, the mystery of the *Cleopatra*'s remarkable discovery and subsequent loss became the talk of the town, and the thief and his missing treasure a source of intrigue and gossip. The culmination of rumour and conjecture would prove tragic: at around 9.30 on the morning of 31 August, the body of thirty-five-year-old pearl dealer Mark Liebglid was washed into the Broome port by the incoming tide. Liebglid was a Polish immigrant who had been in Australia for about fifteen years, working across various parts of the continent. Two men dragged his lifeless body ashore and found that the pearl dealer's skull had been battered and one of his hands so badly bashed that the gold ring on one finger was flattened. In a neatly tied envelope in one of his pockets, the police found more than 450 pounds.

Eventually, in November 1905, after a trial lasting five days, three men were found guilty of Liebglid's murder. One of them was Simeon Espada, the *Toniko Toko* crewman who had been one of the few to see the infamous pearl. He was arrested along with a Norwegian man named Charles Hagen and another 'Manila-man', Pablo Marquez. The trial found that the three men had lured their victim onto a derelict lugger called the *Mist* late at night, with the promise of selling him the stolen pearl around which so much rumour and speculation had circulated. Sensing a trap, Liebglid had managed to scream 'Murder!' before blows to his head silenced him and he slid beneath the water. All three assailants were hanged at Fremantle Prison on 14 December the same year.

A few days later, Victor Nabor was convicted by the Broome Court of initially stealing the pearl and hiding it on the *Toniko Toko*; he was sentenced to three years' jail.[8] The court acknowledged that the identity of the person or persons who had stolen the pearl the second time were unknown, and no reliable sighting of the pearl was ever made again.

AN OMINOUS START

By the time of Nabor's sentencing the newlywed John and Georgina Travers had arrived back in Broome to begin their married life, and in January 1906—possibly influenced by the violent events of the previous year—they sold their share in the *Cleopatra* to Ulbrich. Later that same month their first child, a boy whom they named John, was born, but he survived only two days and was buried at the Broome Cemetery. It was an ominous start to their new life together.

Even so, Georgina soon became pregnant again and John busied himself with various contracts around Broome. Life took on a kind of hope, but the shadows of the mysterious pearl theft, Liebglid's violent murder and their firstborn baby's death hung like a pall over the couple's new life. There was a sense of marking time in a place that now held little appeal for the young couple, and they decided to begin afresh in the southern port town of Carnarvon, some fifteen hundred kilometres away.

And so it was that on the first day of May 1907 the SS *Minilya*, carrying John, Georgina and their newborn baby Sheila Travers, pulled alongside the wooden jetty at the mouth of the Gascoyne River. Carnarvon by this time was thriving largely on the back of the wool industry, and from the deck John and Georgina gazed with interest at the scene below them. Steam and sailing vessels were loading and unloading people and goods, and there were even whaling ships taking on stores for their way north.

The jetty onto which the *Minilya*'s passengers stepped was barely six years old, having replaced the original one built in 1889. A tramway had also been constructed in 1900, to carry the wool from the townsite over the scrub and dunes of Babbage Island to where ships lay berthed and waiting to transport it. The young Travers family climbed aboard one of the horse-drawn trams that carried people to and from the jetty, along the tramway that had only just been reopened after sustaining severe flood damage two months earlier. A shortage of workers had seen Aboriginal prisoners taken from their cells and put to work on the repairs.[9]

TRAGEDY STRIKES AGAIN

John and Georgina seemed to settle in to Carnarvon quickly, and soon established a tentative commercial foothold in the growing community. By the end of their first month in the town, John had already won a local government tender to build part of Stuart Street at the centre of the business district.[10] He completed this job while, at around the same time, opening a small shop on the corner of Egan and Robinson Streets.

The memories of their ill-fated start to married life in Broome were beginning to recede when, on 1 July, exactly two months after they had arrived in Carnarvon, tragedy struck anew.

Late on that Monday afternoon, John Travers set out for the jetty where the *Minilya* had docked and was unloading some goods he had ordered. To get there, he climbed aboard the small horse-drawn tram as it left the holding yards and warehouses just off the wide main street, leaving the faint smell of sheep, camel and horse dung behind him. The tram rattled across the wooden bridge that joined the town to the scrubby excuse for an island called Whitlock, and then curved gently through the equally sparse and sandy scrubland of Babbage Island.

At the end of the tramline lay the start of the wooden jetty, which made its way out in a straight line across an expanse of pallid green mangroves, their roots pointing crookedly upwards like drowned men's fingers. Crabs darted sideways across the mud and birds stood languidly in the warm shallow water below, ignoring the horses and trams making their way across the trembling planks above. The jetty continued beyond the mangroves, casting its shadow briefly on a beach of coarse, windblown sand before reaching the deeper water where it met the ships bringing supplies, exchanging travellers and taking away wool. It was here that Travers alighted from the tram onto the sunlit boards and gazed out to where the *Minilya* was moored, watching it rock gently in the afternoon swell.

It wasn't until the next morning that the alarm was raised that Mr Travers had not returned from the jetty on the trams with the other men. At first it was assumed that he had simply—albeit for reasons unknown—embarked and stayed onboard the ship, which was now making its way south to the ports of Geraldton and Fremantle. But telegraphs received from both ports in the following days reported no sign of the lost man when the ship was searched at each destination. Perth police then stated that they believed Travers had left the ship while it was still docked at the jetty in Carnarvon. Due in part to this confusion, it was Friday before local police began searching and dragging the waters and mangroves around the jetty.

As time progressed, rumours and theories abounded in the small town. It became known that, on the day of his disappearance, Travers had been tired from his day's work and had told people he was not going to wait for the trams to leave but would walk back to town instead. Despite this, the police soon found witnesses who said they had seen him still on the jetty after the trams had left. No-one on the ship said they had ever seen him get aboard the *Minilya*.

Ten days later, officers were still patrolling the beach daily and dragging the waters north and south of the jetty. Nothing was found—no body, no shoes, no clothing, no clues. It was as if John Travers had simply evaporated into the pale northern skies. Questions were still being asked and rumours whispered at the hotel bars and kitchen tables of the township. Why had Mrs Travers not notified the police of her husband's disappearance until the day after he had failed to return home? Why had he told people he would walk back to town rather than waiting for the tram but then remained until after the tram had left the jetty?

There were those who believed that John Travers was just one more victim of the lost pearl, while others suspected his disappearance was a carefully choreographed escape with the stolen prize. Perhaps he simply fell into the sea and drowned.

ONLY THE MUTE

The disappearance of John Travers in 1907 was never solved, and it left in its wake a woman and child to survive alone at the edges of the ocean that had swallowed up their husband and father. Stories, theories and innuendo continued to float around Carnarvon.

As the years went by the details of the case gradually blurred into the past, memories faded, the actors moved on and new players took the stage. Stories of the *Cleopatra*'s pearl became the stuff of folklore, and its final location a tantalising mystery.

Travers' widow, Georgina, would remain in that remote settlement of dust, flies, wind and heat for the rest of her life, raising her daughter Sheila there and becoming a successful shopkeeper in the backblocks of Yankee Town. She never remarried.

Only the mute witnesses to the events of the disappearance now remain. The old jetty still points brokenly into an inscrutable Indian Ocean, the mangroves and the breezes that whisper through their salty leaves give nothing away, and the SS *Minilya* lies drowned in a distant sea. The *Cleopatra*'s pearl, John Travers, and the truth are all gone forever.

CHAPTER 8
SPARGO THE KILLER

The final scene in connection with the tragedy which occurred in the mangroves at Broome last January, when Gilbert Pickering Jones was done to death by the man with whom he had formed a chance acquaintance on board the steamer *Western Australia*, for the sake of his personal possessions, took place in Fremantle gaol last Tuesday morning, when Charles Henry [*sic*: his middle name was in fact Herbert] Spargo expiated his crime on the gallows. The community must feel a sense of relief to know that Spargo is now no more, for such a callous, cold-blooded murderer had of his own volition chosen a career of crime, of such a nature as to place him without the pale of human sympathy.

—*The Leader* (Orange, NSW), Saturday 19 July 1913

DISCOVERY AT SOLLY'S DAM

It had been a good year for drover Aubrey Hall. As he moved a mob of sheep northwards from Yaringa Station, he might have reflected that he had seen worse years than 1937. He didn't have to think back too far: 1933 alone had nearly cost him his life—twice.

First there had been a fall from a horse at Wooramel Station—an accident that had landed him in the Carnarvon hospital for a spell. But that was nothing compared to what had happened just a month later, as he and two Aboriginal men, Teddy Edwards and Balby, were droving about a thousand sheep southwards from Quobba Station to Carnarvon.

When Hall and his team had set off they'd had no reason to be concerned. The experienced drover and bushman had planned well for the warm December weather, with drinking-water supplies for the men and horses placed at regular points along the hundred-kilometre stretch of dry coastland, as well as plenty being carried in their waterbags.

At about nine o'clock on that Monday morning, still around forty kilometres out from Carnarvon, the little group had been moving the sheep across Boolathana Station when they'd come across an old petrol drum full of water. The day was warm and, although their waterbags were still full, they each drank their fill from the drum. Soon afterwards poor old Edwards had become ill, and before long the three dogs and one of the horses had died.

A passing truck driver had notified the people back at Quobba Station of the unfolding drama, and word was passed down the telegraph line to the police in Carnarvon. Meanwhile, Hall himself had ridden to the homestead of Boolathana Station and broken the news. But it had all been to no avail: by the time the police had arrived on the scene later that night it was too late for Teddy Edwards. The water was eventually determined to have been poisoned with arsenic and soda to kill blowflies, but the mystery of how it had come to be left there was never solved.[1]

Today, as Hall and his team moved their current mob of sheep northwards, the drover's thoughts meandered through the bush like the sheep before him, until the riders and stock reached Solly's Dam just a few kilometres south of Carnarvon. Hall was gazing across the wide brown claypan when one of his men approached him in a state of excitement. Hall followed the man to a spot about five hundred metres off the Wooramel road and saw that there, clearly visible, were the scattered remains of a human being.

The bones were spread across a small area and, stooping down, Hall noticed that they were charred as if they'd been burnt. Nearby stumps of trees suggested that the area might once have been covered in scrub, and there was no doubt in Hall's mind that the bones had lain there for many years.

Remounting his horse, the drover made his way to Carnarvon to report the grim find to Sergeant Page. The next morning the two men rode back to the scene together with a doctor in tow. The doctor confirmed that the bones were human, but he couldn't say how long they had lain there or the circumstances of the death. The three men carefully and solemnly collected the detritus of an unknown life and returned with it to Carnarvon.

It wasn't long before conjecture began to circulate around the town that Aubrey Hall's find at Solly's Dam was the missing piece of a puzzle nearly twenty-five years old. Indeed, as it would turn out, the bones would serve to close the final chapter of a bloody narrative that had begun in the north of Western Australia in 1912, when the state's first-known serial killer had stepped ashore at Carnarvon.

AN APPRENTICESHIP IN CRIME

Charles Herbert (Charlie) Spargo was born in Forbes, New South Wales, in around 1876. He grew up in the small town of Narrabri in the north-west of that colony, and spent his early working life in Queensland where he learned to drove cattle and sink dams. He had moved on to Broken Hill in far western New South Wales when gold was found in the Western Australian town of Coolgardie and, aged only twenty, he set off like so many others to make his fortune there.

A tall, slim man, Charlie Spargo was literate by the standards of his times—a keen reader of Steele Rudd's sketches of rural Australian life—and a talented horseman who spoke knowledgeably of the many parts of the country he proclaimed to know. In Coolgardie he took up work driving the coach north to nearby Bonnie Vale, but it wasn't long before, in August of 1896, he came to the notice of police for the first time.

The young man was arrested for false pretences, having obtained goods to the value of four pounds and fifteen shillings by passing a valueless cheque, and was detained in nearby Kalgoorlie. But if he was dismayed by his capture, it didn't show: within a few days he and a fellow inmate had escaped from the Kalgoorlie lock-up and were heading quickly southwards. The two men were soon caught, but not before they had made their way as far as the port of Esperance almost four hundred kilometres away.

Returned to Kalgoorlie, Spargo stood trial for the original offence. Although the magistrate dismissed that case against him, he was again remanded in custody for a separate but similar allegation. Perhaps emboldened by his first breakout, within ten days he had almost succeeded in a second escape attempt: when guards found the hole he had begun to bore through the prison wall it was already three-quarters of the way to freedom. Barely perturbed at having been discovered in the act of attempting to re-abscond, Spargo simply remarked laconically that he should only be charged for half the damage, his cellmate having worked with him on gouging the hole. The judge, not impressed, sentenced him to two months' jail for the attempted breakout; not long afterwards he was also found guilty of the second charge of false pretences and twelve further months were added to his sentence.

Spargo seemed wholly undeterred by these experiences, and shortly after his release was once more in trouble with the law. The year by now was 1898, and this time he and a friend named William Riley were charged with stealing leather harnessing, rope and chaff from a Kalgoorlie business. For this crime Spargo was sentenced to six months' jail and remanded in custody to appear for a further charge of theft.

True to form, it was only three months before the budding career criminal was again on the run, this time breaking out with a fellow renegade by the name of James Ryan. The two men gathered provisions and began walking north through the bush towards Menzies. They were recaptured within a few days but once more seemed unconcerned about their fate; for Spargo at least it must have seemed like familiar territory. However, this time the twice-burned police made sure he stayed put for the remainder of his sentence, and there were no more escapes.

Charlie Spargo's next bout of freedom didn't last long. By 1900 he was again in the news, this time for stealing a horse and cart. Throughout that trial the now hardened lawbreaker seemed philosophical about his fate: after first declaring that he would reserve his defence, he eventually pleaded guilty and asked for the case to be judged as summarily as possible. The judge acceded to the request and Spargo was jailed for another stretch with hard labour.[2]

With two more years in the lock-up to contemplate his thwarted life of crime, the twenty-four-year-old appeared finally to have learned his lesson. Upon his release he spent 1903 working hard around Kalgoorlie and generally keeping his nose clean. But old habits die hard, and at the end of that year he was once again in court.

The charge this time was failing to pay for his board and lodging at the Duke of York Hotel. But at least one man still seemed to think Charlie Spargo was capable of redemption. A detective involved in the case spoke in court on Spargo's behalf, successfully convincing the judge that the prisoner before him was now a changed man and deserved a second chance. The judge, against his better judgement, accepted the detective's entreaty and allowed Spargo to go free on the condition that he paid the money owed. It would prove a fatefully misguided decision.

GRADUATION TO VIOLENCE

Charlie Spargo must have figured that he had just made his first successful escape. But he must also have known that his local notoriety meant it was unlikely to happen again while he remained in the Goldfields. Perhaps he had genuinely decided to start again, away from the influences that had brought him so much trouble so young. Whatever his reasons, in 1904 the petty criminal made his way to the young state's capital, Perth.

In November of that year, a youthful-looking man knocked on the door of a stable-keeper, Thomas Hooper, in the inner-Perth municipality of Leederville. Hooper had recently advertised that he was looking to buy some new horses.[3] The friendly newcomer introduced himself as Mr Jones, and a deal was soon struck between the two men for Hooper to buy some horses that Jones said he had grazing in the Perth hills near Parkerville. Hooper and Jones set off by train that same afternoon to view the animals. As the train pulled away from the station, the stable-keeper had no way of knowing that his congenial companion was none other than renowned Goldfields crook Charlie Spargo.

Disembarking at the small rural settlement of Parkerville, nestled within the Darling Range, the two men walked together into the surrounding bush. After about a kilometre there was still no sign of the horses, and a weary Hooper bent down briefly to retie his shoelaces. As he did so he felt a sudden sharp blow to his head. Rising bewildered to his feet, Hooper found the hitherto friendly Jones now transformed into the sinister form of Spargo, who was calmly holding out a pen and demanding that Hooper write him a cheque for one pound. The bush crowded around them, a silent witness to Hooper's plight.

The liveryman hesitantly wrote out the cheque, but no sooner had he done so than he was commanded to write another one, this time for fifty pounds. Hooper's mind raced and, as Spargo took the second cheque from him, Hooper took his chance and fled into the trees. Spargo, taken by surprise, lost his quarry quickly in the thick woods and, giving up after a short chase, settled for swearing softly while throwing stones after the escaping man. Hooper staggered through the bush until he finally emerged with the Swan View train station in sight. Soon the stationmaster had raised the alarm and the two men were waiting for the arrival of the police.

Meanwhile, Charlie Spargo calmly hitched a ride back to Perth on a passing horse and cart. He was in an amiable mood, and when he and the driver stopped for a drink at the Ozone Hotel on Adelaide Terrace in the city, Spargo bought the beer with his one-pound cheque. He then gave his new friend ten shillings for the ride. It was not until the next day, when he tried to cash the second cheque at a Chinese furniture store in West Perth, that the police closed in. Arrest and capture once again followed swiftly for the swindler. He was now twenty-eight years old and looking down the barrel of another three-year stretch in prison.

'I KNEW HE WAS A BORN KILLER'

Seven years passed. Spargo did his time and then worked around the state, generally doing labouring jobs, often on remote stations. Although for the most part he managed to keep his darker side to himself, it sometimes made a public appearance despite his efforts. One man who knew him in those days would later recall:

> When I first saw Charley [sic] Spargo working on a mill at Donnybrook a few years ago, I knew he was a born killer. One day my little spaniel dog, just a nipper, bit his hand. Cool as you like, Spargo waited for the little chap to come into his tent an hour later, then split his head open from the crown of his skull to the tip of his nose with one swing of an axe. When I sees [sic] that I said to myself: 'Any man who'd do a thing like that wouldn't have no scruples about murdering humans.'[4]

In December 1912, Spargo arrived by ship at the long jetty that marked the entrance to the Gascoyne River. The tram took him the short distance into the town of Carnarvon, where he no doubt hoped to find work. This time the repeat lawbreaker was accompanied by a sturdily built, dark-complexioned, moustachioed man in stylish boots.[5] Stories swirled around town that Antonio—soon known by the locals simply as Jonesy—hailed from Italian parents somewhere in Victoria. Whatever his provenance, the two men took up lodging at Mrs Williams' boarding house, which had only just recently opened for business in Stuart Street.

Ten days before Christmas, Charlie Spargo presented himself at a local livery seeking to hire a horse and sulky. He explained to the ostler that his friend, Jonesy, had picked up work on a sheep station to the south of the town and he planned to drive him to his new job. The two men were seen leaving town the same day. Antonio, carrying about twenty pounds in cash, was wearing brown pants, a green shirt and his usual flashy boots. It was the last time anyone other than Spargo would see him alive.

Later that same day, only three hours after having hired them, Spargo returned the horse and sulky to their surprised owner. He explained that he and Jonesy had met a wool teamster who had offered to take Jonesy the remainder of the way to the station. Only later did it emerge that there was no such teamster and that the station-owner in question had no knowledge of either man. But by then, events had moved on quickly and violently and Charlie Spargo was long gone.

From Carnarvon's long jetty Spargo set sail for the North again. Unlike many of the other passengers he was familiar with the ships that plied the northern coast, and he knew each and every port along the way. His modus operandi—still developing at the time of the Parkerville incident with Thomas Hooper, but since refined with the hapless Antonio—was now well formed. The vast distances between towns and the empty, desolate country lent a kind of passive complicity to the crimes that would follow.

With Carnarvon behind him and Antonio's body lying as yet undiscovered in the scrub near Solly's Dam, Spargo was soon establishing a new life in Broome. Less than three weeks after his most recent crime he had already found a new companion, twenty-two-year-old Reginald Dickerson, and the two men were staying together at the Continental Hotel.

DEATH OF AN ENGLISHMAN

Reginald Dickerson, six feet tall and fair-haired,[6] had travelled halfway around the world from Derby in England, where he had worked for a firm of wine and spirits merchants. Once in Australia the young adventurer spent some time employed at Taylor's Store in Pinjarra, before making his way to the harsh and oppressively hot northern settlement of Marble Bar some time in June 1912. There the Englishman found employment as an assistant shopkeeper.

While Dickerson appeared quite at home in a range of menial jobs, those who got to know him well believed that his parents back in England were well off, and that the new immigrant received regular remittances from his distant family.

In December of 1912, on a ship somewhere off the coast of Western Australia, the paths of Charlie Spargo and Reginald Dickerson merged. Their meeting and the brief friendship that followed would prove fatal for both. It was clear to anyone who saw the men onboard the ship, or later at Broome's Continental Hotel, that the two men had formed a close bond. But for some reason that soon changed and, in the early evening of 4 January 1913, passers-by saw the companions arguing on a Broome street.

One of those who came across the scene was a Carnarvon man called Mackey, who later reported that he thought Spargo was trying earnestly to convince his companion of something to which Dickerson would not agree. Later, at about eight o'clock that evening, Mackey again saw them, now apparently reconciled, walking together towards Roebuck Bay. This was the last known sighting of Dickerson by anyone other than Spargo. An hour later Spargo returned alone, looking, according to Mackey, a little excited.

The following day Spargo boarded the SS *Paroo*, a passenger vessel which at the time serviced the far-flung Western Australian coastal ports as well as making a regular run to Singapore, on its journey southwards to its home port of Fremantle. No-one in Broome raised the alarm about Dickerson's disappearance, most people assuming that he had boarded the *Paroo* with his friend.

Meanwhile Mackey, who was making his way home to Carnarvon onboard the same ship, struck up a conversation with the man he had seen the previous day arguing with Dickerson. By the end of their discussion Spargo had exchanged a finely tailored overcoat, made in England, for Mackey's shoes. He also sold the Carnarvon man an English motoring cap. Later, one of the ship's stewards was happily surprised to receive a set of smart English-tailored clothes from one generous passenger, a Mr Spargo.

Mackey and the steward were not to know that all of these pieces of clothing had been retrieved from an ominous green trunk in Spargo's cabin. The killer would soon paint it blue but, even then, the initials H.R.D. would remain faintly discernible beneath the clumsy attempt at disguise. It was not the only item on which the telltale initials appeared: in Spargo's pocket was a metal lighter with those same letters scratched almost beyond recognition but still declaring that it was once the property of Reginald Dickerson.

The SS *Paroo* and the killer Spargo steamed steadily south.

THE FINAL VICTIM

Two weeks later, and almost a month after the mysterious disappearance of Spargo's friend Antonio in Carnarvon, another young Englishman by the name of Gilbert Pickering-Jones was boarding the SS *Western*

Australia in Fremantle. The steamer was bound for northern ports, including Carnarvon, Broome and Derby.

Pickering-Jones was seen off at Fremantle by his friend Ed Miller, a leatherworker whom he had known for a few months as a workmate in Perth. A quiet and educated man, Pickering-Jones had sailed, in 1910, from Tilbury Docks in London as a steerage passenger on the mail steamer SS *Orsova*. Arriving in Western Australia thirty-two days later, the bespectacled Englishman had stayed for a while at the Immigrants' Home in Perth's Pier Street, then made his way east where he had worked on farms around Merredin.

For most of 1911 he had worked for the Nancarrow family in the Murray district. Some in the area believed him to be an engineer; others suggested he had a medical background, a conclusion deduced from the small kit of surgical instruments he often carried and his apparent knowledge of medicines.[7] He was not without prospects, he had told the Nancarrows: his mother sent him regular ten-pound remittances from Dublin, and he fully expected to inherit three hundred pounds from his father some time in September. Whatever the truth of his past or the hopes for his future, people found him even-natured and difficult to quarrel with. He was generally reserved, only becoming expansive during occasional drinking bouts, when he had been heard to claim that he had once owned a farm in Canada.

Pickering-Jones and his friend Miller had spent the second week of 1913 living above the Imperial Restaurant in Fremantle. It had been an eventful week: the companions had been robbed and Pickering-Jones had lost his silver-cased hunting watch and sovereign belt, as well as a revolver, a razor, some cartridges and his spectacles.[8] The goods were later recovered, however, and the event might have amounted to nothing had several of those objects not reappeared shortly afterwards as evidence of a far more gruesome crime.

After vacating their lodgings on the day of Pickering-Jones's departure, Ed Miller waved goodbye to his friend, a man he would later describe as good-tempered and good-hearted. Pickering-Jones was wearing khaki trousers that he had recently had turned up for a better fit, and a grey flannel singlet under a khaki coat buttoned up to the neck. On his head he wore a grey felt slouch hat with a wide rim. He also carried a khaki helmet, which he had stuffed with paper to fit his distinctively narrow head. His boots, as always, were turned up at the toes—a deformity of one of his small toes required him to wear shoes a size too large—and in the summer sunshine a gold tooth flashed beneath his ginger moustache.

The *Western Australia* made its way north and, stopping first at Carnarvon, took on more passengers. One of them was Charlie Spargo. He and Pickering-Jones, both second-class passengers, soon struck up a friendship, and when the ship moored in Broome it was Spargo who waited at the head of the gangplank to help carry his new companion's luggage ashore.

Broome by now was well known to Spargo, and his face was likewise increasingly familiar to those who lived there. On the day of the *Western Australia*'s arrival in the pearling port, a local man named John McMurtrie was approached by Spargo, whom he had met out at Whim Creek about six months earlier. Broome in 1913 was a wild town in a wild time, and McMurtrie didn't think it odd when his acquaintance asked whether he had a gun for sale. He showed him a Smith & Wesson .32 revolver for which he was asking twenty pounds, but Spargo shook his head. 'That's too much,' he said, adding, 'I don't want it for myself; I want it for my mate.'[9]

In the end, McMurtrie agreed to lend the gun to Spargo if he could supply his own ammunition. Spargo left in search of the appropriate bullets, returning shortly afterwards with several nickel-coated cartridges which, though not Smith & Wesson, McMurtrie believed would fit the gun. By now it was nearly noon.

At midday, Spargo and Pickering-Jones were walking through Broome's streets and had reached the corner of Napier Street when they ran into Alexander Hart, an old friend of Pickering-Jones's who had travelled with him from London on the *Orsova*. Hart was now in business in Broome as a carrier, and when he mentioned this fact, his old travelling companion told him, 'Well, I've got some luggage at the goods shed. You can bring it up for me.'[10]

Hart told Pickering-Jones that the job would cost four shillings. Spargo, who had been growing increasingly agitated as the two friends exchanged their cheerful banter, at this point quickly interjected, 'Four shillings is too much! I've been up here before and I know the price of things.'

An argument developed, and eventually an exasperated Hart turned away with a gesture of disgust, leaving the other two men to continue walking towards the Broome foreshore.

Half an hour after this encounter Charlie Wright, the local pound-keeper and ranger for the Broome Common,[11] was riding his horse along the fringes of the mangrove swamps nearly two kilometres from the township when he saw Spargo and Pickering-Jones walking over the tidal plain not far from the racecourse. He called out a brief greeting before riding on, leaving the two men to continue walking into the mangroves.

At about two-thirty that same afternoon, a local gardener called Joe Bacci was hailed by a voice outside the Broome post office. He turned to find an agitated Charlie Spargo, looking as if he had just returned from a long walk.

'Listen, Joe,' Spargo asked, 'how do you manage to get money out of the Savings Bank?' He took from his pocket a Savings Bank passbook as he spoke.

When Bacci replied that any large amount would take some days to become available, Spargo replied impatiently, 'I can't wait—I have to go to Derby! Anyhow, two pounds is no good to me. I want to draw ten or twenty pounds. Or the lot!' Then he strode off in the direction of the port, where the steamer *Western Australia* was still docked.

If John McMurtrie was surprised when Charlie Spargo returned the revolver to him just a few hours after he had borrowed it, he didn't say so, and he didn't check the gun's chambers.

The day faded to dusk, and that evening found Spargo drinking in the bar of the SS *Western Australia*. At first, his demeanour was so excitable that those around him assumed he was already intoxicated. Then they noticed that, rather than making him drunker, each successive drink seemed to bring the man a greater measure of calm. As the evening wore on he steadily regained control of his emotions and became quieter as he joined the other passengers in one last night on the town.

The next day, Spargo resumed his journey northwards aboard the same ship on which he had arrived. But Pickering-Jones was nowhere to be seen.

'MY NAME IS NOT SPARGO AT ALL'

As the *Western Australia* made its way north to Derby, Spargo's waking hours were consumed by the dilemma of how to get his hands on his latest victim's savings. He was fairly sure that Pickering-Jones's remains, like those of Antonio and Dickerson before him, would never be found, but how was he to access the more than one hundred pounds in Pickering-Jones's bank account? As it turned out, he need not have worried. The problem would soon be solved by a combination of good luck and cunning.

The *Western Australia* arrived at Derby without incident and Louis Grant, a supervisor for the state government's public works department, watched as the assortment of passengers disembarked from the deck. Suddenly his attention was caught by a familiar face.

'How are you getting on, Charlie?' he asked as Spargo walked past him.

Spargo, having been deep in thought and obviously disconcerted, searched the supervisor's face for a clue to his identity.

'I sold you a horse ten or eleven years back,' explained Grant.

'You've a good memory,' Spargo smiled. Then he added, 'Do you remember my last name too?'

Grant was momentarily taken aback and then admitted that, for the moment, the horse buyer's surname escaped him.

'Well, it's Jones,' Spargo said. The two men exchanged a few more pleasantries and then parted.

As he stood and watched his old acquaintance walk away from him along the wharf, something about the conversation—he couldn't say exactly what—began to puzzle Louis Grant. The business about his surname just didn't add up.

By the time Grant had returned to town, he still couldn't remember what the man's surname was but he sure as hell knew it wasn't Jones. Later that day he came across the passenger again in the hotel where both men was staying and, in a flash, the answer came to him.

The two men greeted each other and then Grant asked, 'Did you tell me your name was Jones?'

When the answer came in the affirmative, Louis Grant was ready for it. 'It's a funny thing,' he said. 'When I knew you it was Spargo.'

If Charlie Spargo was surprised or unnerved, it didn't show. He explained casually that it was a simple matter: Spargo had been his stepfather's name; when the old man had died, Charlie had reverted to his biological father's name. 'And that name was Jones,' he told Grant.

Both men were staying at Sack's Hotel in the long, straggling main street that lay more than a kilometre from the Derby jetty, which could be reached by horse tram. Most days they bumped into each other and exchanged a few words as they went about their business. One morning, at one of these meetings, Spargo casually asked his fellow guest if he would do him a favour.

'Not if it means lending you money,' Grant answered jokingly.

'I just need you to identify me to the police,' Spargo replied.

Still joking, and unsuspicious, Grant remarked, 'Don't the police know you sufficiently well?'

Spargo smiled. 'They don't know me well enough for what I want. I want to get some money out of the Savings Bank, and the corporal of police is the agent. They've shifted the bank from the post office.'

Grant said he was busy at present but would come later if that would help. 'Any time this morning will do,' answered the grateful Spargo.

Later, the two men walked to where Corporal West had his station. On the way, Grant asked his friend if he wanted to be known as Spargo or Jones. The answer was as emphatic as it was clear: 'Jones. My name is not Spargo at all.'

Corporal West lifted his head as the pair entered his room in the Derby courthouse. Grant spoke first: 'This man has asked me to come along and say I know him. As a matter of fact, I knew him ten or eleven years ago, and had a business transaction with him.'

The corporal looked at Spargo, and said to the man beside him, 'Are you sure this is the same man you knew before?'

Grant replied, 'Oh, yes. I sold him a horse.'[12]

Then Spargo explained that he needed to withdraw money from his passbook account, and that his friend could vouch for his identity.

A form was completed, money handed over and both men left. At no time had the corporal thought to query under what name Grant had known the man presenting himself as Jones. For the moment, Spargo's luck was intact, and he placed the comforting folds of eighty pounds into his pocket. In fact, he was luckier than even he knew: the corporal, being new to the job, had neglected to demand a signature that could be compared with one on file.

Relaxed and confident, Spargo stayed a few more days in Derby unaware that, as he made plans to sail back to Perth, the warm ocean tides that lapped the shores of Broome were finally giving up a gruesome secret.

'THERE WAS A HOLE EXTENDING THROUGH THE EYE'

On 8 February 1913, an Aboriginal horse driver named Jim Lee was collecting a load of coal by the Broome racecourse when he noticed a bad smell coming from the nearby mangroves. Stepping carefully between the gnarled roots that protruded sharply from the mud, Lee sent crabs scurrying as he pushed his way through the low green trees. The mangroves were so dense that it wasn't until he was within a metre of the smell that he discovered what caused it.

Jim Lee stumbled back onto dry land and turned his horse quickly to town. There he raised the alarm, and then he and Constable Pallet rode back to where a man's decaying body lay floating between the salty branches and leaves that fringed the wide tidal plain.

The corpse was removed, and the next day more policemen and two Aboriginal trackers returned to search the site. It wasn't long before they found an open pocketknife and a revolver, some cartridges and a sovereign belt. Floating nearby, caught up in the branches of the mangroves, an upturned khaki helmet glistened softly in the tropical light.

Meanwhile, at the Broome morgue, Dr Goldstein had begun his autopsy. Despite the internal organs being practically gone, Goldstein was able to determine that death had taken place probably fourteen or fifteen days previously. Later, he would testify, 'There was a hole extending through the eye. The bridge of the deceased's nose was marked by the use of spectacles.' Further forensic examination would reveal a bullet still lodged in the skull. 'It was,' said the doctor, 'highly improbable that the bullet wound, which had an inward, backward and slightly downward run, could have been self-inflicted.'

The last moments of Gilbert Pickering-Jones were further deduced by the finding that there was also a fracture on the left temple. While the doctor believed that the temple wound alone would not have caused death, he had no doubt that it would stun an unsuspecting victim.

A HAGGARD FIGURE, HANDCUFFED

There was enough evidence now to suggest foul play and, as reports came in to the police about the last known movements of Pickering-Jones and his friend Spargo, the investigation moved quickly. A month after the recovery of the body, Charlie Spargo was arrested in Perth and charged with uttering a false cheque in Derby earlier that year. The police sought that he be remanded in custody pending the possibility of further charges, and the judge acceded.

In April 1913, an inquiry into the death in the mangroves was held in Broome and, under the watchful custody of Criminal Investigation Branch Sub-Inspector John Joseph Walsh,[13] the suspect Spargo was delivered by ship to give evidence. The inquiry would return four main findings: that the dead man was indeed Gilbert Pickering-Jones; that he had died on 23 February 1913; that the cause of death was a bullet wound to the head; and, finally, that the man who pulled the trigger was Charles Herbert Spargo.

Spargo listened with apparent shock to the verdict, his face the picture of a man wrongly accused. It was a demeanour he had adopted throughout the inquiry, during which he had stubbornly—in the face of overwhelming evidence to the contrary—denied any knowledge of the dead man and any involvement in his death. His story was as simple as it was untruthful. He had, he said, boarded the *Western Australia* in Carnarvon and worked his passage north, adding:

> I did anything I was told by the officers. We called at Port Sampson, Hedland, Broome and Derby. I went ashore at Hedland but not at Broome. I left the ship at Derby. Passengers and crew were all strangers to me. Nobody was with me.[14]

He made no mention of Louis Grant or Sack's Hotel or Corporal West. Instead he insisted he had camped at a bore a mile from Derby.

When it came to the matter of the savings account, Spargo adopted a position so brazen that even he must have known it would be laughable in the face of the thirty-seven alternative eyewitness accounts presented to the court. Even so, he proclaimed desperately:

> I did not have anything to do or say to a man named Jones ... I am positive of it. I got no money at Derby. I only had about one pound when I left there. I did not meet anyone at Derby I knew. It was the first time I was ever in Derby. I knew a man named Grant who used to be a contractor at Perth. I did not meet him at Derby. I got no money at the post office there; I had none to draw. I drew my last money in Perth—eighteen pounds and nineteen shillings—and I left one shilling. Then I opened an account at Hedland and took twenty pounds out when leaving. I never had any money at the Savings Bank in Derby. I am certain I did not draw eighty pounds at Derby in the name of G.P. Jones. Anybody who says so is telling a deliberate lie.[15]

Too many witnesses, too much evidence to the contrary steadily unpicked Spargo's desperate parade of falsehoods. The jury bought none of it. Even his counsel, Judah Moss Solomon, was unable to find a single witness to speak in his client's defence. After a visit to the site where the body had been found, the jury returned a unanimous guilty verdict after just ten minutes' deliberation. When Justice Robert Bruce Burnside asked the prisoner whether he had any words to say before his sentence was passed,

Spargo told him, 'I am as innocent as what you are.' Unmoved by this assertion, Burnside then condemned Charlie Spargo to death.

Once more, but now for the last time, the killer found himself onboard the SS *Western Australia*; this time as it headed south to the waiting gallows of Fremantle Prison. Finally there were no more protestations from the prisoner, there was no more bravado or faux indignation. It was as if Spargo, increasingly sullen and depressed, had at last realised that the drama of his life was drawing to an end. Forbidden from leaving his cabin and guarded day and night, it was not until the day before he arrived in Fremantle that he was even able to face food. He passed most of his time playing at euchre with Detective McConnell.

The case had by now gained widespread public notoriety and a large crowd gathered to witness Spargo's arrival as his ship pulled alongside the quay at Fremantle's F Shed. *The West Australian* newspaper reported the scene as the murderer and his police guard disembarked:

> He passed with downcast eyes, a haggard figure, handcuffed by the wrist to Detective McConnell, in the way that had been cleared between the foot of the gangway and the shed. He was wearing a long dark overcoat and a Panama hat was pressed tightly over his brows. Tall, straight and thin, and apparently of powerful build, he walked swiftly and unfalteringly through the crowd. His pale unshaven face revealed the severe nervous strain which the journey had cost him.[16]

Spargo now found himself in the condemned cell at Fremantle Prison. There he was given the small concessions a doomed man was permitted to enjoy in the days leading up to his execution. Each day he read the Bible, but he seemed to gain much more pleasure from *On Our Selection* by Steele Rudd, a book he remembered from happier days. He chose not to see any relatives, several of whom lived in Western Australia.

For a while he nursed the hope that the governor might offer him a reprieve. That small seed of optimism was sown on his final voyage from Broome, when fellow passengers on the *Western Australia* had told him that the Labor Party Congress at Bunbury had declared against capital punishment. Surely, they comforted him, this would be the first test of that resolve. Better still, it was known that Attorney-General Thomas Walker, a relatively enlightened man, was an opponent of the death penalty. Spargo's hopes must have been further buoyed when, on the day before his own case was reviewed, he learned of the reprieve of Kurokawa

Fukito, who had been found guilty of the knifing murder of a fellow countryman at Broome. The Japanese man's sentence of death had been commuted to ten years' penal servitude.[17]

But these hopes were to prove fruitless. The attorney-general, while disposed to mercy in general, was not about to extend it to Charlie Spargo.

> I am opposed to hanging, on principle, but the law has to be administered as it stands. In a case like this there is no option but to put it into force.[18]

Walker would also have been aware that, while Spargo had not stood trial for Antonio's or Dickerson's murder, suspicion was rife in the community that Pickering-Jones was but the last of his victims. As if to underscore the point, the governor received not a single plea for mercy on behalf of the condemned man. In his cell, Charlie Spargo received the news that the date for his execution was set for a Tuesday in eight days' time.

The desperate man tried one more throw of the dice. After the governor rejected his plea, he gave his lawyer a personal letter addressed to the attorney-general. Once more he begged for a reprieve, even requesting that Mr Walker visit him in jail. No reply was received, and no visit took place.

'PRAY FOR ME'

As his last lifeline disappeared, the inevitability of Charlie Spargo's fate seemed finally to dawn on him. His recently buoyant and optimistic demeanour collapsed suddenly into deep depression. The prison chaplain, Reverend Howard, reported that the prisoner spent many sleepless nights and lost weight, that his eyes grew sunken and his appetite evaporated.[19] Reverend Howard visited the condemned man in his cell at least twice a day and, while these visits seemed to soothe Spargo somewhat, he balanced precariously on the line between acceptance and sheer terror for most of his final week.

On his last Monday, Spargo finally agreed to meet with his brother, whereupon—with less than twenty-four hours of life remaining and no more to be gained from lying—he broke down and cried, 'I am being hanged for a crime of which I am innocent!' Even now, with all hope gone, no confession passed his lips.

In stark contrast to the terrors of his last week on earth, the final Tuesday morning of Charlie Spargo's life found the prisoner strangely rested and calm in his cell. He had written a final letter to his brother and when, at five minutes to eight, his jailers came for him he was sitting quietly with Reverend Howard. He passively allowed himself to be pinioned but, as the party made its way to the gallows, held tightly to the priest's hand.

'Is it necessary?' Spargo asked the hangman who offered him a blindfold at the entrance to the scaffold. As a small gesture towards this final request, a handkerchief was tied across his eyes instead of the usual white hood. Charles Spargo walked slowly across the platform and, still gripping the reverend's hand, murmured, 'Pray for me.'

The small group of official witnesses to the execution, having learned of the condemned man's behaviour throughout the past week, was surprised that, apart from this mild utterance, the murderer showed little sign of fear. Reverend Howard stepped back and Spargo, in a voice loud enough for the hangman to hear, cried gruffly, 'Get it over quickly.' He made no further sound in this life.

Charles Herbert Spargo's body was buried that same morning in the Fremantle Cemetery. By his own request, his pipe, with which he had found some comfort in his last days, was buried with him.

THE FADING ECHOES OF A MURDEROUS LIFE

More than twenty years after Charlie Spargo paid with his life for the murder of Gilbert Pickering-Jones, the discovery of human bones at Solly's Dam outside Carnarvon saw the newspapers approach a now elderly Detective Sergeant Condon, who had been involved in the Pickering-Jones case, for his thoughts on the mystery. He responded:

> I would not be at all surprised if the remains were those of Jones. Spargo, I know, killed several men. Jones—or Antonio, as he was called at Carnarvon—was very likely one of them.[20]

All that was left was conjecture. The hanged man had left no confession, no hint of his victims' final moments, and certainly no sorrow for their fates. Somewhere in the empty northern expanses of the Western Australian bush, at least one body still lies unmarked and unmourned, more forgotten to the world than the killer Spargo himself.

CHAPTER 9
HOW TOPSY DIED

> A wire received by Sub-Inspector Walsh, the officer in charge of the Criminal Investigation Department, on Tuesday last, announced the arrest at Nannine on the previous day of Harry Varian, alias John Sheehan, on a charge of having on October 8 last, near Carnarvon, murdered Topsy, an infant Aboriginal child.
> —*The Daily News* (Perth, WA), Thursday 13 March 1913

LANDSCAPE WITH FIVE FIGURES
Early one spring morning in October 1912, the mist of darkness rolled gently back to reveal an Aboriginal family walking slowly southwards through the empty tracts of bushland north-east of Carnarvon. Margoo (nicknamed 'Nipper' by the white settlers) and Clara walked alongside their young children Tommy and Topsy, while baby Mary nestled sleepily at her mother's breast. Their soft voices drifted languidly upwards into the wakening sky, their passing leaving only faint footprints and long shadows on the warming earth.

The young family was making its way southwards from Yanyeareddy, the station to which they and their people 'belonged', as Margoo would later have cause to testify in court.

It was common practice at the time for white pastoralists to 'assign' Aboriginal people to their properties, occasionally requiring them to put their mark on papers that formalised the arrangement. By the early 1900s this practice was well established, the viability of many properties having become dependent on the cheap labour of local Aboriginal people. It had been the way of things since at least 1885, when a proposal to establish an Aboriginal mission in the Gascoyne had been met with great alarm by local settlers, who had hastily convened a well-attended public meeting in Carnarvon to protest that the proposal would severely limit pastoralists' access to Aboriginal labour:

> At this stage Mr. Foss resigned the chair to Mr. Bush on account of the following proposition: Proposed by Mr. G.H. Rotten [sic; his surname was Rotton], seconded by Mr. R. Campbell, that the meeting protests against the Government assisting or countenancing the establishment of mission stations, to deal with the aboriginals within this district. Carried unanimously. Discussion was very lengthy on the above proposition, the general feeling being that the mission now about to be established would tamper with the servants of the settlers, which would be ruination to the district. The meeting refused to help the present mission in any way. Great dissatisfaction was shown at the establishment of a mission in the district. Mr. Foss returned to the chair with loud applause.[1]

Conditions for indentured Aboriginal workers varied greatly between stations, with some pastoralists building strong and enduring relationships with local tribespeople while others gained reputations for the opposite. These varying conditions notwithstanding, to Indigenous peoples long used to coming and going at will across their own lands, the finer points of these 'contracts' must have seemed nonsensical and were often disregarded. For either or both of these reasons, sometimes these 'servants' absconded, whereupon the police were dispatched with a warrant issued by Magistrate Foss to hunt them down and return them to the station to which they had been assigned. One local policeman at Gascoyne Junction referred to the capture of escaping Aboriginal people as 'nigger hunting [sic]'.[2] Former police constable Reilly, giving evidence in 1887, elaborated further: 'They always call it nigger hunting [sic] when they go to arrest natives ... whether absconders or not.' Another Gascoyne police officer explained of the practice, 'It made no difference to me whether a native was "signed" or not, so long as I had an arrest warrant'—after all, he went on, Magistrate Foss would not have issued a warrant unless a signed agreement had been produced by the pastoralist.[3]

While broader public opinion on the practice of indenturing Aboriginal people to pastoral stations was mixed, by and large it was seen simply as yet another peculiarity of the northern frontier, as one shearer's account from 1903 illustrates:

> Some of the old hands on the Gascoyne reckon that the indenture system is a fine thing for the district. But for this, it is pointed out, the police and the magistrates would have nothing to do for most of the year. The police work mainly consists of witnessing contracts and, as a consequence, chasing absconding niggers [sic].
>
> If one of the local serangs ['bosses'; landowners] takes a fancy to a young gin [sic], all he has to do is to take her before a J.P., and get her to make a mark on a piece of paper. She then becomes his servant for a year and he can do what he likes with her. Should she clear out with her lawful or tribal husband, the J.P. is rushed for a warrant, and the police bring her back to fulfil her agreement.
>
> A case came to my notice where a station manager had become possessed of a gin [sic] by these means. After a time, she cleared [out] with a native of her tribe. Both were caught and brought back by the police. The man received a term of imprisonment. The gin [sic], sooner than go to gaol, agreed to return to her boss. And when the native [man] had served his sentence, the boss got him indentured to himself, to make certain of the gin [sic]. That's the way they manage things on the Gascoyne.[4]

Whatever the balance of public opinion on the issue, as long as the practice of assigning Aboriginal people to particular stations remained in place, it was left mainly to the ever-pragmatic Carnarvon magistrate C.D.V. Foss to lend the force of law to the practice and to the myriad issues that stemmed from it.

Foss's own views on the matter appear to have been ambivalent at best. While he accepted that the absconding of Aboriginal workers was a 'problem' within his jurisdiction, he also held that it was neither widespread nor harshly punished. In a letter to the colonial secretary in 1886, Foss protested his own leniency in dealing with such cases:

> re Aboriginal natives absconding from their employers and being severely punished, I have the honour to inform you that the number of Aboriginal natives who have been imprisoned for absconding from their employers (since the 1st of June, 1882) amount to thirteen (13) and the maximum term of imprisonment inflicted was fourteen days.[5]

Despite Foss's feeling it necessary even at that time to downplay both the full extent and the full impacts of the indenturing system, six years later it was clear that the practice was still firmly in place. In the Mount Gould police book of 1892, for example, Inspector Lodge would note the large numbers of Aboriginal people still being assigned to stations in the Gascoyne–Murchison, adding that:

> the settler would still consider himself the rightful master of such natives and not expect any other settler to employ them, and this I believe is the sort of unwritten law or mutual agreement between the settlers …[6]

By 1912, while indenturing was still common, much of the early violent subjugation of Aboriginal peoples on the northern frontier had been replaced by an ostensibly more benevolent—but, in fact, equally destructive—legal and social paternalism.[7]

Such was the temper of the times when Margoo and his young family made their way southwards from the Aboriginal camp on Yanyeareddy Station on that spring morning in 1912.

'WHERE YOU GOING?'

Yanyeareddy Station had been one of the earliest established in the Gascoyne region, set up in the face of a desolate, indifferent outback by the Lefroy brothers in the early 1880s. Back then, Henry Gerald Lefroy (father of Frank) and his brother William Gerald Lefroy had taken possession of the land and stocked it with two thousand sheep and a few cattle and horses, which they had overlanded from Boolathana Station further south. By 1914 they would be shearing twelve thousand sheep and contracting eight blade-shearers.[8]

Moving away from the station homestead and crossing the nearby dry, sandy bed of the Lyndon River, Margoo and his family came across two white men who were camping on the bank. John (Jack) Sheehan—whose real name was Harry Varian—was a shearer who just the previous evening had thrown in his lot with a fifty-six-year-old kangaroo shooter from New Zealander who called himself Maori Bill—his own real name being William Williams. Sheehan was around thirty-seven years of age at the time and had worked on stations in the North-West for thirteen years. His new companion was making his way south to Bunbury with a cartload of fresh kangaroo skins, and the shearer had arranged to travel with him.

Margoo called out to the two men, 'You chaps lose anything last night?'

The pair looked at each other, and then Sheehan replied, 'Yes, two bottles of wine: one full and one half-full. I lost them down the creek.'

Margoo handed the bottles, which he had found earlier that morning, to the grateful men.

'Where you going?' Maori Bill asked the family.

When Margoo replied that they were making their away to Middalya Station to the south-west, Sheehan said, 'Well, put your swag into the cart.'

The two horses were hitched, and a swag was laid out on the cart for the two older children. Clara chose to walk behind with the baby in her arms.

MARGOO AND CLARA'S STORY

The small party moved on through the bush. When they reached Five Mile Gate, Sheehan offered Margoo a sip of whisky. The Aboriginal man took a mouthful, then Sheehan asked him to give some of the spirit to the walking Clara.

The Aboriginal man shrugged: 'Don't think she drink.'

Sheehan became insistent: 'Yes, she will drink.'

Margoo shrugged again. 'She won't, I think. Well, you try it, if you don't believe me.'

This show of perceived belligerence apparently offended Sheehan, who exclaimed, 'What?! If you say that to me, I'll give you a kicking!'

Margoo, sensing that the mood was changing for the worse, said, 'Best thing put my swag down.'

The swag was placed on the ground and the children with it. The cart moved off without the family, who watched it disappear into the low scrub.

Margoo, Clara, Tommy, Topsy and baby Mary now waited a little while, hoping to put some distance between themselves and the two men. When enough time had passed, they set off again through the silent bush. Even so, they had gone only another few kilometres when, at a place called the Beeroi Claypan, they again came across the shearer and the shooter, who had now camped for lunch.

Later, in court, Margoo would recall that the cart was on the right-hand side of the track, its shafts resting on prop sticks, the horses having been turned out to feed. Sheehan was lying under the cart while Maori Bill was sitting on an upturned box nearby.

The New Zealander, perhaps oblivious of the tensions from early in the day, called to the family group, 'Aren't you going to stop and have some dinner?'

Margoo paused. 'I haven't much water or tucker,' he said.

Maori Bill brushed this aside with an amiable, 'Make your fire and I'll give you water and tucker.'

After doing as promised, Maori Bill went to see after the horses while Margoo and his family ate, Margoo standing near the cart while his wife and children sat on the ground on the other side of the track.

Sheltered from the sun, Sheehan remained drinking under the cart. His state, according to his reluctant guest, was 'a bit sober'.

While the family ate, Sheehan called out, 'Margoo!' twice from beneath cart. The Aboriginal man did not answer.

Sheehan persisted: 'Margoo! Going to have a nip?'

This time Margoo replied, 'No, thanks.'

The voice from under the cart came sullenly from the shadow: 'Well, you no good.'

Shortly afterwards Sheehan emerged into the sunlight. Margoo moved back towards where Clara and the children were sitting on the left-hand side of the track. The family watched as Sheehan retrieved a rifle from the cart and walked towards them.

'A man ought to shoot you,' he muttered. 'You'd better clear out.'

Margoo stood still. He was unarmed and vulnerable, but his voice was steady: 'I will go away when I have finished my dinner.'

The family stared at the man with the gun. Clara was sitting on the ground, baby Mary in her arms and toddler Topsy standing alongside her.

Sheehan insisted: 'You'd better clear out now.'

Then, as if suddenly making up his mind, he raised the rifle swiftly to his shoulder and, without further warning, pulled the trigger.

The crack of a single shot shattered the midday calm. In the split second that followed, Sheehan's bullet hit Clara in the right arm, breaking the bone and then passing hot and misshapen into Topsy, lodging in the child's belly cavity in front of her spine, just below the level of her navel.

Margoo reached down desperately and gathered his bloodied daughter into his arms. Clara, in shock, slid prostrate into the dust.

At that moment Maori Bill, arriving on the scene with the two horses, screamed out in horror: 'What in the name of God are you doing, man? Stop that game!'

He grabbed Sheehan and, as he struggled to take the rifle from him, a second shot rent the air. Then the New Zealander punched Sheehan in the face with enough force to knock him down, before moving quickly to bandage the bleeding child.

Sheehan lifted himself awkwardly out of the dust. The blow seemed to have brought him to his senses and, overcome with the enormity of what he had done, the sobbing shearer repeated over and over, 'I'm sorry! I'm sorry!'

Maori Bill ignored him and went about his urgent task quickly. Once Topsy's and Clara's wounds were dressed, he and Sheehan went over and tipped up the cart and pulled the props out. Maori Bill motioned to Margoo that he would lift Clara into the cart, but Margoo wouldn't let him. Instead, carrying his dying daughter, he climbed up into the cart and Clara followed.

Maori Bill hitched the horses and the cart moved slowly back towards the Yanyeareddy homestead. As they once more reached Five Mile Gate, Sheehan offered Margoo a sip of whisky and this time Clara, in a state of shock and pain, also accepted.

It was then that the shearer begged Clara, 'Don't you tell Lefroy that I shot you. You say like this: the cart tipped over and the gun went off.'

Clara said nothing. She remained silent too when Sheehan added in a whisper, 'I kill you if you tell Lefroy that I shoot.'

MAORI BILL'S STORY

The sturdily built kangaroo shooter known as Maori Bill would also be called on some time later, in a court of law, to give his version of the tragic events that had played out at the Beeroi Claypan that day. His recollections of the morning leading up to the events at Five Mile Gate—where Sheehan had first offered Margoo a sip of whisky as the two parties travelled together—were consistent with those of Margoo and Clara, but they diverged markedly from that point on.

All he knew of any argument, he would tell the jury, was that Sheehan and Margoo had been 'speaking in nigger language [sic]',[9] and then suddenly the Aboriginal man's belongings were thrown from the cart.

Later, he said—when the family had arrived at the men's camp at lunchtime—he told Sheehan, who was reading a magazine under the cart, to fix the things on the cart ready for hitching the horses while he fetched them. When he returned with the two horses, he continued, he saw his companion on top of the cart, holding a rifle in one hand and trying to make room for a tuckerbox with the other. As he watched, the cart tipped backwards—he himself having forgotten to place the props there as he would usually have done—and as it did he heard the gun, which he always kept loaded, go off.

The New Zealander claimed that the reason he had called out to Sheehan, 'What in the name of God are you doing?' was that all of his belongings were in the cart. He denied that he had struck Sheehan or taken the rifle from him. Moreover, he told the court, the rifle had always been unstable and had even gone off once while slung over his shoulder.

The story told by Maori Bill continued to differ from that told by Margoo and Clara. During the journey back to Yanyeareddy, the New Zealander said, he was sitting close to both Sheehan and Clara; had Sheehan issued her with threats, Maori Bill would have been sure to hear them. He was adamant that he hadn't heard anything pass between them.

SHEEHAN'S STORY

Like Maori Bill, Jack Sheehan would later describe the events of that day in similar terms as Margoo and Clara—up until the alleged argument at Five Mile Gate.

According to Sheehan's account it was Margoo who had suggested that Clara, too, might like a drink of whisky. Before Sheehan could acquiesce to this request, however, the Aboriginal man seemed to think the better of it and, instead, asked that his children and their swag be placed on the ground. Sheehan couldn't explain this sudden change of mind; he testified that immediately beforehand he and Margoo had been exchanging small talk, with the shooter asking the meaning of different words in 'nigger lingo [sic]',[10] his attempts to pronounce the words causing the Aboriginal man to laugh.

Later, according to Sheehan, he had been reading under the cart at lunchtime when Margoo and his family arrived at the camp. Shortly afterwards, Maori Bill went off to get the horses and Sheehan pulled on his boots, rolled up his swag and climbed up onto the cart to arrange things for their departure. As he reached down to pick up a rifle lying in the cart, a 'cockeye bob'[11] suddenly swept over the cart. The startled shearer stepped backwards onto the tailboard and, as the cart tipped, the butt of the rifle stuck him in the eye.

Then, Sheehan recalled, 'As I was scrambling up, I heard the rifle go off.'

It was at this moment, he continued, that he heard Maori Bill cry out, 'What in the name of God are you doing?'

Sheehan also became aware of the shouting of the family, he said, but took little notice as he did not yet realise anyone had been hurt.

'I DIDN'T MEAN TO DO IT'

By all accounts it was midafternoon by the time the small party arrived back at the Yanyeareddy homestead. Sheehan jumped from the cart and ran ahead to alert Mrs Lefroy, who hurried with him back to the cart shed. There Flora Lefroy found Margoo walking towards her with the injured Topsy in his arms. She noticed the child's stomach protruding through the wound to her belly, and told Margoo to take the little girl straight to the main house. Then she quickly set about bandaging Clara's badly wounded arm.

Meanwhile, Sheehan hovered nearby, trying to help where he could, but his hands were shaking so much that Mrs Lefroy was sure he had been drinking. As she pushed him gently aside she heard him say, 'I didn't mean to do it, Clara.'

The Aboriginal woman ignored him and instead told Mrs Lefroy directly, 'He meant to shoot Margoo but he shot me instead.'

The white woman looked up at Maori Bill for confirmation: 'Is that true?'

But the kangaroo shooter, in direct contradiction of what he would later tell police, only replied, 'I know nothing about it. I wasn't there. I went away after the horses.'

'What happened to your face?' Mrs Lefroy asked Sheehan when she noticed the large bruise on the agitated shearer's cheek.

This time it was Sheehan who would contradict his later evidence: 'I ran into the cart's shaft,' he explained. He made no mention of the gun having struck him in the eye.

Mrs Lefroy now turned her attention to the wounded toddler, but her efforts would be to no avail. At around six o'clock that evening, Margoo and Clara's daughter Topsy slipped quietly away.

'CLEAR OUT!'

The dead child's body was gently wrapped by the two women in some old sacking and a red-and-blue striped shirt. Meanwhile, Margoo had found a bicycle and was riding out to find Mr Lefroy, who was working elsewhere on the property. Maori Bill was also keen to locate William Lefroy, determined to tell him his version of events and then be on his way. He revealed nothing of those details to Mrs Lefroy, however, who was forced to piece together what had happened at the Beeroi Claypan from the fragmented accounts of the distraught Sheehan and the wounded Clara.

When the station-owner arrived back at the homestead with Margoo, shocked and angry at the child's death, he was in no mood to hear the white men's story. Instead, he immediately sent Margoo to the Winning Pool telegraph station some one hundred kilometres away, with a letter to the postmaster outlining the facts as he knew them and recommending that the police be notified.

It was not until ten o'clock the following morning that Maori Bill was able to speak to the pastoralist, and even then Lefroy was sharp: 'Carnarvon is the place for you to make your statement.'

As for the gunman himself, Lefroy, suspecting that Sheehan was still under the influence of drink, refused outright to hear his statement and told him angrily: 'Clear out! Carnarvon is the place where you are wanted. There will also be another charge against you, Sheehan.'

Jack Sheehan must have known that his future, perhaps even his life, hung precariously on there being an alternative version to that of Margoo of what had taken place at the claypan. He was terrified that Maori Bill, his sole supporting witness, would disappear into the empty landscape without first corroborating his account of what had happened. In the end, William Lefroy relented, but only as far as taking Maori Bill into his office to hear his side of the tale. He still would have nothing to do with Sheehan.

The next day, Maori Bill and Jack Sheehan resumed their journey south, stopping once more for lunch at the scene of the shooting.

Back at Yanyeareddy Station, Margoo and another Aboriginal man, Alex, buried Topsy's body. It had been two years and three months since the day of her birth on the station.

'BLOODY LIAR'

Two days after the burial of Topsy, Constable Joseph Fogarty and an Aboriginal tracker known as Limerick set off on horseback from the northern town of Onslow to Yanyeareddy Station to investigate the events surrounding the little girl's death. They would travel southwards for four days, arriving at the station on the evening of 16 October 1912.

The following morning the two men met with Margoo, and all three made their way to the fatal scene at the Beeroi Claypan. There having been no rain, the constable and the tracker were able to undertake a forensic examination of the site, tracking and recording the footprints, bloodstains and wheel marks in the sand. Fogarty believed he could identify signs of a struggle, and a place where a bullet had entered the earth.

The dedicated officer and his offsider then began the task of finding the shearer and the roo shooter, who by then had disappeared into the vast tracts of desolate wilderness. They turned their horses southwards again and headed towards Minilya Station, the last known destination of Sheehan and Maori Bill. Within three days, on 19 November, they found themselves about twenty kilometres from the Minilya homestead where a spring-cart was pulled up alongside a waterhole. Crouched by the cart, making damper in a camp fire, was Jack Sheehan.

Fogarty and Sheehan already knew each other from Onslow. Sheehan visited there often, and only three years before had been at the town's local racetrack preparing his horse Saucy Bee for the Onslow Cup.

The constable said, 'Hello, Jack.' The two men shook hands.

'Are you looking for me?' asked Sheehan.

Fogarty stared into Sheehan's eyes. 'I've come to arrest you for wilful murder.'

'If you'd been a few days later I'd have been at Winning Pool.' It was hard to tell whether Sheehan was being laconic or wistful. Then, as if he had been expecting this moment, he handed the policemen a letter addressed to the resident magistrate in Carnarvon. 'Read it,' he said.

Fogarty didn't share his prisoner's sense of urgency, and it wasn't until after supper—as the men sat waiting for the return of Maori Bill, who was out shooting with the same rifle that had claimed Topsy's life—that he glanced through the letter's contents. It described Topsy's death as an accident caused by of the tipping of the cart.

The constable looked up at Sheehan. The shearer, perhaps suspecting that Margoo had already told the story of Maori Bill struggling to wrest the gun away and striking him to his senses, remarked, 'You're looking at my eye.'

The policeman nodded. It was hard to ignore the fact that the shearer's left eye was bloodshot and black, with a slight swelling underneath.

But Sheehan was ready with his answer: 'When the rifle fell out of the cart, it kicked me in the eye,' he explained.

Half an hour passed, and Maori Bill returned to the camp site. According to the evidence he gave later, he saw Constable Fogarty giving Sheehan whisky in the hope that it would loosen his tongue and see him corroborate Margoo's version of events. But if that was Fogarty's plan then it failed dismally, for Sheehan remained steadfast in his assertion that the whole incident had simply been a tragic accident. Maori Bill would later allege that, in response to Sheehan's statement to that effect, Fogarty called his prisoner a 'bloody liar'. This version of events was later denied by the policeman.

The next morning, Fogarty and Limerick left Maori Bill at the camp site and continued south towards Carnarvon. This time they brought Jack Sheehan with them.

The men reached town a few days later but, having delivered his prisoner to the lock-up, Fogarty knew his job was far from done. He and Limerick now turned their horses north again to revisit the scene of the fatal incident and then retrieve the little girl's body for the inquest that would establish the cause of her death. A Carnarvon police officer, the 'reliable and efficient' Barney McGowan,[12] accompanied them.

Sunset found the three men a few kilometres out of town when, as they made their way across the Bibbawarra Claypan, the figure of Maori Bill sitting atop his spring-cart appeared through the twilight. By now darkness and rain were setting in, and the four men decided to camp together for the night. By the firelight, the two constables used the opportunity to take a statement from the shooter. The night passed without incident and, in the morning, Maori Bill signed the written statement and McGowan added his name as witness.

Fogarty folded the document carefully, inwardly annoyed that it contained a direct contradiction to the New Zealander's original claim that he had been away with the horses and had not witnessed the shooting. Now, he claimed to have seen the whole thing. There was no time to argue about it now, however.

In the cool of the morning Maori Bill once again headed southwards and the police party continued north towards the distant site of the killing of Topsy. Once there, the three men minutely examined the scene. At one stage, Limerick put on Sheehan's hobnailed boots to compare their tracks to those previously left in the sand. Fogarty was keen to prove that a second shot, as described by Margoo, had been fired during the alleged fight between Sheehan and Maori Bill. To test this, McGowan watched as his companion fired a shot into the ground next to the spot where Fogarty believed a bullet had previously entered the earth. According to both men, the two holes matched and the bullet proved untraceable.

Having made notes and maps of the crime scene, the trio continued to Yanyeareddy where, with the help of Margoo, they disinterred Topsy's remains. They then prepared the toddler's body for the journey back to Carnarvon where, on 4 November—twenty-seven days after the shooting—Dr Henchley would carry out the autopsy.

The policemen had done what they could. Now only the inquest remained to determine which version of the events leading to Topsy's death was the truth.

'THE EVIDENCE OF NATIVES'

At the Carnarvon courthouse on Tuesday 12 November 1912, the ex officio coroner—Magistrate C.D.V. Foss—convened the official inquest into the death of the Aboriginal child, Topsy.

First, Margoo took the stand to give his version of what had happened at the Beeroi Claypan. His story was unequivocal: Sheehan had, in a fit of pique, attempted to shoot him and instead had wounded Clara and killed Topsy.

Dr Henchley gave his report of the post-mortem examination of the body of a female child, 'apparently between three and four years of age, wrapped up in some sacking and an old blue-and-red striped shirt; also some reddish earth and scrub mixed up with the clothing'.[13] He tendered as evidence the misshapen bullet removed from the child's abdominal cavity.

After listening to Dr Henchley's report, Topsy's mother, Clara, gave her recollection of the fateful day. Her story echoed the evidence given by Margoo.

Now the only other adult witness took the stand to explain how the child had come to die at Yanyeareddy Station on that October afternoon. Maori Bill's story, albeit now different from his original version, was well formed: the death was an accident, the gun having gone off when it had struck the ground.

Constable Fogarty tried in vain to have the original written statement of the witness presented to the jury. Mr Fitzroy Marmion, appearing as defence for the accused, would have none of it: his client was an illiterate man and the statement transcribed by the policeman and signed by Maori Bill was therefore valueless, he argued. Foss concurred, and the jury withdrew its request for access to the document.

It was now left to the meticulous Constable Fogarty to lay out the findings of his investigations and the content of his conversations with

Sheehan and with Maori Bill. Constable McGowan also appeared briefly, confirming Fogarty's testimony.

Flora Lefroy, who had tended Topsy's wounds after the shooting, then told the story of the small group's arrival at the station homestead a month earlier, and her futile attempts to save the little girl's life.

And then it was time for Jack Sheehan to take the floor. In the main, the gunman's story matched that of the only other white witness to the shooting: Topsy's death had been a tragic accident to which no malice aforethought could be attributed.

Sheehan's barrister now addressed the jury. He began by all but dismissing the evidence given by Margoo and Clara, glibly telling the jury, 'You all know from experience how far the evidence of natives can be taken.'[14]

Instead, Marmion relied heavily on Maori Bill's evidence. The kangaroo shooter, he argued, had nothing to gain by creating a falsehood; after all, he had only met Sheehan for the first time the night before. This was not, in Marmion's opinion, a case of misplaced loyalty to a friend.

As for the alleged argument between Sheehan and Margoo—which Margoo and Clara had cited as the reason the two groups had parted ways at Five Mile Gate—it was entirely feasible that 'the native [had] asked for the swags to be put down as the woman was lagging behind and carrying a baby only three weeks old'.[15]

Marmion now doubled down on his argument. The logic of the case simply did not add up, he claimed. If the tall Aboriginal man, Margoo, was Sheehan's intended target, why would the gun have been aimed so low as to strike a seated woman and a toddler? No, insisted Marmion, this was plainly and clearly an accident 'which might occur to anyone, and the like of which is reported in the newspapers every day'.[16]

The barrister then confidently resumed his seat.

Now Coroner Foss began his summing up of the case for the jury. He began by reiterating Marmion's observation that the evidence of Aboriginal witnesses was not reliable—except when corroborated, he clarified. And in this case, he noted, Margoo's description of the shooting was indeed backed by the investigations of Constable Fogarty.

The coroner continued: he did not consider the marks in the dust to constitute sufficient evidence after such a long interval that a struggle had taken place, but he did believe the bullet hole in the ground contradicted Maori Bill's account of events.

Foss went further: he believed that the kangaroo shooter had, in describing what had happened that day at Yanyeareddy, clearly contradicted himself. Perhaps Foss was acknowledging the discrepancies between the New Zealander's original written and subsequent verbal statements—the former of which, although not made available to the jury, the coroner himself had sighted. Or perhaps he was reflecting on the evidence given by Constable Fogarty and Mrs Lefroy—each of whom had independently reported Maori Bill's having told them that he had not witnessed the shooting as he was tending the horses. In any event, Foss's advice to the jury was unequivocal: 'The evidence of Maori Bill must be discounted to a large measure,' he told them.

Foss, like so many others in the courtroom, was now left with the conundrum of motivation. If, in fact, Sheehan was culpable—that is, if both he and Maori Bill were lying—then what possible reason could lie behind such a crime?

The coroner's attempt to get at the heart of the matter began with his laying out of the distinctions between murder and manslaughter. To his mind, he told the courtroom, the incident was not motivated by a desire to cause harm; of that he was sure. There was simply no conceivable reason produced at the inquest that could incite the deliberate taking of a life.

'But,' he added, 'if a rifle were pointed at a person and it exploded, the person holding the rifle is responsible for the result.'

This remark points to an emerging suggestion by the coroner that this was a case of accidental death triggered by rash behaviour intended to intimidate rather than to injure.

Finally, Magistrate Foss defended Constable Fogarty against the attempts of Maori Bill to discredit him: 'The policeman, while not known to me, has a good reputation and his evidence should carry some weight.'

The jury now retired to consider the evidence put before them. They were gone for barely ninety minutes before returning to their seats. The foreman stood before the court and read the verdict: 'We find that Topsy came to her death from a rifle wound, accidentally inflicted by Jack Sheehan.'[17]

The relieved shearer was immediately released.

'THAT EXTRAORDINARY CONSTABLE'

The tragedy that had begun at the Beeroi Claypan might well have ended in the Carnarvon courthouse, had it not been for a general sense of disquiet that followed the announcement of the verdict—particularly when the news reached Perth. In March 1913, as a result of a report commissioned by the Crown law authorities, Jack Sheehan was arrested and committed for trial at the Perth Criminal Court.

Once more, witnesses were rounded up from across the state and called on to repeat the stories they had told in Carnarvon just a few months earlier. Margoo and Clara were asked yet again to relive the memories of their young daughter's death, and to listen as Maori Bill gave a repeat performance that discredited their version of how she had died. Also in the witness room awaiting their turns in court were Constable Fogarty and two women from the Aboriginal camp at Yanyeareddy Station: in the trial reports, these women are referred to only as 'Black Maggie' and her daughter.

The trial quickly descended into farce. To begin with, both Maggie's and her daughter's evidence was belatedly deemed irrelevant, so was never presented to the jury. Worse was to come when Constable Fogarty took the stand on the first day. His attempts to explain the maps he had drawn of the scene at the Beeroi Claypan proved too abstruse for either the judge or the counsels to interpret. To make matters worse, on the second day of the trial the constable failed to arrive in court for his scheduled reappearance. It was not until fifteen minutes later that he was located elsewhere in the building, having mistakenly been waiting in the witness room. This incident, combined with the apparently confused nature of his evidence, raised the ire of the presiding Justice John Booth as well as that of the defence lawyer, Edmund Drake-Brockman, and even the Crown prosecutor, Francis (Frank) Parker.

In the course of once more trying to make sense of Fogarty's baffling maps, it was the frustrated prosecutor who exclaimed, 'Have you been drinking this morning, Constable Fogarty?'

The startled policeman turned to the judge: 'I ask your Honour if that is a fair question to put.'

But Parker was insistent: '*Have* you been drinking?' he repeated.

Fogarty replied shortly, 'No, I have not been drinking.'

But the damage was already done in terms of the credibility of the Crown's chief witness. The issue of Constable Fogarty's sobriety—first raised in the evidence of Maori Bill—now became a recurring theme throughout the trial. Was it true that Constable Fogarty had been drunk when he had first met Maori Bill? Was it not the case that he had been so drunk that he had had to take the shooter's statement half a dozen times? Had he not gone on a week-long 'bender' after the original inquest? To all these questions, the beleaguered policeman firmly insisted that the opposite was true.

When it came to the description of the crime scene itself, Drake-Brockman continued to press home the image of an incompetent, drunken policeman. He asked Fogarty whether he had been drunk at the time he had inspected the footprints at the Beeroi Claypan.

'I was not,' replied Fogarty, elaborating, 'I did not have an opportunity to get into such a condition.'

The defence counsel was unimpressed. 'If you had, you would have taken advantage of it, I suppose.'

The constable was indignant: 'No, I would not! I have never been drunk in my life.'

The questions continued in the same vein until, finally, Fogarty turned to the judge and, in a hoarse voice, asked whether he might be relieved from giving further evidence due to a bad cold. But Booth would have none of it, warning instead that the constable's conduct was putting him in a serious position and that he had 'better watch himself'. It was clear that frustration was rising in all parties.

Finally, the increasingly annoyed judge, in an effort to resolve the confusion about the crime scene maps, left the bench and attempted to indicate to the jury the various positions of the cart and the characters as explained in the policeman's testimony—even marking in red the salient points of his exposition.

Mr Parker, however, respectfully disagreed with the judge's interpretation and sought permission to obtain further clarification from Fogarty.

Booth replied coolly, 'Certainly, Mr Parker. Do anything that will make it clearer.' Then he returned to his seat.

Margoo and Clara looked on as the Crown's representative made one last attempt to make sense of the map that depicted the scene of their daughter's death. But it was to no avail.

Finally, Parker cried, 'It's worse than ever now! Let us disregard it altogether.'

The judge agreed, and Fogarty's illustration of the events at the Beeroi Claypan was put aside once and for all.

Sheehan and Maori Bill then gave evidence that married with the versions of events they had provided to the inquest in Carnarvon. This time, the two men only contradicted each other once, with Maori Bill claiming the gun went off while in the accused man's hand but Sheehan claiming it went off when it hit the ground.

Maori Bill also firmly denounced the recollections of Mrs Lefroy. It was not true, he said, that he had told her that he did not know how the woman and child had come to be shot. Nor had he told her that he did not want to discuss the matter with her. The New Zealander was adamant about these points.

The trial sometimes lapsed into dark humour, as *The West Australian* would report:

> Amusement was caused in Court when Mr. Parker slung the rifle over his shoulder and found himself unable to take it off again without obtaining his Honour's permission to remove his wig.[18]

The newspaper did not reflect, however, on how much humour was to be found in these moments by Margoo and Clara.

Eventually, the trial took its course and the judge's summation to the jury left little doubt about which way the verdict would fall.

'The principal witness for the prosecution was the man Margoo himself,' Justice Booth explained to the court, 'and, from his story, the accused had practically no motive for the alleged crime.'

It was also, said the judge, difficult to understand how the minor argument alleged to have occurred at the Five Mile Gate could have led to an act of murder.

Then His Honour moved on to 'that extraordinary constable, Fogarty'. On this subject the judge was scathing, and all but laid the Crown's failure to make a case against Sheehan entirely at the feet of the Onslow policeman:

> If he could have supported Nipper as to the tracks he found, if he had come here as a decent witness and shown that there was at all events reasonable grounds for thinking that a struggle had taken place where the murder was alleged to have taken place, the court might have placed some reliance on him … I cannot but say that by making a disgraceful exhibition of himself he has done all he could to weaken the case he was here to support.[19]

Justice Booth then turned to the jury:

> It is not for me to dictate to you as to what your verdict should be, but I feel myself that it would be almost impossible for you to bring in a verdict of wilful murder against the accused practically on the uncorroborated

evidence of the man Margoo, especially in view of the fact that the crime, if crime it was, was absolutely motiveless.[20]

If any reasonable doubt remained about what had occurred at that remote place north of Carnarvon, the judge further cautioned the jury, then a guilty verdict of the charge of wilful murder could not be the outcome of the trial. Booth might not have been dictating the verdict, but he was certainly whispering it.

His guidance would have the desired effect. After just a few minutes' deliberation, the jury brought in a verdict of not guilty and his Honour ordered the accused be discharged.

QUESTIONS OF MOTIVE

Accidents happen. Sometimes they arise from the most unlikely convergence of events, and have the most tragic of consequences. Nonetheless, they are simply accidents. Both a 1912 coronial inquest and a 1913 trial by jury found that Topsy had died from such a series of events, for which no blame could be attributed: a man had stood on a cart, the cart had upset, causing a gun to discharge and a bullet to strike a child and her mother.

But there remains one critical problem: four adult witnesses to the events that unfolded that day on the road south from Yanyeareddy Station told two fundamentally different stories. And only one version can be true.

Once we accept one witness's account over another's, we are then left with the uncomfortable conclusion that the other witnesses—who were also present at the time and who knew exactly what had happened to Topsy—knowingly lied about it. Usually, this means someone has something to gain from lying. To understand why someone would do so under oath, it is necessary to look more closely at the reasons that might underpin each witness's version of events in this case.

At both the inquest and the trial into Topsy's death, the respective presiding lawman placed great emphasis on the issue of motive. What possible reason, they each asked, could Sheehan have had to cold-bloodedly attempt to gun down an Aboriginal man whom he had only just met? Even if one accepts Margoo's report of an earlier argument at the Five Mile Gate, it was not, on the face of it, the kind of major disagreement likely to provoke a murder. Both Foss and Booth agreed on this.

There are other motives to consider too: if Topsy's death was simply a tragic accident, what could Margoo's and Clara's reasons have been for lying that the shooting had been intentional? And if they were not lying, then what could Maori Bill's motive have been for protecting a man he had known for less than twenty-four hours? And what are we to understand was Mrs Lefroy's potential motive for lying about the New Zealander's having asserted to her that he had not seen the events unfold? Or the motive for Sheehan's untruth about his black eye having resulted from walking into the side of the cart?

In attempting to answer these questions, it is worth beginning with the evidence of Maori Bill—the only witness with no apparent vested interest in anything other than the truth, but whose evidence was found by both investigations to be contradictory and untrustworthy. In one version, given to Mrs Lefroy, he claimed he did not see what happened at the camp. He repeated that story in a written statement to Constable Fogarty. Only when he stood at the witness stand did he change it dramatically.

Once under oath, Maori Bill proclaimed he had seen the whole chain of events unfold from about five to ten paces away. And yet what he said he saw varied from what Sheehan himself suggested had happened. There is, for example, no mention of the cockeye bob that Sheehan declared had caused him to lose his balance. More importantly, the New Zealander swore that the gun went off in Sheehan's hand, while Sheehan himself was adamant that it had left his hand and only discharged when it struck the ground.

Then there are the two different stories told by the shearer himself about the bruising to his face. Margoo swore that Sheehan's black cheek and bloodshot eye were the results of a blow from Maori Bill as he'd tried to take the gun from the alleged killer. To Mrs Lefroy, Sheehan explained that he had walked into the side of the cart; to Constable Fogarty he said the butt of the rifle had struck him in the face as he'd fallen from the cart.

Any police officer, lawyer or judge will tell you that memory is a fragile commodity—especially under pressure, and equally so under oath. Even when telling the truth, witnesses often change their stories over time, recalling and forgetting different parts, in some cases becoming convinced of things that never happened. Inconsistent evidence, therefore, is not always a clear indicator of either innocence or guilt.

This might have been why, despite the discrepancies within his accounts, the court placed significant weight on the lack of motive Maori Bill might have had to lie on behalf of a man whom he barely knew. It might also have been why the changing nature of Sheehan's explanations was outweighed by the absence of any probable reason to kill a virtual stranger. This compounding lack of motive provided a powerful tipping point for the verdicts of both the inquest and trial.

To find a possible motive—both for Sheehan's alleged actions and for his companion's supporting evidence—it is necessary to consider some additional information that was provided to both the inquest and the trial by Margoo, Clara and the two other Aboriginal witnesses. That information relates to events of the night preceding Topsy's death.

'I WENT TO THE NATIVE CAMP TOO BUT COULDN'T GET A WOMAN'

At the Carnarvon inquest, Margoo and Clara had both revealed that, on the night before the shooting, they had seen Sheehan at the Aboriginal camp on Yanyeareddy. The shearer, whom Margoo thought seemed drunk, had said to him, 'Any chance of getting a woman?'

The Aboriginal man had replied that there were no women for him, and taken him back to his camp where Maori Bill was waiting. The roo shooter had looked up at the two men and said, 'I went to the native camp too but couldn't get a woman.'

Margoo's allegation that both white men had been at the Aboriginal camp, and that both of them had been looking for women, was backed up by the Aboriginal woman later referred to in the trial records as 'Black Maggie', who also said she 'belonged' to Yanyeareddy Station.

Maggie told the inquest, 'On the night the mail cart came in from Carnarvon, Maori Bill came to the camp and called out, "That you, Maggie? Is Peter there?"'

She added that she had noticed he had a bottle in his pocket.

Maggie's husband, Peter, she said, had called out to the kangaroo shooter, 'What you want Maggie for? You clear out; don't come blackfellow camp.'

Maggie's daughter also testified at the inquest that she had heard the arrival of Sheehan at the camp and seen Margoo leading him away.

Both Sheehan and Maori Bill had hotly denied these claims. Even the assertion that they had been intoxicated that night was refuted. The shearer protested that he and his new companion had only drunk three-quarters of a bottle of whisky that evening, and that neither had gone to the Aboriginal camp.

These alleged events, whether true or not, made no impact on the inquest and were not mentioned in the summing up of Magistrate Foss. In Perth, Maggie had barely taken the stand when Drake-Brockman had appealed to the judge that her evidence was irrelevant to the matter at hand. His Honour had agreed, and Maggie was stood down. In this way, the matter of what was alleged to have happened on the night before the shooting had been dismissed from the considerations of the jury.

There had been no assertion that the evidence was not true—only that it had no bearing on the case. The fact that the state had paid for Maggie to travel from Yanyeareddy to Perth to give her evidence suggests, however, that the Crown prosecutor had seen something in her story that was connected to the events at the Beeroi Claypan. Given the cost alone, it is surprising then that even Mr Parker failed to challenge the judgement that Maggie's account was irrelevant to the matters at hand.

And yet it is possible that these alleged events at the Aboriginal camp the previous night—and the period of Western Australia's history within which they occurred—go to the heart of a possible motive for both Sheehan's alleged actions and the witness testimony of Maori Bill.

'IT SHALL NOT BE LAWFUL'

In 1904, some eight years before the death of Topsy and the alleged events at the Yanyeareddy Aboriginal camp, a royal commission was held into the treatment of Aboriginal people in the north of Western Australia. It was prompted by a litany of allegations about exploitation, injustice and cruelty that had been filtering southwards for many years.

The royal commission was headed by former Queensland Protector of Aborigines Mr Walter Edmund Roth. Among other findings, his report was damning with respect to the sexual abuse of Aboriginal women, particularly at the hands of itinerant white men.

Roth's report ushered in Western Australia's *Aborigines Act 1905*, which instituted unprecedented control over a wide range of aspects of the lives of Aboriginal people in the state, including their 'welfare', the 'custody, maintenance and education' of their children, their right to work, their access to alcohol and to firearms, where they could live and who they could marry.

Importantly, the Act also made interracial sexual relations illegal without the express permission of the state's Chief Protector of Aborigines. Furthermore, to reduce opportunities for such relations, it stated categorically, 'It shall not be lawful for any person ... without lawful excuse, to enter or remain or be within or upon any place where Aborigines or female half-castes are camped'.

These statutes were well established by the time of the events at Yanyeareddy Station. The alleged behaviour of Sheehan and Maori Bill in seeking women for sex at the Aboriginal camp the night before was illegal. It would not have been something either man would want brought to general notice or, worse still, affirmed through a public trial.

It is also possible that the alleged events of the night before Topsy's death fed into an undercurrent of ill-feeling that flowed unspoken and invisible between each of the players in the tragedy that unfolded. This might explain the simmering resentment of Sheehan towards the man who had escorted him from the Aboriginal camp the night before. It could well account for Clara's decision to walk some distance behind the cart on which her husband and two elder children were riding to the Five Mile Gate.

At face value, it might also provide a reason for Maori Bill's unwillingness to stand by his original statement that he had not seen the events unfold later that day. If the New Zealander were to confirm Margoo's version of events at Beeroi Claypan, then he would also have to affirm that part of the Aboriginal man's evidence that placed him illegally in the Aboriginal camp the night before.

Whatever the case, and for whatever the reason, the circumstances of the night before the death of Topsy did not enter into the considerations of either Foss or Booth as they pondered the potential motives that might lie behind the tragedy.

The two lawmen seemed even more unwilling to consider the motives that Margoo and Clara might have had for their apparent lies about what had taken place that day. By virtue of the not guilty verdict, the court was effectively upholding Sheehan's and Maori Bill's accounts and, by implication, discrediting those of Topsy's parents. The two stories were worlds apart. In one account, Sheehan purposely aimed the gun at Margoo and accidentally shot Clara and Topsy; in the other, the death arose from a chain of unhappy and inconsistently recalled coincidences.

No-one seemed to question what motive the couple might have had to invent a story that, if believed, would have had dire consequences for an innocent man. Had their grief become malice? Were the devastated parents hell-bent on making someone pay for the death of their child, irrespective of the truth?

Corporal Fogarty didn't think so. The policeman had gone to great effort to bring the accused killer to justice. He had believed that the evidence supported the Aboriginal couple's version of events. His alleged drunkenness while taking Sheehan's statement was a fabrication of the two men who had most to gain from telling such a tale. It could easily have been dismissed by Constable McGowan, who had accompanied Fogarty when taking Maori Bill's statement and when making maps of the crime scene.

While Fogarty's investigations were commended—albeit to little effect—at the Carnarvon inquest, the court in Perth seems to have been quick to discredit the only man who could have shed professional and objective light on the death of an innocent child.

Even more strangely, the court seemed more content to accept the possibility of a drunken policeman who denied drinking than that of two drunken white men who admitted to drinking on the day of the events and on the night before.

'FOR HUMAN LIFE IS NOT TO BE PLAYED WITH'

After the trial, both Jack Sheehan and Maori Bill were interviewed by *The Sunday Times*. A relieved Sheehan openly acknowledged his debt to the only other white witness to the shooting, telling the sympathetic reporter, 'If it weren't for him, I'd have had my neck stretched.'[21]

Once more, Sheehan's version of events strayed quickly from the evidence he had earlier given under oath. This time he added a particularly cruel twist: in describing the scene after the shooting, he attributed Topsy's death in part to Margoo's 'bounding about' uncontrollably with the child in his arms while the two white men tried to treat her wounds.

Both men, as well as the newspaper itself, continued to pillory Constable Fogarty who, they declared, had tutored the Aboriginal witnesses, had been drunk at various times and had tried to convince Maori Bill to change his version of events. Sheehan and Maori Bill argued that the constable's behaviour warranted financial and moral redress by the state, and *The Sunday Times* agreed:

> If there has been any hanky-panky, then let the offenders be punished with all the rigour of the law, for human life is not to be played with. The most humble member of the community is just as much entitled to protection as the highest in the land, and, in the present case, we hope to see that principle vindicated.[22]

For two humble members of the community there would be no such protection, no financial redress nor moral vindication. Unlike for Sheehan and Maori Bill, there would be no public outpourings of sympathy for Margoo and Clara and their two remaining children. After the trial, they were simply returned by ship to Carnarvon. From there they walked back into the obscurity of the vast northern interior from which the violent death of Topsy had briefly wrenched them.

EPILOGUE
THE 'GRAND OLD MAN OF THE GASCOYNE'

> It is announced that magistrates A.S. Roe and J. Cowan of Perth, and C.D.V. Foss of Carnarvon, are to be retired from the magisterial bench. In future men only [sic] who have passed the prescribed examination in law or legal practitioners will be appointed to the Bench. It does not necessarily follow that the man who is chock full of law makes the best beak. On the contrary, the man who has a bit of common sense, and uses it, is invariably the one who has the fewer decisions quashed on appeal.
> —*Truth* (Perth, WA), Saturday 23 May 1914

'ONLY THE ABLE, FEARLESS AND IMPARTIAL'

In the spring of 1915, the end of the long legal career of Magistrate C.D.V. Foss was being marked at a small ceremony in Carnarvon. At the conclusion of the magistrate's heartfelt speech of thanks to those gathered around him, council secretary Bill Newman rose to his feet. In his hand he held a letter from the parliamentary member for the Gascoyne, Mr Archibald Gilchrist MLA.

Gilchrist had enjoyed a long association with Magistrate Foss since arriving in Western Australia from Victoria as a young Presbyterian pastor in 1904. While he was unable to attend the day's festivities, his letter was now read aloud to an appreciative audience:

> I respect Mr. Foss for the lack of bias and for the genial common sense he invariably brought to bear on cases brought before him. Those qualities

of geniality and impartiality have also been evident in his private life, and have won him the esteem and attachment of all ... My wish is that the 'Grand Old Man of the Gascoyne' may live many years to enjoy the good opinion of the district.

Seventy-four-year-old Foss was humble in his response: 'I thank you all for the great honour you paid me, and for the kindness and support I have always received from everybody in the district'—he paused for effect—'even the drunks.' Laughter now joined the sound of clapping. 'I hope that you extend the same kindness to my successor, Mr [John Elton] Geary.'

More speeches followed until, eventually, the small party of local dignitaries that had gathered to honour the retiring magistrate began to disperse with laughter, handshakes and hearty farewells. Mayor Frank Whitlock, pleased with the valedictory celebration, watched the retired magistrate walk out into the bright September day, little suspecting that within a few short months the old man would replace him as the new mayor of Carnarvon.

Foss paused for a moment at the open doorway, gazing out at the town that lay softly shining in the mild spring sunshine, the faint smell of ocean and mangroves carried along on a light breeze.

The old man might have reflected with pride on a job well done, a game well played. Before his arrival, the region's settlers had been struggling to gain a tenuous foothold on this north-western frontier of the great terra 'nullius'—this flyblown, barren, scorched continent of 'nobody'. On both sides of the long river, law and order now reigned where once there had been only a refractory people, ungovernable and unsubdued; along with treacherous Asians and white scoundrels. Here, now, was a place made safe for teamsters and drovers, for pastoralists and pearlers; a wharf where ships calmly loaded sheep and wool bound for southern ports; a settlement of pubs and churches; a region where settlers were the masters of every inch of land they surveyed. The frontier town was now full-born and the law—wielded with deadly efficacy by Magistrate C.D.V. Foss himself—had been its expert midwife.

The words of Gilchrist's speech rang through Charles Foss's head:

> The position you have held for so long is a difficult one to fulfil, and only the able, fearless and impartial manner in which you have carried out its functions could permit you to retire, as you do, with the esteem

and goodwill of the whole community. As citizens we also have to thank you as our Chief Magistrate for the many acts of kindness, courtesy and assistance in all matters pertaining to the welfare of the community, and the prosperity and advancement of the town and district.

The Grand Old Man of the Gascoyne stepped nimbly into the street, adjusted his hat, and set out for his home by the sea.

ENDNOTES

PROLOGUE
1. *The Northern Times* (Carnarvon), 3 July 1915; *The Western Mail* (Perth), 24 September 1915.
2. *The Northern Times* (Carnarvon), 9 June 1906.
3. *The Northern Times*, 25 September 1915.
4. Irwin District Historical Society, 'World War I', irwinhistory.org.au/?cat=12.
5. *The Victorian Express* (Geraldton), 11 October 1882.
6. ibid.
7. *The West Australian* (Perth), 14 November 1882.
8. *The West Australian* (Perth), 26 December 1882.
9. *The Victorian Express* (Geraldton), 27 December 1882.
10. *The West Australian* (Perth), 28 February 1885.

CHAPTER 1
1. *The Victorian Express* (Geraldton), 5 October 1881.
2. *The Herald* (Fremantle), 21 April 1883.
3. *The Victorian Express* (Geraldton), 7 March 1883.
4. *The Northern Times* (Carnarvon), 17 July 1925.
5. *The West Australian* (Perth), 25 August 1882.
6. *The Victorian Express* (Geraldton), 7 March 1883. The Port Inn, originally built near the site of the current Carnarvon Hotel, was later renamed the Port Hotel. It was seriously damaged in the floods of the late 1890s and early 1900s, and by 1908 had been demolished and rebuilt at the corner of Robinson and Alexandra streets. The Port Hotel was again destroyed in 1925, this time by fire, and was once more demolished and a new building reconstructed from the remains of the last (*The Northern Times*, Thursday 21 March 1940; State Heritage Office WA, inHerit, inherit.stateheritage.wa.gov.au).
7. *The Daily News* (Perth), 4 December 1883.
8. *The Herald* (Fremantle), 6 September 1879.
9. *Bulletin* (Sydney), cited in *The Victorian Express* (Geraldton), 26 August 1892.
10. ibid.
11. ibid.
12. *The West Australian* (Perth), 31 October 1882.
13. *The West Australian* (Perth), 30 May 1882.
14. Bush (1855–1939) was an intrepid explorer of the Gascoyne as well as a successful pastoralist (founder of Bidgemia, Mount Clere and Clifton Downs Stations), a gold prospector, a justice of the peace and member of Western Australia's first legislative council.
15. Cameron, 1982, p. 60.
16. *The West Australian* (Perth), 22 August 1882.
17. *The Inquirer and Commercial News* (Perth), 31 May 1882.
18. Green, 2007, p. 78.
19. *The West Australian* (Perth), 16 June 1882.

20 The site where the two rivers met became a town in 1912 and was named Killilli, after a local Aboriginal word for bulrushes. In 1939 its name was changed to Gascoyne Junction.
21 *The West Australian* (Perth), 16 June 1882.
22 Hansard, 21 September 1882, p. 434.
23 Drake-Brockman, 1969.
24 ibid.
25 *The West Australian* (Perth), 14 December 1922.
26 ibid.
27 WA Government Parliamentary Debates, September 1882, pp. 430–431.
28 ibid., p. 437. There is some uncertainty about the circumstances described in this letter since, a year later on 3 August 1883, an Aboriginal man named Nanacaroo was tried for the murder of Charles Brackell, in circumstances very similar to those of the murder of Redfern. At Nanacaroo's trial, no mention was made of the shooting of Aboriginal people at the time of his arrest.
29 *The West Australian* (Perth), 8 December 1882.
30 WA Government Parliamentary Debates, September 1882, p. 437.
31 *The West Australian* (Perth), 27 April 1883.
32 *The South Australian Register* (Adelaide), 26 April 1883.
33 *The West Australian* (Perth), 31 October 1882.
34 *The West Australian* (Perth), 27 April 1883.
35 Sometimes reported as Milli Milli in the newspapers of the time.
36 *The West Australian* (Perth), 27 April 1883.
37 *The South Australian Register* (Adelaide), 27 April 1883.
38 Adams, 2009, p. 12.
39 ibid.
40 *The West Australian* (Perth), 11 May 1883.
41 *The Herald* (Fremantle), 23 June 1883.
42 *The Inquirer and Commercial News* (Perth), 27 June 1883.
43 ibid.
44 Convict Records, 'Robert Grundy', convictrecords.com.au/convicts/grundy/robert/9740.
45 *The Victorian Express* (Geraldton), 10 December 1884.
46 Nowaraba was sometimes also referred to in the press as Nowarabiddy.
47 *The Inquirer and Commercial News* (Perth), 18 June 1884.
48 *The West Australian* (Perth), 10 June 1884.
49 *The Victorian Express* (Geraldton), 10 December 1884.
50 ibid.
51 ibid.
52 *Eastern Districts' Chronicle* (York, WA), 22 December 1884.
53 *The West Australian* (Perth), 8 December 1882.
54 WA Government Parliamentary Debates, 21 September 1882, pp. 426–440.
55 ibid.
56 G.S. Olivet, Travelling Inspector, Carnarvon, article dated 24 April 1900, in *Aborigines Department Report 1901*, p. 26.
57 A 'bardie' (bardi in the local Aboriginal language) is a particular edible insect.
58 P. Traynor, in *The Northern Times* (Carnarvon), 10 September 1910.
59 *The Western Mail* (Perth), 18 February 1905.
60 ibid.
61 *The Victorian Express* (Geraldton), 14 January 1885.
62 Finnane, 2011.
63 Green, 2007, p. 78.

CHAPTER 2

1 *The West Australian* (Perth), 11 July 1931.
2 *The West Australian* (Perth), 9 February 1935.
3 *The West Australian* (Perth), 5 August 1925.
4 Cameron, 1982, p. 63.
5 *The West Australian* (Perth), 9 February 1935.
6 *The Western Mail* (Perth), 25 July 1935.
7 *The West Australian* (Perth), 11 July 1931.
8 ibid.
9 *The West Australian* (Perth), 9 February 1935.
10 ibid.
11 *The West Australian* (Perth), 11 July 1931.
12 *The Herald* (Fremantle), 14 July 1883.
13 Purdue, 1993, p. 30; *The West Australian* (Perth), 17 July 1883.
14 *The Herald* (Fremantle), 4 August 1883.
15 *The West Australian* (Perth), 15 July 1884.
16 *The West Australian* (Perth), 12 January 1884.
17 ibid.
18 *The Victorian Express* (Geraldton), 19 December 1883.
19 Birman, 1972.
20 ibid.
21 Birman and Bolton, 1988.
22 Kimberly, 1897.
23 Robinson, 1990.
24 *The West Australian* (Perth), 12 January 1884.
25 ibid.
26 ibid.
27 ibid.
28 ibid.
29 ibid.
30 In Western Australia, women were not eligible to serve on juries until 1957.
31 *The West Australian* (Perth), 12 January 1884.
32 ibid.
33 ibid.
34 ibid.
35 Finnane, 2011, p. 5.
36 ibid.
37 *The Inquirer and Commercial News* (Perth), 19 October 1859.
38 Zitzer, 2016.
39 *The Age* (Melbourne), 22 February 1884.
40 *The Telegraph* (Brisbane), 7 February 1884, p. 5
41 *The Herald* (Fremantle), 26 January 1884.
42 *The Victorian Express* (Geraldton), 13 February 1884.

CHAPTER 3

1 *The Victorian Express* (Geraldton), 11 October 1882.
2 *The Victorian Express* (Geraldton), 10 August 1889.
3 ibid.
4 *The Herald* (Fremantle), 30 December 1882.
5 Bennett, 2004, p. 51.
6 Green, 2007.
7 Hansard, 1883.
8 Bennett, 2004, p. 52.
9 ibid.

10 Green, 2007.
11 *The Victorian Express* (Geraldton), 7 March 1883.
12 Cited in *Report of a Commission Appointed by his Excellency the Governor to Inquire into the Treatment of Aboriginal Native Prisoners of the Crown in this Colony: And Also into Certain Other Matters Relative to Aboriginal Natives*, 1884.
13 *The Daily News* (Perth), 9 August 1889.
14 The prison at Rottnest Island was a hell on earth for Aboriginal people. In 1882, as Foss began his 'pacification' of the North, the punishment of whipping—already abolished for non-Aboriginal people—was introduced for the island's Aboriginal prisoners through the *Aboriginal Offenders Act (Amendment)* 1892 (Green, 2007). Malnutrition, measles and influenza also wrought fatal consequences on the Indigenous people imprisoned there, with some 369 dying over the years. Five were hanged (Watson, 2012).
15 Reynolds, 1990.
16 Nettelbeck, 2015.
17 Reynolds, 1990.
18 *The WA Record* (Perth), 25 July 1889.
19 Green, 2007, p. 80.
20 *The Inquirer and Commercial News* (Perth), 11 October 1889.
21 *The Victorian Express* (Geraldton), 10 August 1889.
22 *Eastern Districts' Chronicle* (York, WA), 10 August 1889.
23 *The WA Record* (Perth), 17 October 1889.
24 *The West Australian* (Perth), 11 October 1889.
25 ibid.
26 *The Western Mail* (Perth), 12 October 1889.
27 ibid.
28 *The Daily News* (Perth), 10 October 1889.
29 *The Victorian Express* (Geraldton), 19 October 1889.
30 *The Western Mail* (Perth), 30 November 1889.
31 Trackers were essential to the work of police in the outback. A 1904 report indicates that they were paid around three shillings a day, but most of this went to the local policeman to cover incidentals. There was little evidence that the balance made its way to the trackers themselves.
32 *The Inquirer and Commercial News* (Perth), 12 January 1876.
33 *The Western Australian Times* (Perth), 25 January 1876.
34 *The West Australian* (Perth), 3 June 1885.
35 *The West Australian* (Perth), 30 May 1882.
36 *The Inquirer and Commercial News* (Perth), 4 March 1868.
37 *The Western Argus* (Kalgoorlie), 18 May 1899.
38 Reynolds, 1990.
39 ibid.
40 *The West Australian* (Perth), 9 May 1899.
41 ibid.
42 ibid.
43 *The West Australian Sunday Times* (Perth), 14 May 1899.
44 *The Sunday Times* (Perth), 29 July 1906.
45 *The Sunday Times* (Perth), 6 July 1913.
46 *The Sunday Times* (Perth), 13 September 1903. Foss later publicly repudiated this, claiming, 'I rode in one [a train] before the "tothersiders" ever came to this country' (*The Sunday Times* (Perth), 25 February 1906). The accusation, nevertheless, seemed to stick over the years.
47 *Geraldton Express*, 30 August 1912.
48 *The Geraldton Guardian*, 29 August 1912.
49 Government of Western Australia, *Annual Report of the Aborigines Department 1901–02*, Perth, p. 8.

CHAPTER 4

1 In the nineteenth century the area was referred to as Shark's Bay, before later becoming Shark Bay.
2 Now Useless Loop.
3 Reynolds, Steve, 2001, 'Nicolas Baudin's Scientific Expedition to the Terres Australes', *Marine Life Society of South Australia Journal*, No. 12, December.
4 *The Inquirer and Commercial News* (Perth), 22 October 1873.
5 ibid.
6 Useless Inlet is the twelve kilometre stretch of water on the western side of Cape Heirisson, and is not to be confused with Useless Loop, a place containing a set of solar ponds established on the other side of the cape in the 1960s.
7 *The Herald* (Fremantle), 13 June 1874.
8 *The Inquirer and Commercial News* (Perth), 25 February 1874.
9 Bagnall, 2006, p. 37.
10 Australian Bureau of Statistics, 1925, 'The Chinese in Australia', in Year Book Australia, 1925, cat. no. 1301.0, www.abs.gov.au/ausstats/abs@.nsf/featurearticlesby title/4A6A63F3D85F7770CA2569DE00200137?OpenDocument.
11 *The Inquirer and Commercial News* (Perth), 25 March 1874.
12 ibid.
13 *The West Australian* (Perth), 4 July 1885.
14 *The West Australian* (Perth), 17 July 1884.
15 *The Inquirer and Commercial News* (Perth), 19 March 1884.
16 McGann, 1999, p. 44.
17 *The West Australian* (Perth), 4 September 1884.
18 *The Daily News* (Perth), 2 August 1884.
19 The prefix 'Ah', commonly used with Chinese names at this time, usually signified a shortening of the name to express familiarity, roughly equivalent to the English use of 'Mister'.
20 *The West Australian* (Perth), 4 September 1884.
21 *The Daily News* (Perth), 1 September 1884.
22 *The Daily News* (Perth), 22 November 1884.
23 *The Victorian Express* (Geraldton), 10 September 1884.
24 ibid.
25 *The Inquirer and Commercial News* (Perth), 19 November 1884.
26 *The Inquirer and Commercial News* (Perth), 5 November 1884.
27 Nyman and von Bibra, 1996, p. 96.
28 Dickson, 1996.
29 *The West Australian* (Perth), 30 May 1908.
30 Western Australian Museum, n.d., 'Notch Point', museum.wa.gov.au/research/research-areas/maritime-archaeology/batavia-cape-inscription/cape-inscription/notch-point.
31 *The Western Mail* (Perth), 27 June 1919.
32 Stanbury, 1986, p. 6.
33 Nyman and von Bibra, 1996, pp. 96–97.
34 Atkinson, 1991, p. 2.
35 *The Victorian Express* (Geraldton), 3 July 1886.
36 ibid.
37 James Barratt—who two years earlier had unsuccessfully defended Nowaraba, Gnalbee and Geeler against the charge of murdering Robert Grundy—was an able solicitor well known from Geraldton to Cue in the last decades of the nineteenth century. He was a larger-than-life character who had once been fined six pounds or three days imprisonment 'for using insulting remarks towards the Bench' (*The Western Mail* (Perth), 11 June 1897). He also made unedifying appearances on the wrong side of the bench relating to the visiting of prostitutes in Perth's Roe Street, and in 1897 was charged with issuing a false cheque for various items of

jewellery. The judge, in declaring his decision, spoke plainly to the disgraced man: 'Look here, Mr. Barratt, I am going to discharge you, but in doing so I want to give you a word or two of warning. You must remember your former scrape and the circumstances connected with it. You are a clever and well educated man, and as a pleader in criminal cases you have distinguished yourself in a high degree. You are now lowering yourself in the eyes of society, but if you avoided the consequences of drink you would be an ornament to the profession to which you belong. If you go on doing as you are now you will find yourself one of these days, in the criminal court. You have had a severe lesson. Now take my advice and leave drink alone altogether. Wine and women are the cause of all the trouble in your case—avoid both' (ibid.).

38 *The Victorian Express* (Geraldton), 3 July 1886.
39 It had been Robert's brother, George, who had once been fined for non-registration of the death of Chinese man in his employ.
40 *The West Australian* (Perth), 28 April 1886.
41 *The Victorian Express* (Geraldton), 8 July 1892.
42 WA Museum, n.d., Welcome Walls, 'Rowe, Thomas & Sarah', museum.wa.gov.au/welcomewalls/names/rowe-thomas-sarah.
43 *The Victorian Express* (Geraldton), 3 July 1886.
44 ibid.
45 ibid.
46 ibid.
47 ibid.
48 ibid.
49 ibid.
50 ibid.
51 ibid.
52 ibid.
53 ibid.
54 ibid.
55 ibid.
56 *The Daily News* (Perth), 21 May 1886.
57 *The West Australian* (Perth), 19 September 1885.
58 *The Daily News* (Perth), 21 May 1886.
59 Bach, 1955.
60 Western Australian Museum, n.d., 'Notch Point', museum.wa.gov.au/research/research-areas/maritime-archaeology/batavia-cape-inscription/cape-inscription/notch-point.
61 *The Victorian Express* (Geraldton), 29 May 1886.
62 ibid.
63 *The Geraldton Guardian*, 20 March 1909.
64 Western Australian Museum, n.d., 'Notch Point', museum.wa.gov.au/research/research-areas/maritime-archaeology/batavia-cape-inscription/cape-inscription/notch-point.
65 *The Western Mail* (Perth), 14 August 1886.
66 *Eastern Districts' Chronicle* (York, WA), 27 November 1886.
67 This is an apparent reference to the skin tones of the Aboriginal people living at Warangesda Mission in New South Wales, which was established by Reverend Gribble.
68 *The Victorian Express* (Geraldton, WA), 4 December 1886.
69 *The Western Mail* (Perth), 11 December 1886.
70 *The Victorian Express* (Geraldton), 4 December 1886.
71 *The West Australian* (Perth), 2 July 1886.
72 Bach, 1955, p. 51.
73 Atkinson, 1991, p. ii.

CHAPTER 5

1. *The West Australian* (Perth), 12 January 1904.
2. *The Western Mail* (Perth), 16 January 1904.
3. *The Western Mail* (Perth), 23 June 1900.
4. *The Daily News* (Perth), 3 December 1903.
5. *The Daily News* (Perth), 11 January 1904.
6. *The West Australian* (Perth), 15 June 1909.
7. The Settler's Hotel was known locally as Skinner's, after owner Charles Skinner.
8. This conversation is reproduced here as it was presented (in English) at the subsequent inquest.
9. *The Western Mail* (Perth), 2 April 1897.
10. Western Australia Now and Then, n.d., 'Chinese in Western Australia', www.wanowandthen.com/Chinese-in-Western-Australia.html.
11. Atkinson, 1991.
12. *The West Australian* (Perth), 25 December 1896.
13. *The West Australian* (Perth), 21 December 1896.
14. The wife and family of Thomas Bird, the original owner of the Port Hotel who had died some years earlier in 1887, lived in Yankee Town for many years.
15. This was not uncommon at the time, the habit of opium smoking having been brought to Australia with successive waves of Chinese immigrants.
16. Stannage, 1983.
17. *The Western Mail* (Perth), 16 January 1904.
18. *The West Australian* (Perth), 12 January 1904.
19. The novice executioner, although vowing never to do the job again, had performed his task well and Ah Hook died instantly.

CHAPTER 6

1. Poole and Grigg, 1999.
2. *The Northern Times* (Carnarvon), 28 September 1907.
3. A.H. (Harry) Hearn, in *The Northern Times* (Carnarvon), 20 October 1906. Hearn was the licensee of the Carnarvon Hotel, an active member of the local council and a well-known sportsman.
4. *The Sunday Times* (Perth), 29 April 1906. The Ashburton Goldfield was a short-lived goldmining region from around 1890 to 1900; it encompassed several widely spaced locations within the Capricorn Ranges.
5. *The Northern Times* (Carnarvon), 13 October 1906.
6. A.H. (Harry) Hearn, in *The Northern Times* (Carnarvon), 20 October 1906.
7. *The Newcastle Chronicle* (NSW), 20 January 1874.
8. *The Daily News* (Perth), 5 October 1906.
9. *The Northern Times* (Carnarvon), 10 February 1906.
10. Also known as Dick Vickers.
11. *The Northern Times* (Carnarvon), 17 February 1906. Eight years later, after several days of heavy drinking, Vann would take his own life by swallowing strychnine (*The Western Mail* [Perth], 6 November 1914).
12. *The West Australian* (Perth), 5 October 1906.
13. *The Daily News* (Perth), 5 October 1906.
14. Dr Hickinbotham would later testify that he believed the bullet had entered at the sixth rib and exited at the tenth, passing through the left lung and eventually causing death (*The Daily News* [Perth], 4 October 1906).
15. *The Northern Times* (Carnarvon), 10 February 1906.
16. The telegraph station at Winning Pool was an important link to the port at Carnarvon (*The Daily News* [Perth], 19 August 1896).
17. Bunbury left each member of the Foss family 250 pounds in his will (*The Northern Times* [Carnarvon], 26 February 1910).

18 *The Northern Times* (Carnarvon), 2 December 1905.
19 The letter was probably sent by Dave Johnson, who admitted during the second inquiry into the matter that he 'wrote two statements to *The Sunday Times* … My object in sending the letters to *The Sunday Times* was that it had been stated I was hiding from the police, and was shielding Fleming. I was blamed for hiding from the police' (*The Northern Times* [Carnarvon], 7 July 1906).
20 Magisterial inquiries were generally undertaken by resident magistrates acting as ex officio coroners at a time when Australia's vast size and the isolation of many of its locations where sudden or unexplained deaths occurred meant that a state coroner could not be present. They carried the same authorities as a coroner, including the power to summons witnesses, to compel the answering of questions and the provision of documents, and to issue a warrant for a person's arrest in order to give evidence.
21 *The Northern Times* (Carnarvon), 10 February 1906.
22 In fact, Vann had arrived at the campsite after the will had been drawn up. Ewing may have been implying that the dying man had had time to amend the will in favour of his friend, had he so desired.
23 *The West Australian* (Perth), 6 October 1906.
24 ibid.
25 ibid.
26 *Geraldton Express*, 12 October 1906.
27 *The Sunday Times* (Perth), 7 October 1906.
28 *The Northern Times* (Carnarvon), 20 October 1906.
29 *Geraldton Express*, 25 November 1908.

CHAPTER 7

1 Population estimates at the time were often unreliable due to the disregard of Aboriginal people and Asian immigrants. See this example from Perth's *The Western Mail* (1 December 1906): 'Carnarvon proper has a white population of some 300 souls, besides Japs, Chinese, and native blacks, whilst at Yankee Town there are some 60 whites, as well as a dozen Chinese gardens, and some blacks'. The town was also growing steadily: on 6 March 1909 *The Northern Times* (Carnarvon) would report: 'Census of the local population has just been concluded by the police which gives the population of Carnarvon and Yankee Town as follows: Whites: males 344, females 266. Asiatics and others: males 29, females 1. Grand total: 640.'
2 These were Dalgety and Company, Whitlock and Company, and Barton and Company.
3 These were the Port Hotel (run by R. McAllister), the Carnarvon Hotel (Harry Hearn) and the Settler's Hotel (Charles Skinner).
4 German-Australian Aliens of Militarism, germanaustralianalianstomilitarism. blogspot.com/2011/09/t-surnames-germanic-emigrants-1870-1920.html.
5 Georgina Campbell was thirty-two years old when she married 'Cecil John Wilks' in Fulham, London in April 1905, Mr Wilks once more becoming John Travers on their return to Australia. Georgina had already spent time in Australia as housekeeper to Sir Rupert Clarke in Melbourne.
6 *Dampier Despatch* (Broome), 30 September 1905, issue 231, pp. 353–354.
7 Boyd, Annie, 2013, *Koombana Days*, Fremantle Press, p. 307.
8 *Goulburn Evening Penny Post* (NSW), 23 December 1905.
9 *The Northern Times* (Carnarvon), 23 March 1907.
10 *The Northern Times* (Carnarvon), 25 May 1907.

CHAPTER 8

1. The tainted water would claim one other victim. Two days before Christmas that same year, a drover found the body of thirty-five-year-old itinerant Richard Blake just fifty metres from the fatal tin. Blake's skeleton and belongings suggested he had died while setting up camp for the night. Thought to be from England, he had left Carnarvon 'sundowning' (looking for work) in April 1933. His body was buried where it was found.
2. *The Herald* (Coolgardie & Kalgoorlie), 13 June 1900.
3. *The West Australian* (Perth), 19 November 1904.
4. *The Mirror* (Perth), 5 January 1952.
5. *The Kalgoorlie Miner*, 20 April 1913.
6. *Government Gazette of Western Australian*, 30 May 1913.
7. *The Western Mail* (Perth), 2 May 1913.
8. ibid.
9. *The Sunday Times* (Perth), 27 April 1913.
10. *The Kalgoorlie Miner*, 26 April 1913.
11. Many country towns at the time had a common—an area of government-owned land designated for public use such as the grazing and watering of animals and collecting of firewood.
12. *The Daily News* (Perth), 26 March 1913.
13. In 1926, Walsh and a colleague named Pitman would become part of WA criminal folklore when, on discovering an illegal gold treatment plant south of Kalgoorlie, they were murdered and dismembered and their bodies thrown down a disused mine shaft. A monument to them now stands at the WA Police Academy in Joondalup.
14. *The West Australian* (Perth), 28 April 1913.
15. ibid.
16. *The West Australian* (Perth), 6 June 1913.
17. Justice Burnside later said that, in the case of Fukito, the death sentence was merely a formality and that extenuating circumstances had led him to recommend leniency.
18. *The Murchison Times and Day Dawn Gazette* (Cue), 28 June 1913.
19. *The Bunbury Herald*, 1 July 1913.
20. *The Daily News* (Perth), 29 October 1937. In later years there was also talk that Spargo had left Donnybrook early in 1912 with a man named Bryant, who was never seen again; this has never been verified.

CHAPTER 9

1. *The West Australian* (Perth), 24 November 1885.
2. *The West Australian* (Perth), 29 June 1887.
3. *The West Australian* (Perth), 4 June 1887.
4. *The Sunday Times* (Perth), 16 August 1903.
5. *The Western Mail* (Perth), 26 October 1886.
6. Green, 2007, p. 83.
7. This took the form of increasing control over every aspect of Aboriginal people's lives, as enabled by the *Aborigines Act 1905* (WA) and enacted largely by the Department of Aborigines and Fisheries (formed in 1909). Government interventions were complemented by the establishment of Christian missions across the state.
8. *The Northern Times* (Carnarvon), 26 September 1914.
9. *The Northern Times* (Carnarvon), 16 November 1912.
10. ibid.
11. A cockeye bob is a sudden, spiralling wind.
12. *The Northern Times* (Carnarvon), 7 July 1917.

13 *The Northern Times* (Carnarvon), 16 November 1912.
14 ibid.
15 ibid.
16 ibid.
17 ibid.
18 *The West Australian* (Perth), 8 May 1913.
19 ibid.
20 ibid.
21 *The Sunday Times* (Perth), 11 May 1913.
22 ibid.

EPILOGUE
1 *The Northern Times*, 25 September 1915, p. 2.
2 ibid.

REFERENCES

Aborigines Department, 1901, *Report for Financial Year Ending 30 June 1901*, Alfred Watson, Government Printer, Perth.
Adams, Simon, 2009, *The Unforgiving Rope: Murder and Hanging on Australia's Western Frontier*, UWA Publishing, Perth.
Atkinson, Anne, 1991, 'Chinese Labour and Capital in Western Australia, 1847–1947', PhD thesis, Murdoch University, Perth.
Bach, J.P.S., 1955, *The Pearling Industry of Australia: An Account of its Social and Economic Development*, NSW University of Technology, Newcastle.
Bagnall, Kate, 2006, *Golden Shadows on a White Land*, Department of History, Faculty of Arts, University of Sydney.
Battye, J.S., 1912, *The Cyclopedia of Western Australia: An Historical and Commercial Review, Descriptive and Biographical Facts, Figures and Illustrations: An Epitome of Progress*, nla.gov.au/nla.obj-116156597.
Bennett, John Michael, 2004, *Lives of the Australian Chief Justices*, Federation Press, Sydney.
Birman, Wendy, 1972, 'Hensman, Alfred Peach (1834–1902)', *Australian Dictionary of Biography*, National Centre of Biography, Australian National University, adb.anu.edu.au/biography/hensman-alfred-peach-3756/text5917.
Birman, Wendy and Bolton, G.C., 1988, 'Parker, Sir Stephen Henry (1846–1927)', Australian Dictionary of Biography, National Centre of Biography, Australian National University, adb.anu.edu.au/biography/parker-sir-stephen-henry-7957/text13853.
Black, D. and Bolton G. (eds), 2010, 'Biographical Register of Members of the Parliament of Western Australia: Volume One 1870–1930', Parliamentary History Project, Perth.
Boston, Paquita, 2004, *What's in a Name? Place Names of the Gascoyne*, Western Australian Museum, Perth.
'Brockman, George (Julius)', Brockman and Drake-Brockman Family Tree, www.brockman.net.au/Brockman,%20George%20Julius.pdf.
Cameron, C.W.M., 1982, 'R.E. Bush, Gascoyne Explorer and Pastoralist', *Journal and Proceedings of the Royal Western Australian Historical Society*, Perth.
Dickson, Rod, 1996, *Ships Registered in Western Australia 1956–1969: Their Details, Their Owners and Their Fate*, Fremantle, www.maritimeheritage.org.au/documents/Shipping%20Register.pdf.
Drake-Brockman, H., 1969, 'Brown, Maitland (1843–1905)', *Australian Dictionary of Biography*, National Centre of Biography, Australian National University, adb.anu.edu.au/biography/brown-maitland-3080.
Findlay, Merril, 1983, *Reflections of a Country Town*, Carnarvon Shire Council.
Finnane, Mark, 2011, 'Settler Justice and Aboriginal Homicide in Late Colonial Australia', *Australian Historical Studies*, Griffith University.
Green, Neville, 2007, 'Aboriginal Sentencing in Western Australia in the Late 19th Century, with Reference to Rottnest Island Prison', *Records of the Western Australian Museum*, Supplement 79, Perth.
Gregory, A.C. and F.T., 1884, *Journals of Australian Explorations*, Government Printers, Brisbane.

Kimberly, W.B., 1897, *History of West Australia: A Narrative of Her Past Together with Biographies of Her Leading Men*, W. Niven & Co., Melbourne and Ballarat.

Konishi, Shino (ed.), 2014, *Aboriginal History*, Vol. 38, ANU Press, Australian National University, Canberra.

McGann, Sally, 1999, 'Wilyah Miah' (master's thesis, Centre for Archaeology, UWA), Report No. 33 for the Department of Maritime Archaeology, Western Australian Maritime Museum, Fremantle, museum.wa.gov.au/maritime-archaeology-db/sites/default/files/no._033_wilyah_miah_shark_bay_pearling.pdf.

Nettelbeck, Amanda, 2015, '"Keep the Magistrates Straight": Magistrates and Aboriginal "management" on Australia's North-west Frontiers, 1883–1905', *Aboriginal History Journal*, 38, 10.22459/AH.38.2015.02.

Nyman, Lois and von Bibra, Graeme, 1996, *The von Bibra Story*, Foot and Playsted, Launceston, Tasmania (available at www.vonbibra.net).

Poole, Tony and Grigg, Gordon, 1999, *Harvesting of Kangaroos in Australia*, Department of Zoology, University of Queensland, for Environment Australia.

Purdue, Brian, 1993, *Legal Executions in Western Australia*, Foundation Press, Perth.

Reynolds, Henry, 1990, *With the White People*, Penguin, Melbourne.

Richardson, A.R., 1909, *Early Memories of the Great Nor-West and a Chapter in History of WA*, E.S. Wigg & Son, Perth, nla.gov.au/nla.obj-201134973.

Robinson, F.M., 1990, 'Stone, Sir Edward Albert (1844–1920)', *Australian Dictionary of Biography*, National Centre of Biography, Australian National University, adb.anu.edu.au/biography/stone-sir-edward-albert-8675/text15173.

Stanbury, Myra, 1986, *Historic Sites in Shark Bay*, Report No. 199 for the Department of Maritime Archaeology, Western Australian Maritime Museum, Fremantle.

Stannage, Tom, 1983, 'Richard Septimus Haynes (1857–1922)', *Australian Dictionary of Biography, National Centre of Biography*, Australian National University, adb.anu.edu.au/biography/haynes-richard-septimus-6615/text11389.

Watson, Bronwyn, 15 December 2012, 'Rottnest Island's Dark Past', *The Australian*.

Zitzer, Leon, 2016, *Darwin's Racism: The Definitive Case, Along with a Close Look at Some of the Forgotten, Genuine Humanitarians of that Time*, iUniverse, Bloomington, Indiana, USA.

ACKNOWLEDGEMENTS

This book is unlikely to have been written without Trove, that outstanding online database of the National Library of Australia. I am only one of the tens of thousands of users who access this peerless Australian resource every day. Our country is smarter and richer for its existence.

Locally, I am much indebted to the State Records Office of Western Australia, the Battye Library and the Maritime Museum of Western Australia.

The team at Fremantle Press deserves special thanks for their unequivocal support of this book, and for guiding it through the publishing process, in particular Jane Fraser, Claire Miller and Armelle Davies. Special mention must also be made of Leila Jabbour, who edited the manuscript with such professionalism, sensitivity and patience.

On a personal level, I am grateful to many people for their support and encouragement. The first of these are my son and daughter, Jai and Holly Price, who first enjoyed hearing the dark tales over coffee every Sunday morning and made me think that others might enjoy them too. And I am thankful to the many friends and family who, usually without even knowing it, once said something that kept me writing—they include, among others, Bob and Lyn Price, Perette Minciullo, Jim and Jenny Caunt, Robynn Offer, John West, Peter Jeans, Kevin O'Keefe, Debbie Boon, Dan and Jill Norton, Sharyn O'Neill, Franklin White, Nick Palmer and Leanne Potter.

Finally, I would like to acknowledge my great grandmother, Georgina Travers (nee Campbell), who features in the story of the *Cleopatra*'s pearl. When her husband disappeared in 1907, this courageous Scottish woman remained in the outback settlement of Carnarvon, where she single-handedly raised her daughter, established herself as a formidable businesswoman and dedicated herself to the public good for the rest of her life.

I hope that, when the full history of our country is finally written—the one that includes Aboriginal people and Asian migrants, that records the things we got wrong as well as the things we got right—pioneer women like Georgina can also take their rightful place.

INDEX

Notes:

Index entries in *italics* refer to names of ships, titles of legislation, newspapers, books or reports.

Chinese and Japanese names are filed as written, e.g. Ah Sing files under A.

Aboriginal people
 assaulted by station owners 18–19, 55–9, 61–72
 before white settlement 7
 friendship with Asian labourers 13
 impact of white settlement on 32–4
 imprisonment on Rottnest Island 12, 14, 20, 26, 34, 53–4
 as indentured labourers 162–5
 in pearling industry 75
 as police constables 53
 prostitution of 77
 rumours of cannibalism among 19
 sexual mistreatment of 22, 32–4, 68–9, 164
 skirmishes with settlers 18, 20
 as trackers 60, 99, 157, 171–3
Aborigines Act 1905 183–4
Afghan cameleers 13
Ah Chew 104
Ah Fa 88
Ah Foo 78–80
Ah Hook 100–12
Ah Kee 102, 107–10
Ah Lee 103–4, 107
Ah Ling *see* Ah Hook
Ah Saw 102–7
Ah Sing 104–5
Ah Tong 81–91
Ah Tue 102, 105–7

Angelo, Edward 120, 125
anti-Asian sentiment 74, 83, 93
Arthur River Station 134
Asian labourers
 community distrust of 74, 83, 93
 friendship with Aboriginal people 13
 loneliness of 76, 104
 in pearling industry 76–99
 relationship with settlers 13, 14, 77
 see also Chinese labourers

Babbage Island 99, 141–2
Bacci, Joe 154
Balby 144–5
Barker, A.E. 129
Barrabong 26
Barratt, James 31, 82–92
Baston, George Jr 16–17, 19
Beeroi Claypan 166–86
Beewar 29, 30
Beringarra Station 56
Bibbey, Richard 49
Bibra, Francis von 80, 81
Bibra, Leopold von 80–99, 138
Billamarra 49
Billie 62, 64
Billy 82, 90
Bird, Constable 55
Bird family 106
Bird, Thomas 17

Black Maggie 177, 182–3
Blackall 70
blackbirding 59–61
Boolathana Station 37, 145, 165
Booth, John 177–80, 184
Boulay, Arthur Houssemayne du 79, 84–8
Brackell, Charles (Charlie) 22, 38–9
Bramston, John 54
Brickhouse Station 105, 115, 119, 122
Brockman, George Julius 37, 59–72
Brockman, Joanna Elizabeth 66
Brockman, John 61
Broome, Frederick Napier 93–4
Broome 139–40, 153–4, 156–7
Brown, Aubrey 94
Brown, Maitland 20–1, 32, 94
Brown, Stephen 116, 119, 123
Brown, Thomas 90–1
Bryant, Mrs 138
Buck, Constable 120, 125
Bullarra (steamer) 129
Bunbury, M.C.R. 119
Bungegoora 53
Bungurdie 57–9
Burnside, Robert Bruce 135, 158–9
Burt, Septimus 58
Bush, Robert Edwin (Bob) 19

Carnarvon 8, 17–18, 138–9
  see also Port Gascoyne
Carnarvon jetty 17, 141–2, 149
Cawabila 62–4
Charon (steamer) 133
Chief Protector of Aborigines 72, 183
Chinese labourers
  community distrust of 74, 83, 93
  disappearance of 19
  loneliness of 76, 104
  murders of 100–12
  as pearlers 92–8
  relationship with settlers 13–14, 74–99
  violence among 100–12
  see also Asian labourers
Clara 162, 165–86

Cleopatra (lugger) 139–41
Clifford, Charles (Charlie) 39–50
Cocking, Sam 113–24
Condon, Detective Sergeant 161
Coonthenmungajarra 57–9
Cooper, Fred 59–61
Coordie 61–72
Cowan, J. 187
Cox, Reverend 136
Criminal Investigation Branch (WA Police) 157, 162
Crowther and Baston (merchants) 16–17, 19
Crowther, Charles Jr 16–17

Dalgety and Company 11
Dark Deeds in a Sunny Land (Gribble) 8, 52
Darlot, Everard Firebrace 56
De Grey Station 59–61
Denham 74
Derby 154–6
Dickerson, Reginald 150–1
Dickie 24
Dirk Hartog Island 80, 96
disease
  in Rottnest Island Prison 34
  in Shark Bay settlements 75–7
Doodjeep 26
Doorawarrah Station 37
Drake-Brockman, Edmund 177–8, 182
du Boulay, Arthur Houssemayne see Boulay, Arthur Houssemayne du
Dunn, Mr 82

Early Memories of the Great Nor-West (Richardson) 9
Edwards, Teddy 144–5
Eliot, George 43
Erivella 56
Espada, Simeon 135–40
Ewing, Claude 120–8

Fairbairn, Robert 21–2, 26, 32
Fane, Charles 12

Index

Farrelly, Alfred 83, 90
Filipino labourers 139–40
Five Mile Gate 166, 180
Fleming, John 114–34
flogging, guidelines for 18–19
Fogarty, Joseph 171–9, 181, 184–5
Foss, Charles Denroche Vaughan
   appointment as magistrate 9, 11–15
   Brockman trial 62–72
   buys Chinese pearling fleet 96–7
   criticised by *Sunday Times* 52, 71–2, 125, 132
   exceeds authority 53, 54–6
   as head of Carnarvon police 32, 53, 138–9
   imposes two-pound fine for death of Chinese man 77
   inquest into Grundy's death 29
   inquest into Jim Chu's death 84–90
   inquest into Thackabiddy's death 42
   inquest into Topsy's death 174–82
   life before Carnarvon 11–12
   magisterial inquiry into Lonton's death 120–8
   opinion on treatment of Aboriginal people 34
   retirement as magistrate 10–11, 187–9
   returns indentured workers to stations 163–5
   sends Aboriginal prisoners to Rottnest Island 20, 53–5
   uses law to protect settlers' interests 13–15, 35, 51, 163–5
Foss, Vaughan 101
Fremantle Prison 111–12, 140, 159–61
Freshwater Camp (Denham) 74
Freycinet, Louis-Henri de Saulces de 74
Fry, George 77
Fry, Robert 82–91

Gale, Richard 40
gambling 76

Gascoyne Junction 55
Gascoyne River, naming of 8
Geary, John Elton 188
Geeler 29–31, 34
Georgie 82, 89–90, 92
Gibbons, Percy 29
Gilchrist, Archibald 187–9
Gnalbee 29–31, 34
goldfields 93, 114, 146, 148
Goldstein, Dr 157
Gooch, George Joseph 22, 36–47, 69
Gooroonoo 12
Grant, Louis 155–6, 158
Gray, Constable 133
Greenough 37
Gregory, Francis (Frank) 21
Gregory, R.T., expedition to Gascoyne region 8
Grey, George 8
Grey, Richard (Dick) 116, 118–19, 122–3
Gribble, John Brown, *Dark Deeds in a Sunny Land* 8, 52
Grundy, Robert 28–35
Guerhilla 27–8

Hagen, Charles 135–40
Hall, Aubrey 144–5
Hart, Alexander 153
Haynes, Richard Septimus 110
Hearn, A.H. (Harry) 132–3
Henchley, Dr 174
Hensman, Alfred Peach 43–7
Herbert, Robert 54
Hickinbotham, James Ryland 108–10, 120, 138
Holden, Ed 11
Hooper, Thomas 148
Hough, Sam 65
Houlihan, Thomas 33–4, 56, 108–10
Howard, Reverend 160–1
Hubble, George Yorke 103

interpreters 23, 31, 82–8, 92, 110
Isles, Mr 138

Jackie 62–4
Jacob 36
Jenny 56
Jenuethenbean 56
Jim Chu 81–92
Johnson, David Charles (Dave) 117–19, 125–30, 133
Jones, Antonio (Jonesy) 149–50, 151, 154, 161
Judy 56

Kalgoorlie 146–7
Kaluman 23–4
kangaroo shooters 113–34
Kata Tukenei 108–9
Katie 64
Keane 39–40, 46
Keen, Lance Corporal 29
Keenan, Norbert 125, 133
Kitty 64
Kurokawa Fukito 159–60
Kuwinywardu 7

Laurence, Edward Hayes 37
Leake, George 23
Lee, Jim 156–7
Lefroy, Flora 170, 175–6, 178–9, 181
Lefroy, Frank 114, 116–20, 165
Lefroy, Henry Gerald 165
Lefroy, William Gerald 165, 170–1
Liebglid, Mark 135–40
Limerick 171–4
Lodge, Inspector 164
loneliness
    of Chinese labourers 76, 104
    of Gascoyne workers 113
Lonton, James (Queenslander) 114–30
Loughhead, Reverend 138
Lyndon River 114, 165

McCloud, Charlotte 72–3
McCloud, Donald 72–3
McConnell, Detective 159
McGowan, Barney 173–4, 175
Mackey, Mr 151

Mackintosh, James Drummond 23, 25, 26
McMurtrie, John 153, 154
Maggie 64
magisterial inquiries 120–8
mail coaches 114
Mainland, Lance Corporal 76–7
Malay labourers 13
    see also Asian labourers
Mansfield, John Harman 120, 125
Maori Bill see Williams, William
Mardathuna Station 98
Margoo (Nipper) 162, 165–86
Marmion, Fitzroy Francis 11, 174–5
Maroonah Station 120
Marquez, Pablo 135–40
Marshall, Reverend 112
Mead, Thomas 56–9
Mendik 26
Middalya Station 166
Miller, Ed 152
Millie Millie Pool 28
Mills, Mr 138
Minilya River 19, 36–9, 116
Minilya (steamer) 137–43
Minilya Station 60–73, 114, 172
missions 163
Monkey's Well 113–34
Mount Gould 56, 58, 164
Mount Wittenoom 13

Nabor, Victor 139–40
Nanacaroo 22, 38–9
Nannine 162
Natives Convictions Validity Bill (1883) 54
Newman, William (Bill) 11, 103, 187
Nowaraba 29–31, 34

Odling, Enoch 81–2, 90, 95
O'Halloran, Reverend 112
O'Loughlin, Edward 108–9
On Our Selection (Rudd) 159
Onslow 114, 115, 172
opium 76, 104, 107
Orsova (steamer) 152, 153

Page, Sergeant 145
Pallet, Constable 157
Parker, Francis (Frank) 177–9, 183
Parker, Stephen Henry 43–6
Paroo (steamer) 129, 151
Pass, Henry 23, 31
pearling industry 59, 74–99, 139–40
Pennefather, R.W. 72
Penny, C.R. 129
Pickering-Jones, Gilbert 144, 151–4, 157, 160–1
Point Cloates 61
police
  Aboriginal constables 53
  at Carnarvon 13, 29, 32, 33–4, 42, 53
  at Mount Wittenoom 53
  at Shark Bay 75, 76–7
  Central Intelligence Bureau 83–4
  coaching witnesses 44
  Criminal Investigation Branch 157, 162
  report skirmishes with Aboriginal people 18
  rounding up of Aboriginal indentured workers 163–5
  see also names of individual officers, e.g. Troy, Patrick
Port Gascoyne 17
  see also Carnarvon
Port Inn 17
Prinsep, Henry Charles (Harry) 72–3
prostitution, in Shark Bay 77
Purkiss, William Morton 110

Quobba Station 144–5

Raghib, Edmund 91–2
Redfern, Charlie 20, 22–8
Reilly, Constable 163
Richardson, Alexander Robert, *Early Memories of the Great Nor-West* 9
Riley, William 147
Roach, Ted 40–1, 44–6
Roe, A.S. 187
Roe, J.B. 27

roo shooters *see* kangaroo shooters
Rooth, Justice 129–32
Roth, Walter Edmund 33, 183
Rottnest Island Prison 12, 14, 20, 26, 34, 53–4
Rotton, Gilbert 59
Rowe, Thomas 79, 83–5, 88–9, 96–7
Royal Commission on the Condition of the Natives 33–4, 183
Rudd, Steele, *On Our Selection* 146, 159
Russell, Alfred 28
Ryan, James 147

sandalwood trade 17, 81
Saunders, George 120
Scott, Edward 44–5
Settler's Hotel 108, 138
Sewell, John Edgar 25
Shark Bay 74–99
Sharks Bay Pearl Shell Fishery Act 1886 95–8
Sharp, J.W. 138
Shaw, Arthur Miller 56–9
Shaw, Gordon Douglas 56–9
Shea, Jack 81–92
Shea, John 59–61
Sheard, Paul 138
Sheehan, John (Jack) 162, 165–86
Silver, William 91
Sing Hay 78
Sing Ong 78–80
Smith, Constable 56
Smith, Lance Corporal 95
Smyth, Sergeant 120
Snook, W.S. 69
Solly's Dam 144–6, 150, 161
Solomon, Judah Moss 158
Spargo, Charles Herbert (Charlie) 144–61
Spry, Constable 133
Stone, Edward 43–9
Stone, Frank Mends 23, 26, 43
Sunday Times (newspaper) 52, 71, 125, 132, 136, 185

Taylor, Corporal 95
Thackabiddy 39–49
Toniko Toko (lugger) 139–40
Topsy 162, 165–86
Travers, Georgina 138–43
Travers, John 138–43
Travers, Sheila 138–43
Tribe, Samuel 94–5
Troy, Patrick 26
Troy, Richard 25
Tunnie 102, 105–8, 111
Turner, William (Bill) 42, 61–70

Ulbrich, Gustav Anton (Tony) 139–41
Union Bank 120
Useless Harbour 74, 76, 92–8

Vann, George 117–19, 122–3, 128
Varian, Harry *see* Sheehan, John
von Bibra, Francis *see* Bibra, Francis von
von Bibra, Leopold *see* Bibra, Leopold von

Walker, Constable 55
Walker, Thomas 159–60
Wall, Lance Corporal 29, 95
Walsh, John Joseph 157, 162
Wandagee 37–40
Wangabiddy 20, 23–8
Warribee 29, 30–1
Warton, Charles Nicholas 55–9
Webster, Chief Warder 137
West Australian (newspaper) 22, 27, 52, 74, 83, 137, 159, 179
West Australian Sunday Times (newspaper) *see Sunday Times* (newspaper)
West, Corporal 156, 158
Western Australia (steamer) 144, 153–5, 158, 159
Wheelock, Charles Thomas (Charlie) 22, 36–9
Whitlock, Frank 10–11, 188
Whitlock Island 142

Wilks, Cecil John *see* Travers, John
Williambury Station 70, 119–20
Williams, William (Maori Bill) 165–86
Willy Willy 23, 25
Wilyah Miah 75
Winning Pool 119, 171
Wood, George Tuthill 125–9
Woodegar 24, 25–6
Woods, Sergeant 61–2, 66
Wooramel Station 80–4, 87, 144
Wrensfordsley, Henry 54
Wright, Charlie 153
Wurry 24

Yanget Pool 107
Yankee Town 11, 100–12, 143
Yanoo 108–10
Yanyeareddy Station 113–23, 162–86
Yaringa Station 144
Yorilba 29, 30
Youngyu 56
Yu Chi 78–9
Yu Quong 81–91

www.ingramcontent.com/pod-product-compliance
Lightning Source LLC
Chambersburg PA
CBHW031427150426
43191CB00006B/429